IMAGES
of America

BURRILLVILLE

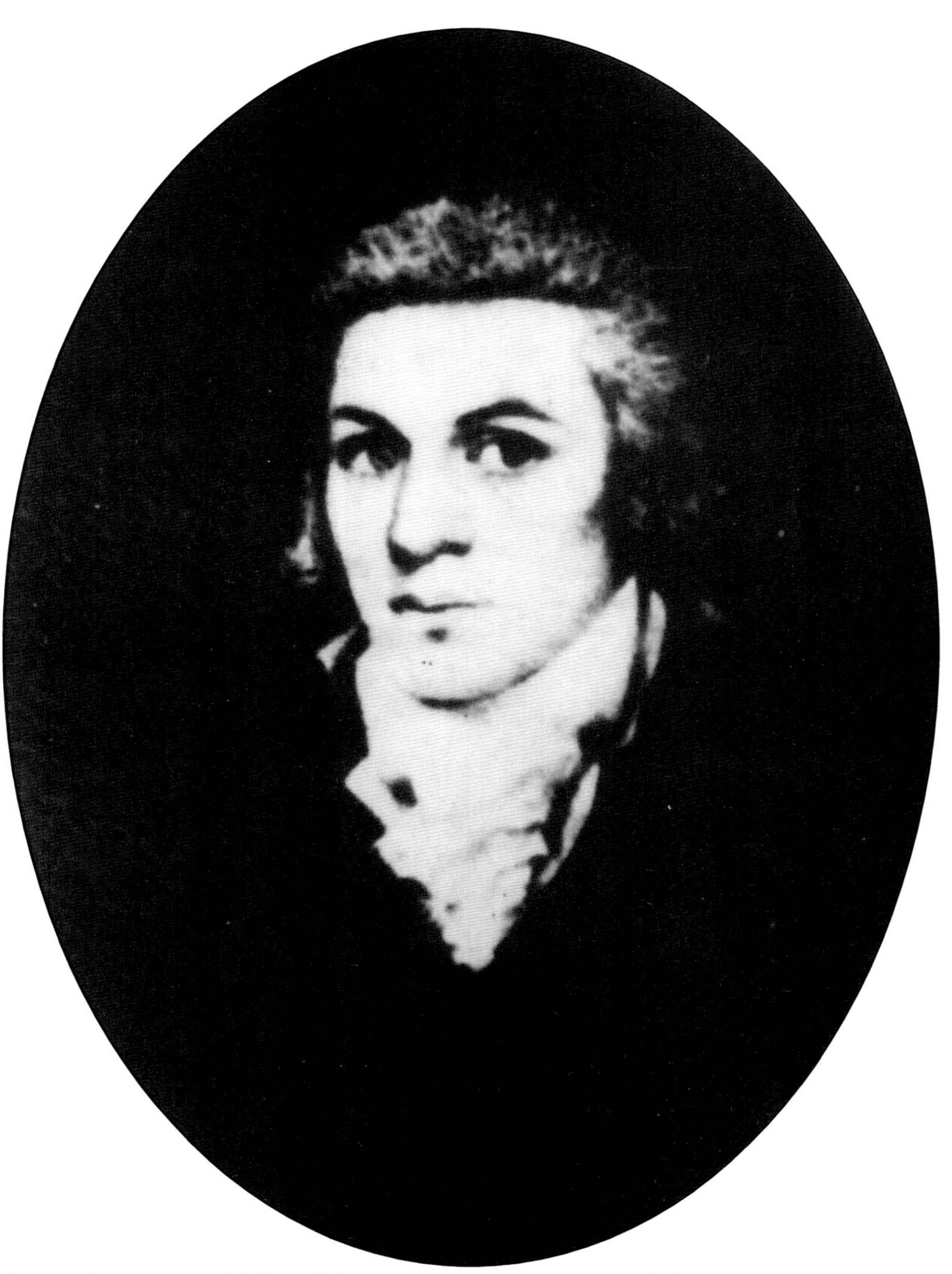

Senator James Burrill (1772–1820), for whom the town of Burrillville is named, was a man of many talents. He was the Rhode Island Attorney General from 1797 to 1813, the Speaker of the Rhode Island House of Representatives in 1814, a Chief Justice of the Supreme Judicial Court from 1816 to 1817, and represented Rhode Island in the Senate from 1817 to 1820.

IMAGES of America

BURRILLVILLE

Patricia Zifchock Mehrtens

ARCADIA PUBLISHING

ISBN 978-0-7385-6391-6

Published by Arcadia Publishing
Charleston, South Carolina

Printed in the United States of America

Library of Congress Catalog Card Number: 2009920850

For all general information contact Arcadia Publishing at:
Telephone 843-853-2070
Fax 843-853-0044
E-mail sales@arcadiapublishing.com
For customer service and orders:
Toll-Free 1-888-313-2665

Visit us on the Internet at www.arcadiapublishing.com

Contents

Acknowledgments

This photographic history of Burrillville could never have been completed without the help and cooperation of the many people who loaned and/or donated their precious photographs to me over the past thirty years. If your name is not included, please forgive the omission. This occurred only because in the early years I failed to record who gave what material, but you can be assured that your help was certainly appreciated.

Many sources of research materials were used, including: early books giving their views of the history of Burrillville; bits and pieces of information gathered over the years; town records where applicable; and ultimately, information from my own private collection.

In particular I would like to thank the following: Mrs. Kenneth E. Bailey, Blanche Robillard Gonyea, Esther Sherman Hoyle, Etta Mowry Jacobs, Michael and Mary Jarvis, John Kaczynski Jr., Edna Whitaker Kent, Millie Legg, Rita Jarvis Mikulis, Helen Fairbrother Moroney, Robert Pascoe, Barton St. Amant, Milton Sherman, Mildred Bailey Gunther Smith, Vern Smith, Lillian J. Steere, Loretta Stratford Steere, Ruth Tourtellot, J. Oscar and Raymond Trinque, and Dennis Whitman, all of whom contributed to this collection of Burrillville photographs. Thanks also go to my brother George Zifchock who helped in the hunt for "new" photographs just for this publication.

Introduction

"Ours is a city of hills and mills. We sit on the hills and watch the busy mills the while we scratch with our quills."

From a *Pascoag Herald* editorial of April 9, 1892

The above quote tells it all. Burrillville, which separated from Glocester in 1806, is certainly a place of hills and mills. It has the second highest hill in Rhode Island and all its rivers and streams run downhill to the east. Burrillville is located in the northwest corner of the state of Rhode Island with Connecticut on the western border, Massachusetts on the north, North Smithfield on the east, and Glocester on its southern border.

Our plentiful lakes, streams, and rivers lent themselves to the development not only of the mills but of the many small villages which supported them. In those days, you were from Buck Hill, Wallum Lake, Bridgeton, Pascoag, Harrisville, Whipple, Glendale, Spring Lake, Oakland, Mapleville, Gazza, Nasonville, Mohegan, or Tarkiln. Some of the names have disappeared, but the village identities are still important to the people who live here.

Burrillville was a booming town right from the start. In its early years, farming was the prominent occupation even though the soil was rocky and not very suitable. Saw and grist mills began our growth, with cotton and woolen mills following. It was because of the availability of water power that cotton-spinning operations started in the Tarkiln and Pascoag areas in 1807. The woolen industry began in 1814 at the site of the Sayles Mill in Pascoag. In the early 1850s, Burrillville became the largest producer of woolen goods in Rhode Island. During the Civil War, several of our mills produced cloth for uniforms for the Union soldiers. The tradition continued throughout World Wars I and II with our mills and workers operating around the clock to support the war efforts. Sadly, all that vanished when the mills closed and went south in the 1950s.

Railroads and trolleys made transportation to and from Burrillville easy, and many people took advantage of this to travel to other parts of the state. Granite from our quarries was shipped by train to Providence along with most of our trees, which were used as fuel to warm the folks there at the turn of the century. Thankfully, the trees have grown back since that time.

Entertainment was provided by small local groups at the various halls around the town. Church groups and fraternal organizations were an active part of our history. Baseball teams competed with each other as they still do today. We even had a well-known race track which flourished for many years. Picnicking, boating, and swimming were other entertainments that are still available on our lakes and rivers today.

These photographs from the 1890s through the 1940s can only give you a taste of what life was like in those days. Every little village had its own school, churches, and mills, which made it unique. The choice of which pictures to use to represent them was a difficult one. But in the end it all comes down to people—the people who made Burrillville what it was and what it is. I hope you enjoy this collection of old Burrillville memories.

Patricia Zifchock Mehrtens
Burrillville Historian and Author

One

Farms, Homes, and Businesses

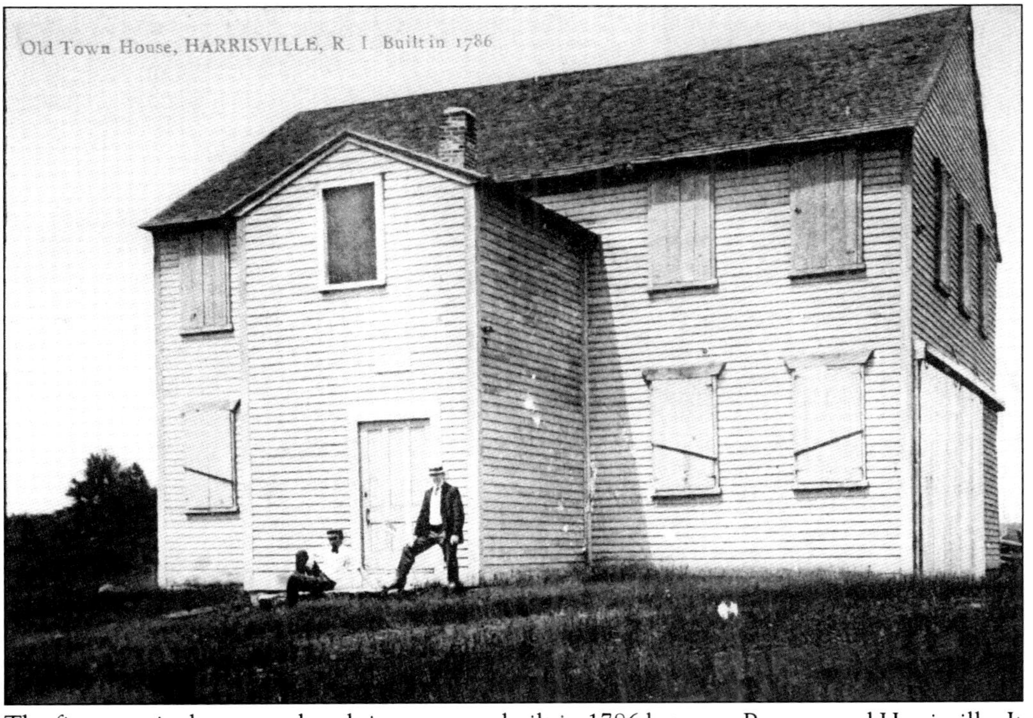

The first meetinghouse or church in town was built in 1786 between Pascoag and Harrisville. It was originally used as a place of worship by several denominations, and then became the town house or town hall (where the town records were kept) and the town clerk's office. It was last used to store highway equipment for the town of Burrillville before being razed.

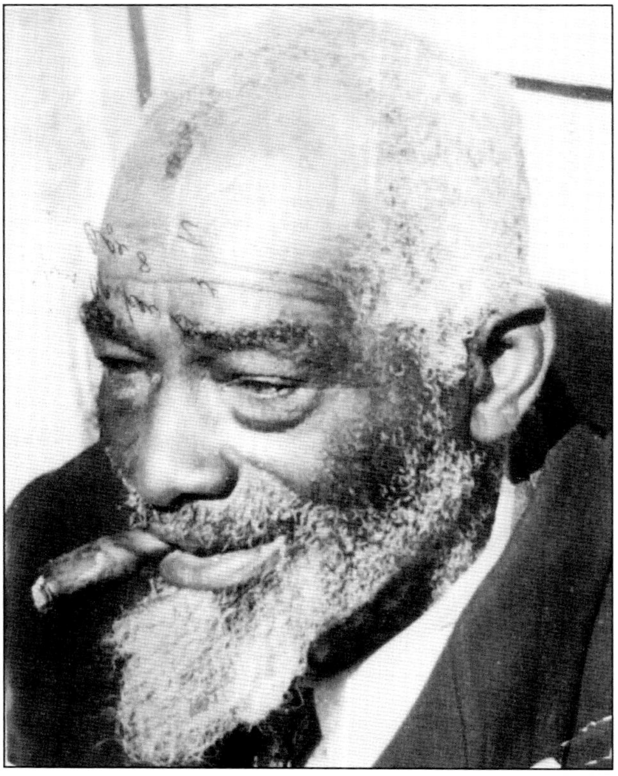

Henry Johnson was born near Richmond, Virginia, in 1834 and died in 1943 at the age of 109. He liked to recount shaking hands with President Abraham Lincoln after being freed from slavery. Mr. Johnson charged the photographer, Harry Weintraub, 25¢ for permission to take this picture in front of the old First National Store in Pascoag by the entrance to the Odd Fellows Hall.

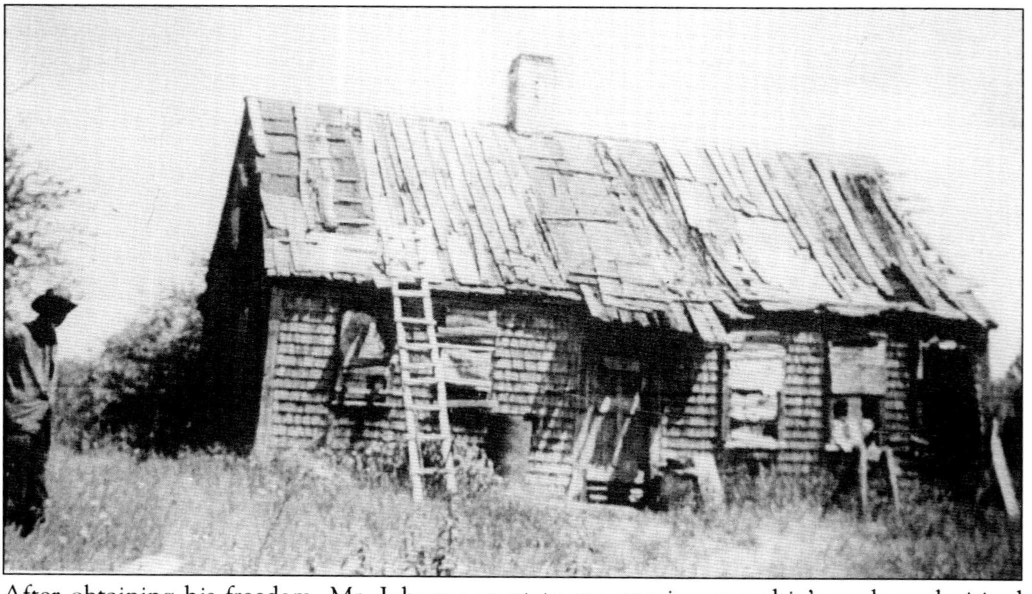

After obtaining his freedom, Mr. Johnson went to sea, serving as a ship's cook, and visited many ports throughout the world. He eventually quit the seafaring life and cut wood, worked on farms, and toiled in mines. When he finally came to Burrillville he was hired to work on the old Wells Farm on Wallum Lake Road. Henry Johnson was a well-known and beloved addition to our town.

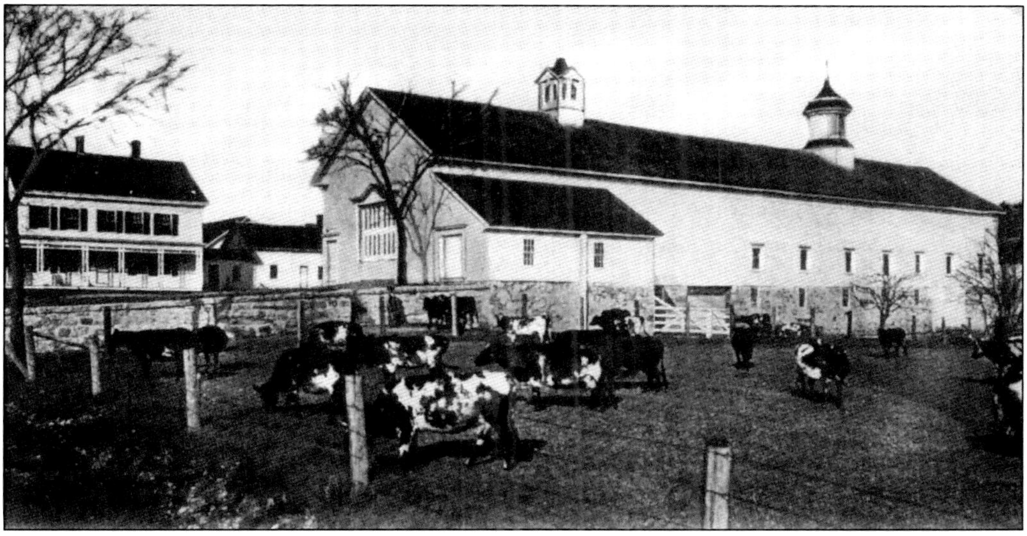

Sherman Stock Farm in Harrisville was owned by Sumner Sherman. In later years, Mr. Levy raised cattle here for shipping to his plantation in the Bahamas. The barn was built in 1876 and burned to the ground one hundred years later.

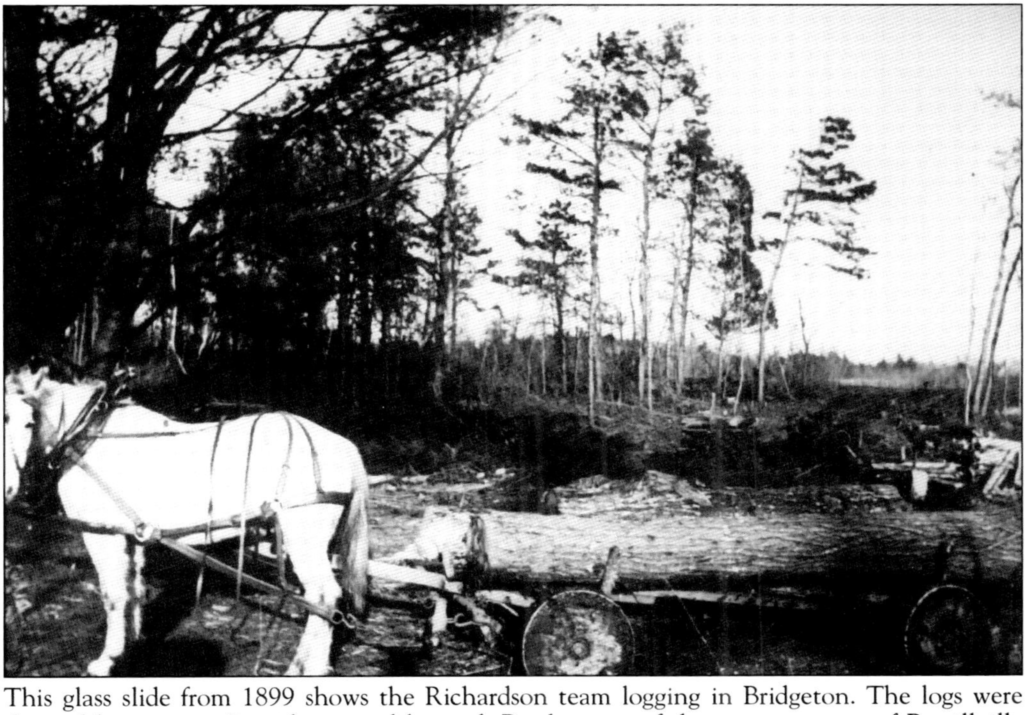

This glass slide from 1899 shows the Richardson team logging in Bridgeton. The logs were shipped by train to Providence and beyond. By the turn of the century, most of Burrillville timber had been cut and sold; open fields and stone walls were all that remained.

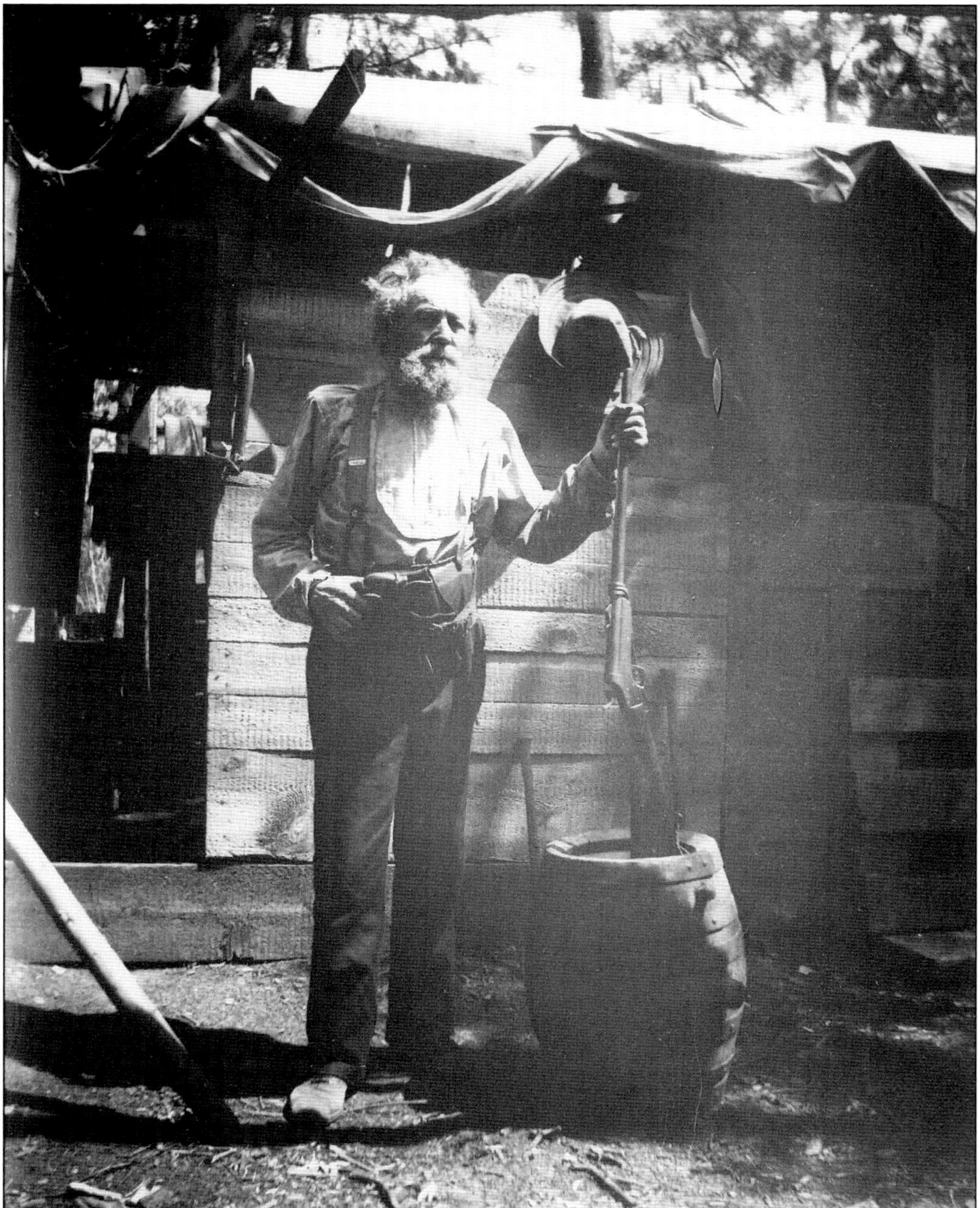

An old man and his gun—standing in front of his home. Typical Burrillville woodcutters at the turn of the century lived in sparsely-settled areas and made their living by hunting, fishing, and cutting wood. If supplies were needed, a walk to the nearest village was the order of the day.

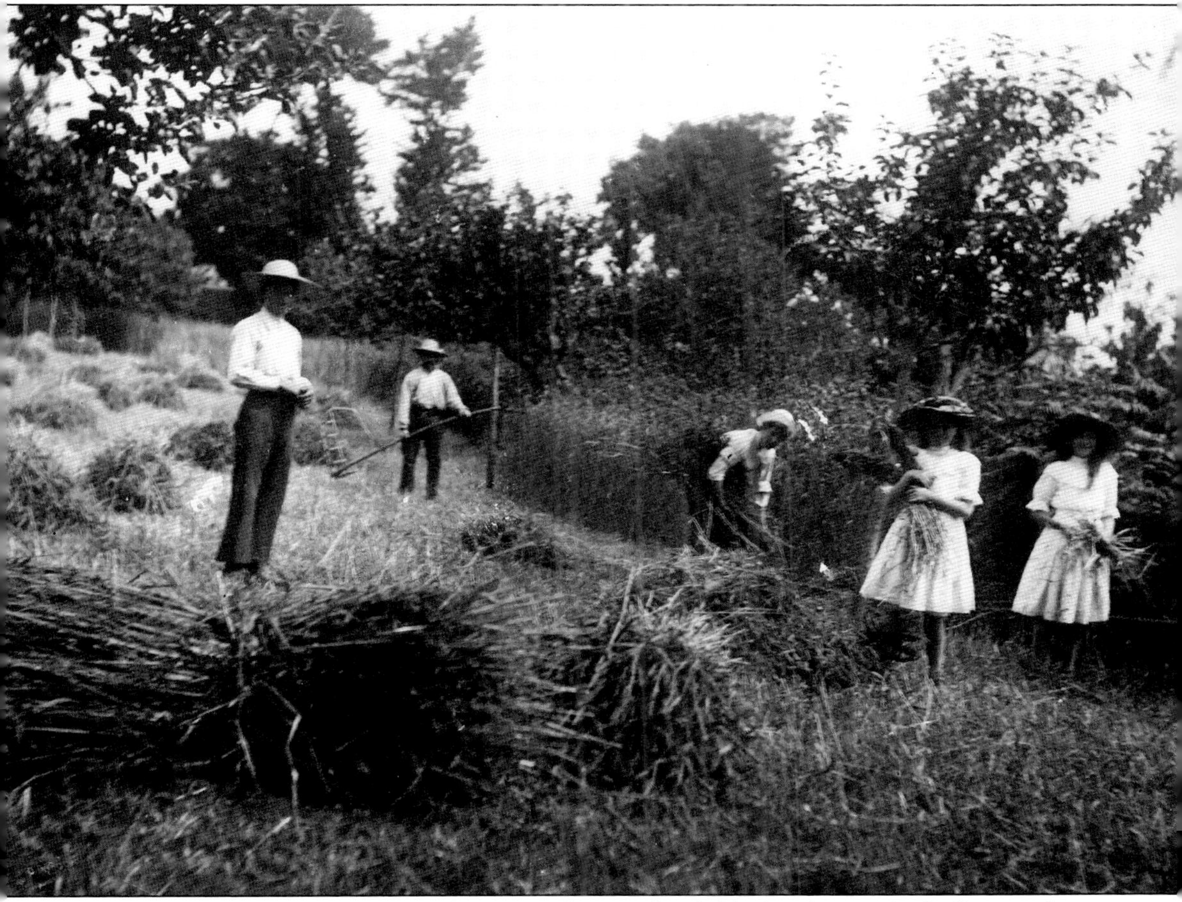

This fine example of a family working together in the fields for the good of all was taken from a 1900 glass slide. In the early days, children would attend small schools within walking distance of their farms, usually during the winter months. Spring was for planting and fall was for harvesting the mature crops.

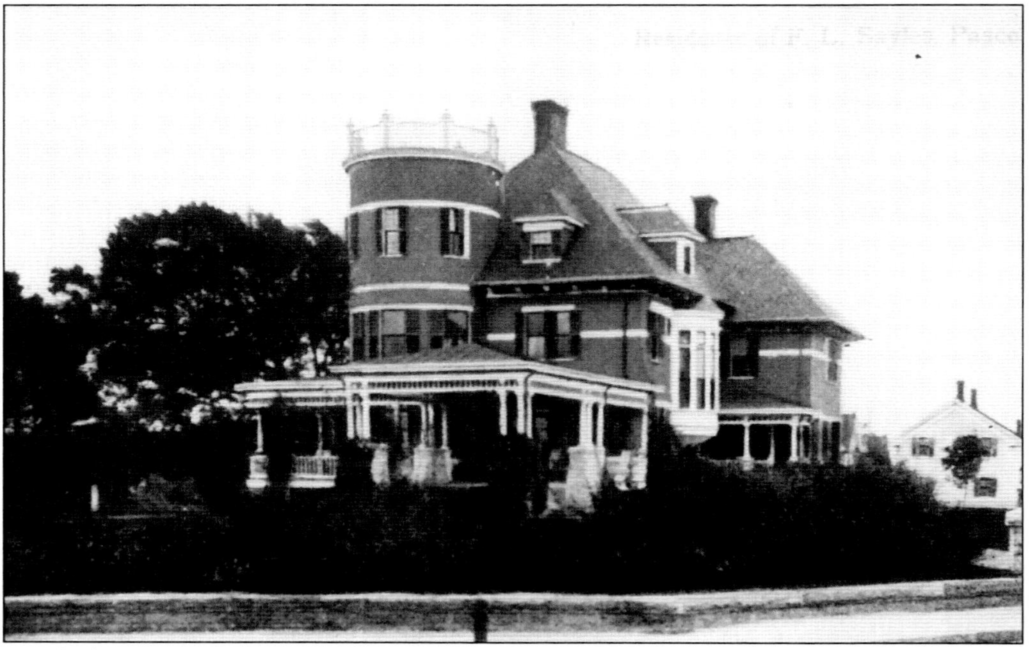

Overlook Mansion in Pascoag was built in 1896 by Fred L. Sayles. In 1964 it was converted into a nursing home and in 1979 it was demolished and replaced by the new building.

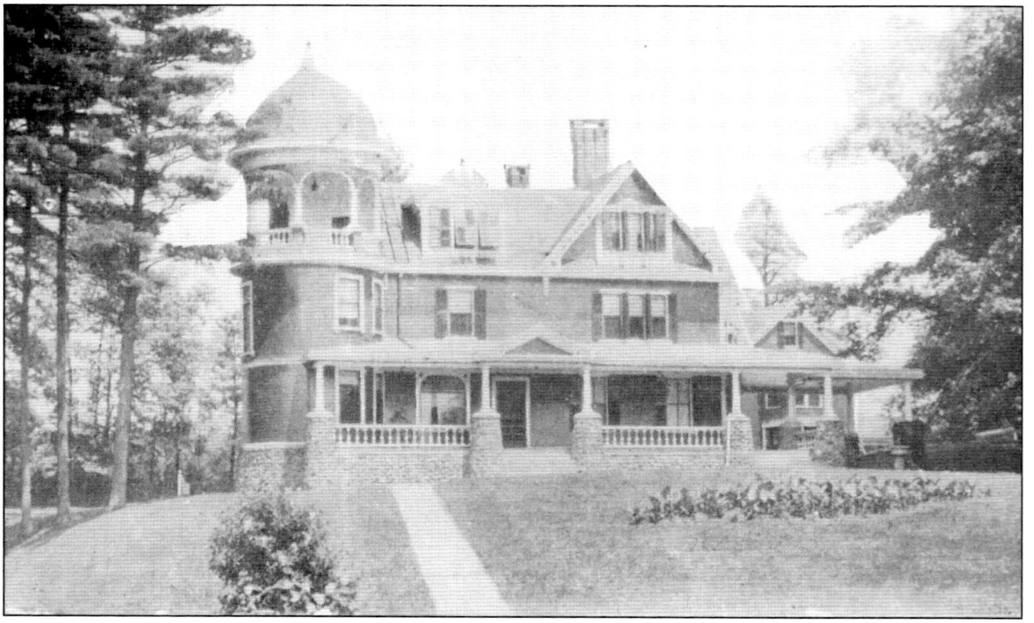

The Tinkham Residence on East Avenue, Harrisville, was renovated for William Tinkham, who died in 1914. Tinkham, a mill owner, brought the Providence and Springfield Railroad out to the northwest corner of the state along with the help of Albert Sayles of Pascoag, also a mill owner. Members of Tinkham's immediate family still reside in the family homestead.

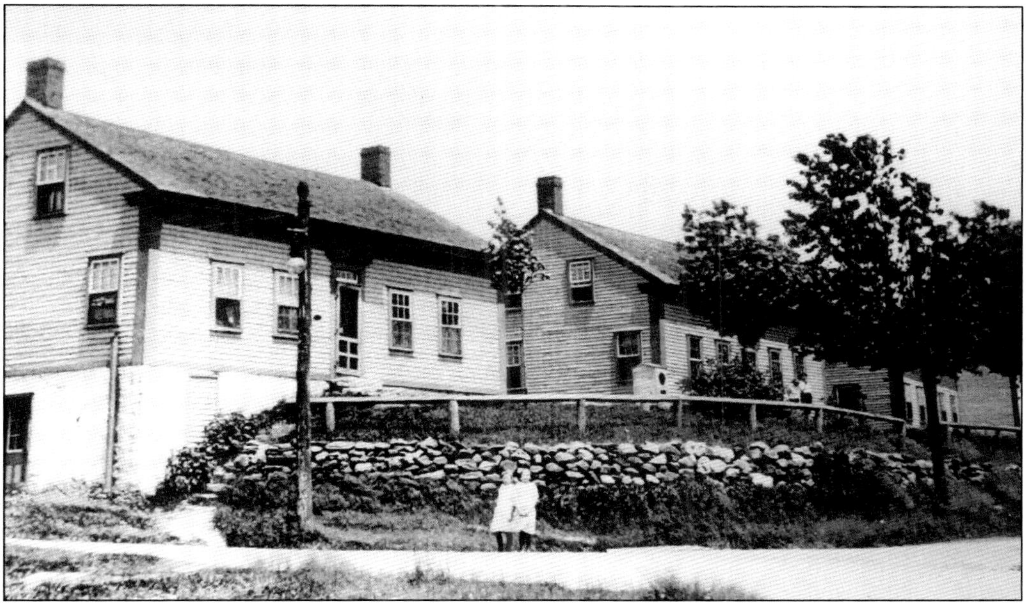

These mill houses in Glendale were associated with the Orrell Mills. When Mr. Levy purchased the mills, he wanted to demolish these houses. Before obtaining permission from the Town, he had to promise to build the same amount of housing for his workers. As a result, the area known as New Village in Glendale came into being in 1936.

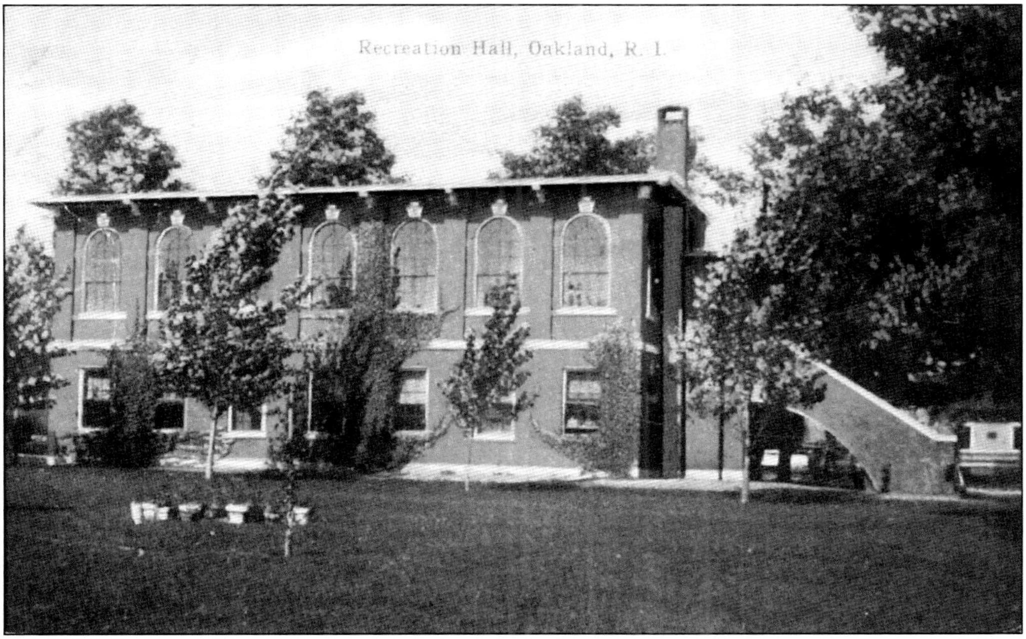

Recreation Hall in Oakland was built in 1898 by the Metcalfs. Weddings, dances, meetings, and other celebrations were held here along with a tonsil clinic in the 1940s. Lee's Variety Store was on the first floor for many years.

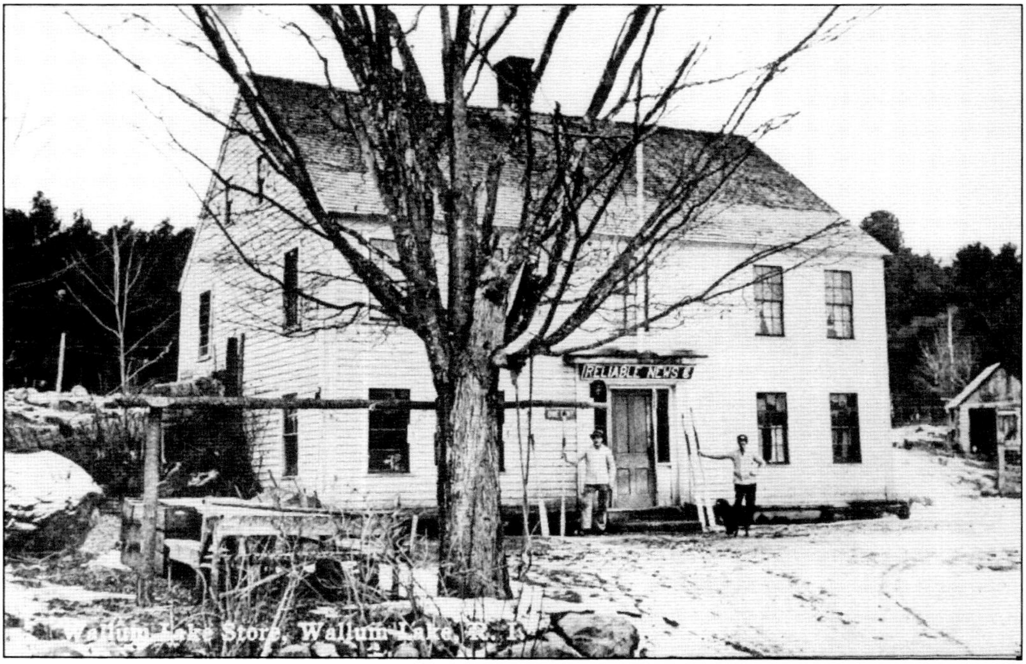

The Reliable News Company store was run by the Angell family at Wallum Lake. They sold everything from newspapers, sundries, and tobacco to fireworks and fishing lures. Like many of the older buildings, it is now a private residence.

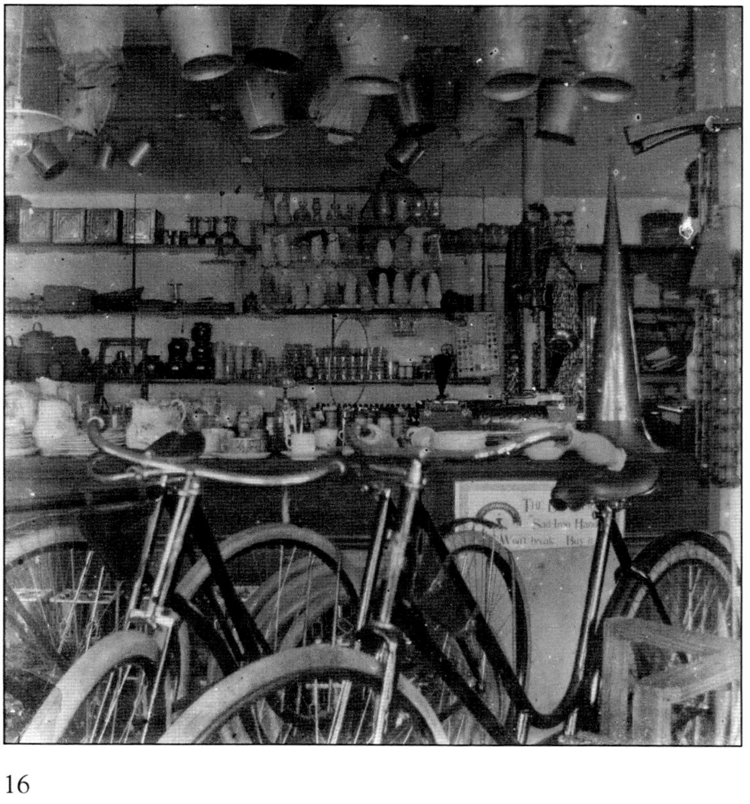

This view is of the interior of a typical store during the late 1890s. An 1891 advertisement shows bicycles selling from $33 to $133 each.

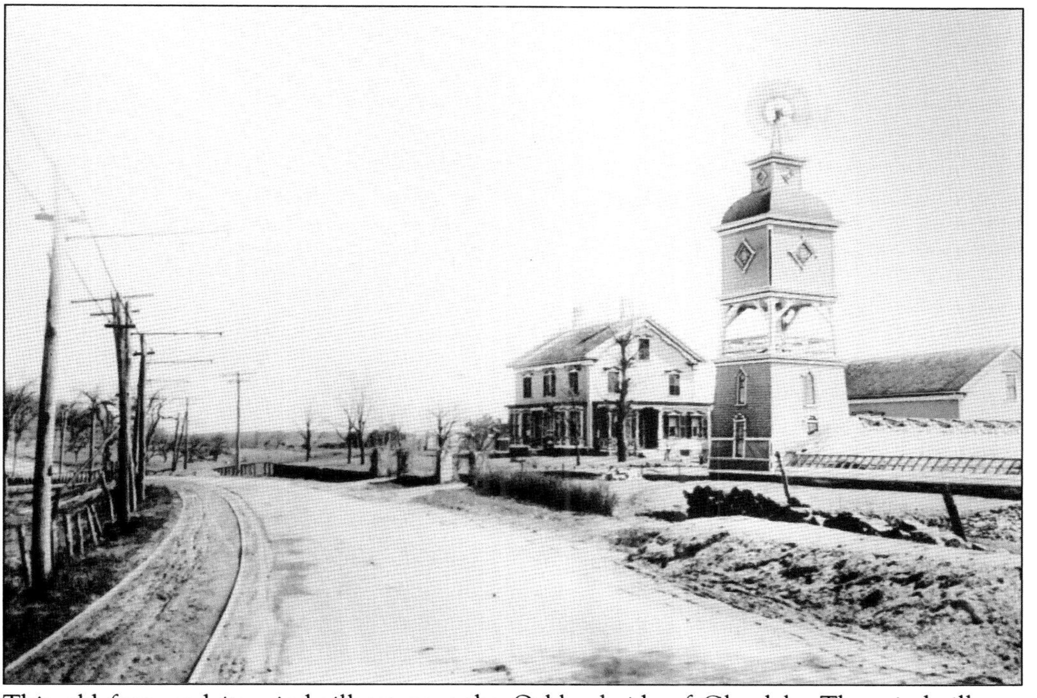

This old farm and its windmill sat near the Oakland side of Glendale. The windmill was typical of the ones used all over town for pumping water from the wells. Only the house is standing today.

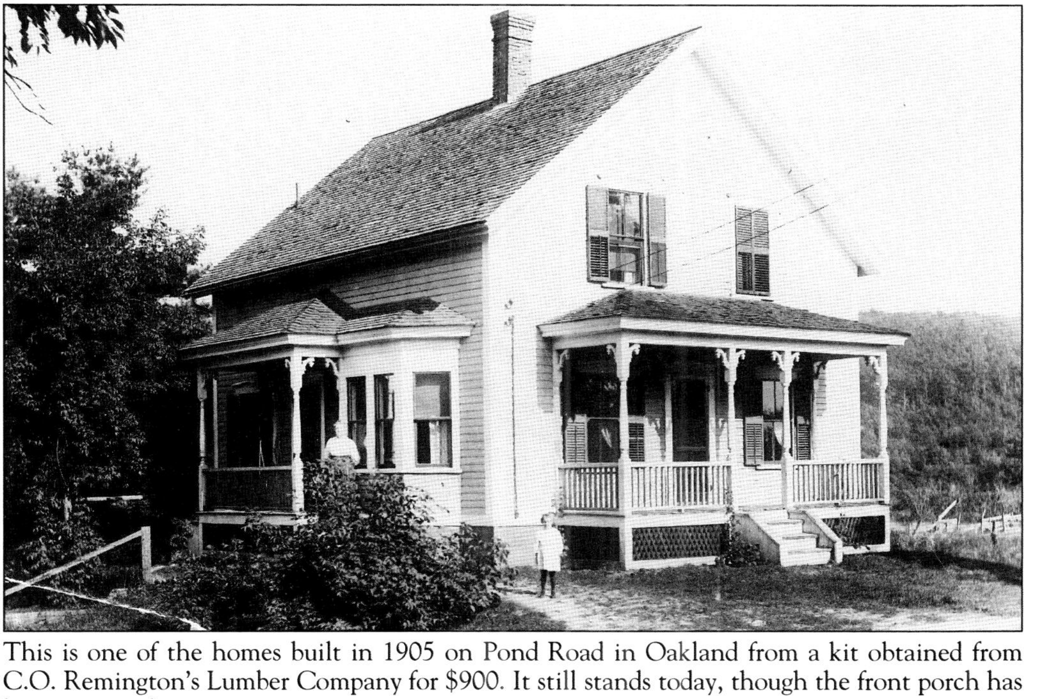

This is one of the homes built in 1905 on Pond Road in Oakland from a kit obtained from C.O. Remington's Lumber Company for $900. It still stands today, though the front porch has been removed.

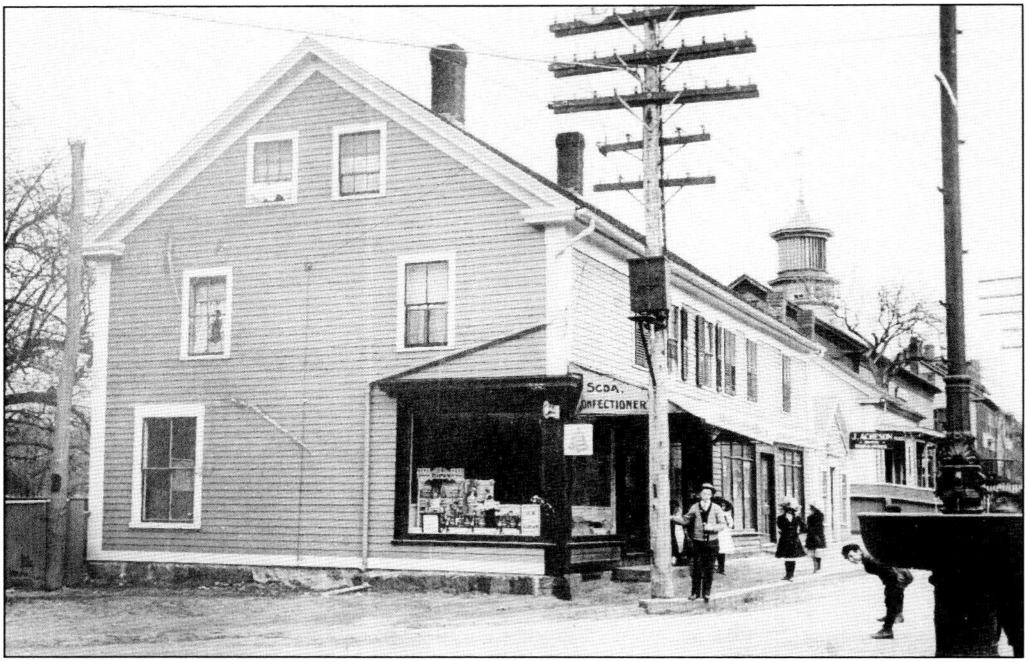

Legg's Store was located at the corner of Main and South Main Streets at Fountain Square in Pascoag. At the time this photograph was taken, cobblestones were just beginning to be laid around the fountain. After being sold to Industrial Bank (Fleet) in 1975, the building was razed and is now their parking lot. Millie Legg was born in the second-floor apartment.

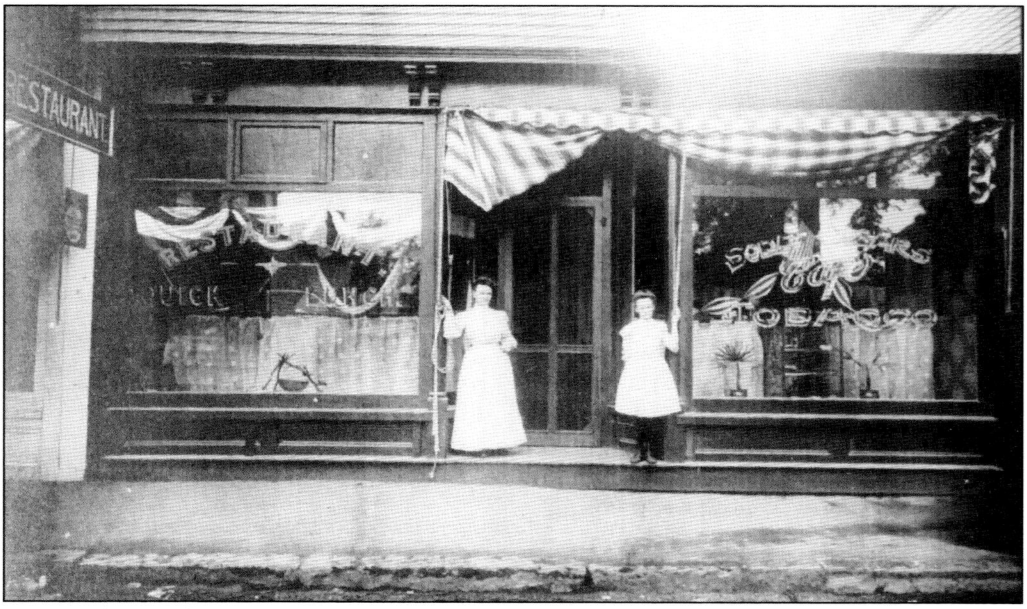

Mrs. Emily Brearley and her daughter Ida, who later married Mr. Legg, are shown here around 1905. At that time, there was a restaurant on one side of the building and a variety store on the other. Over the years it has housed the post office, a restaurant, a bakery, a cobbler shop, and other business enterprises.

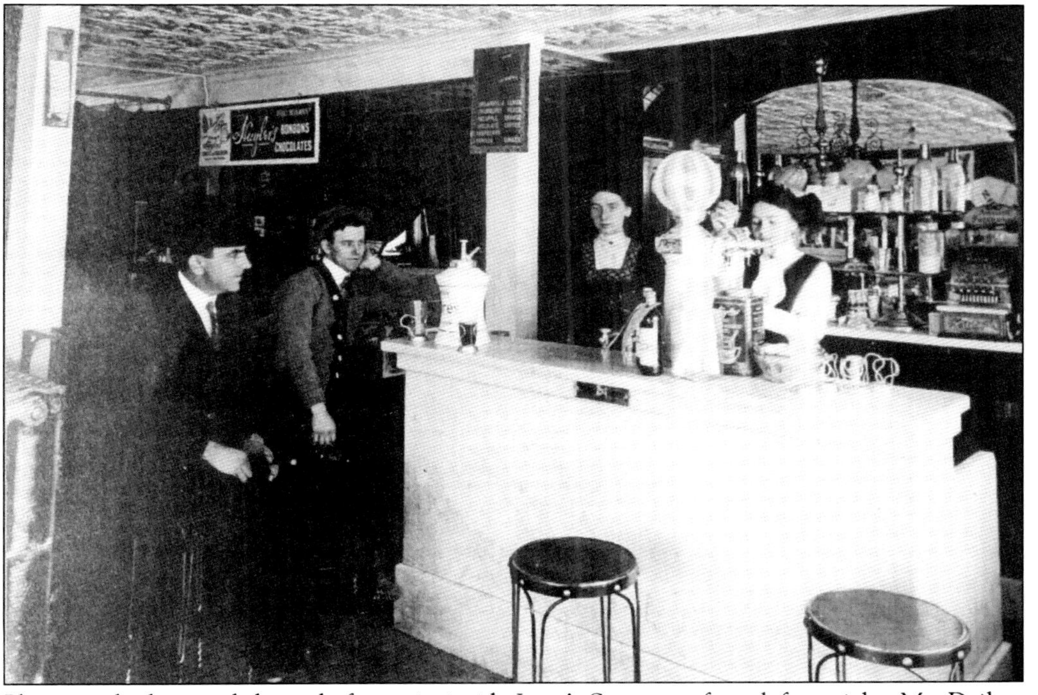

Photographed around the soda fountain inside Legg's Store are, from left to right, Mr. Dailey, Mr. Edward Legg (proprietor), Margaret Smith, and Kitty Kirby. In the early years, Mr. Legg made his own ice cream using a gasoline-driven engine.

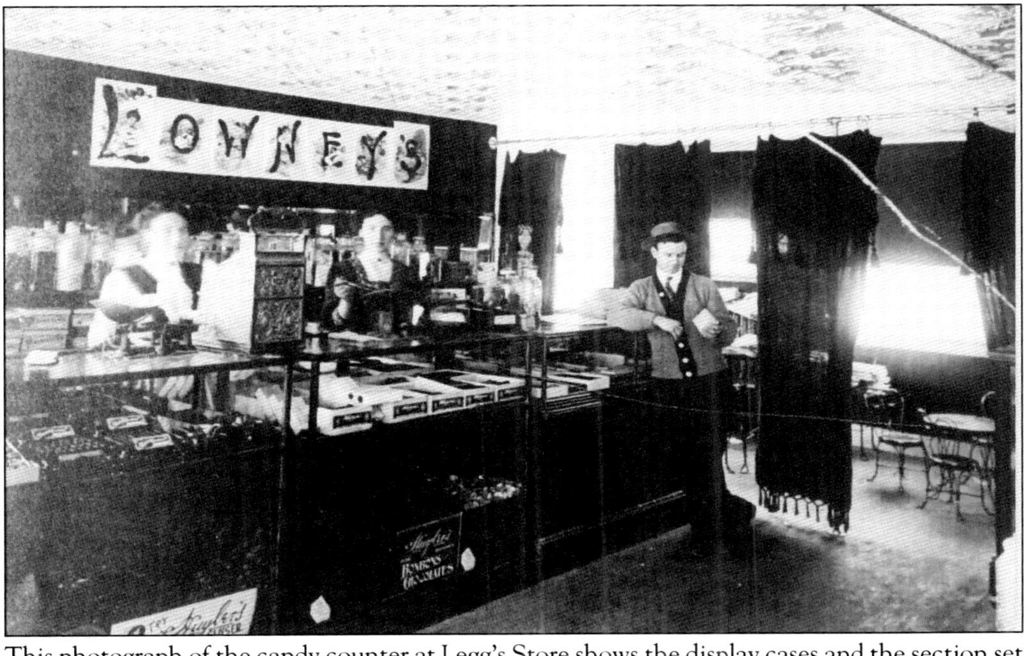

This photograph of the candy counter at Legg's Store shows the display cases and the section set aside for enjoying the ice cream which was also sold here. In later years, Millie's was the favorite place for children to obtain penny candy and for the Granite Mill workers to have lunch.

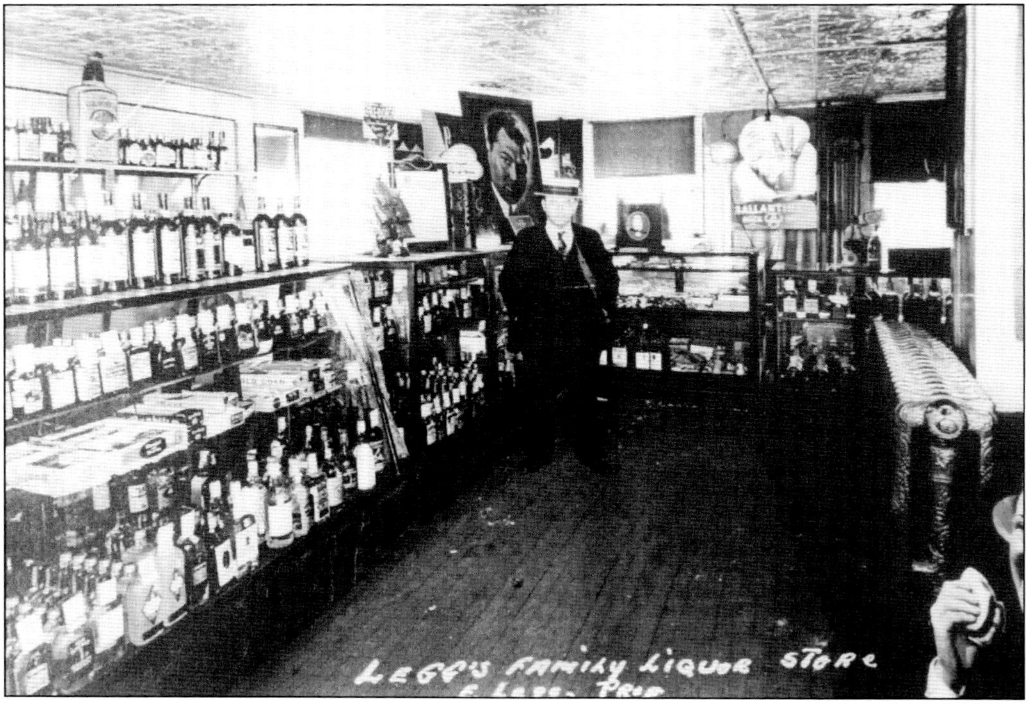

Edward Legg, proprietor, was photographed in 1934 inside his liquor store.

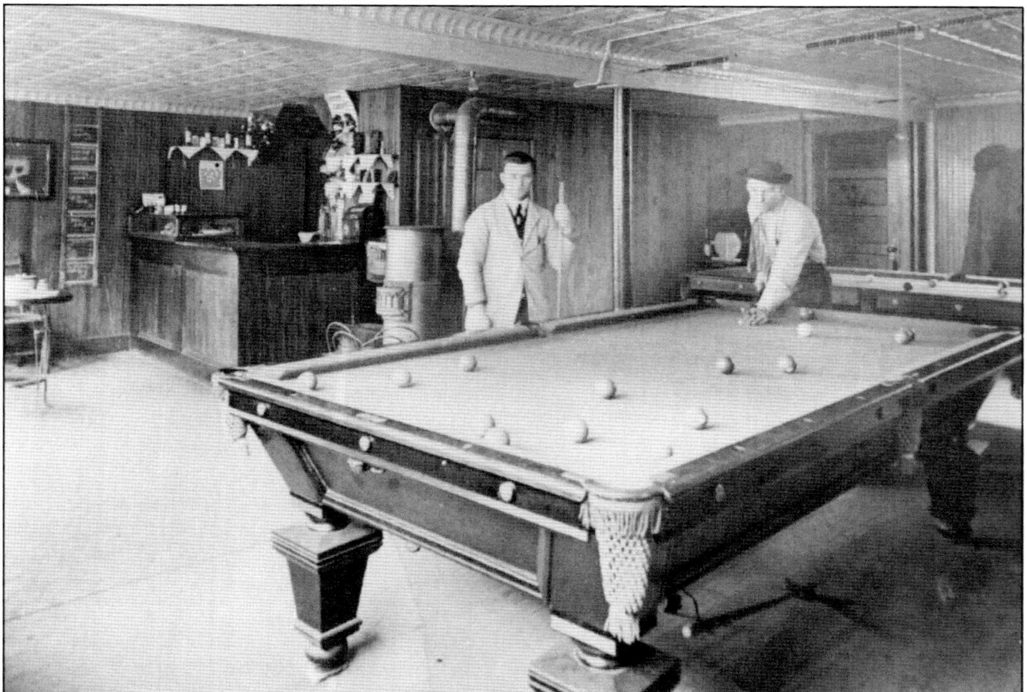
The pool table on the liquor store side of Legg's was a convenient place for the workers to relax after a long day in the mill.

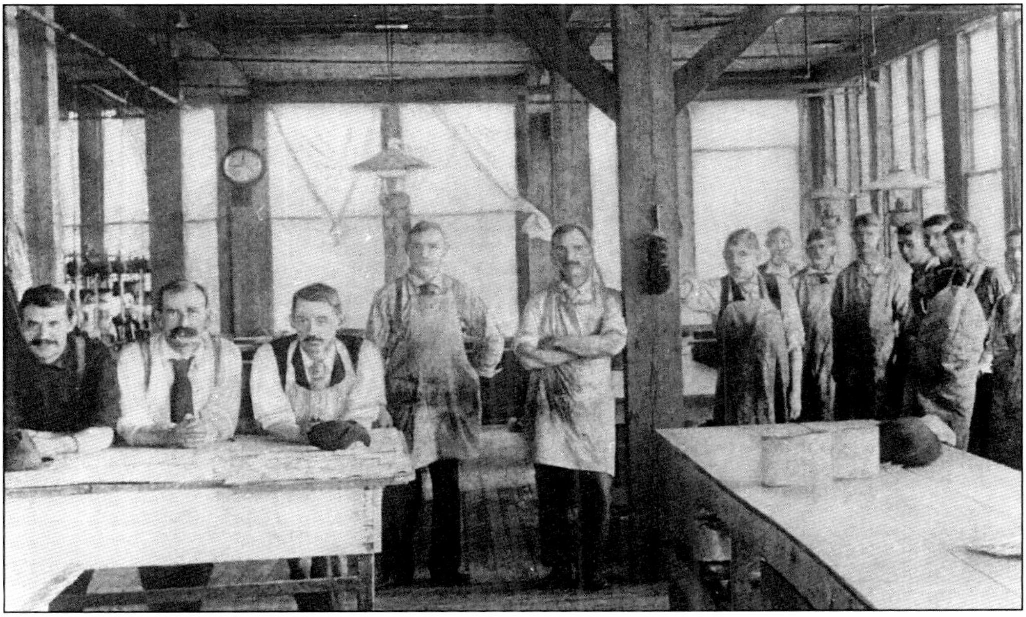

The interior of Louis Lariviere's Bakery on Cherry Farm Road in Harrisville was photographed prior to 1893. Bakery goods were delivered first by horse and wagon and later by truck. Three consecutive generations of bakers owned and operated this bakery.

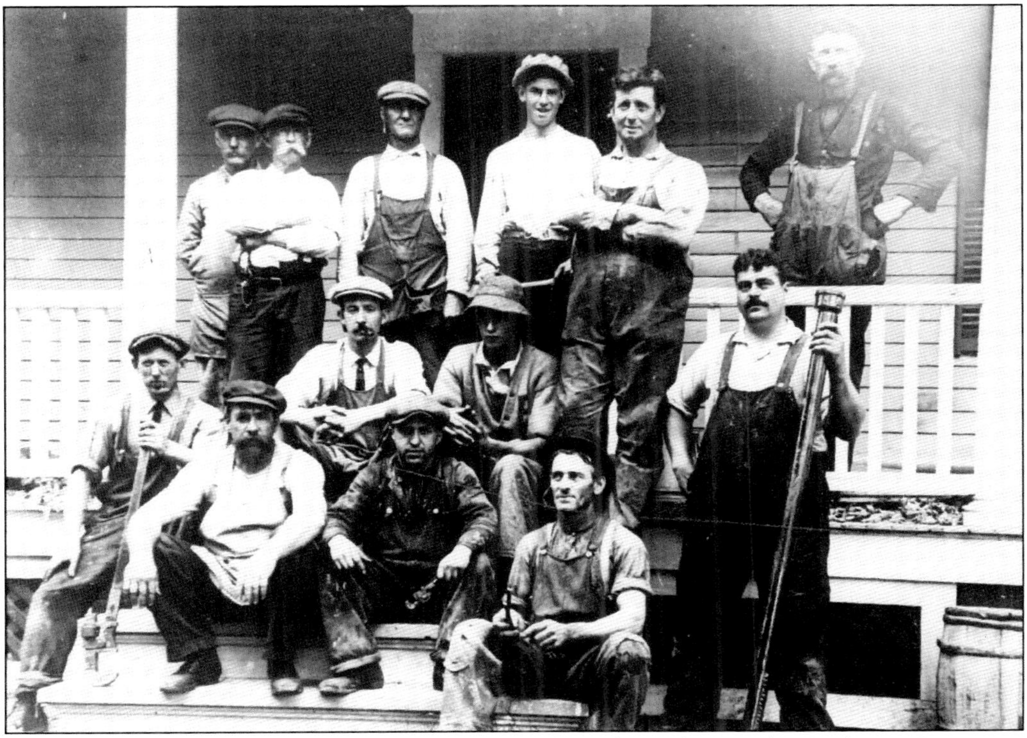

This photograph, taken around 1915, shows workers from the Smith Hardware Company, which had businesses in both Pascoag and Harrisville.

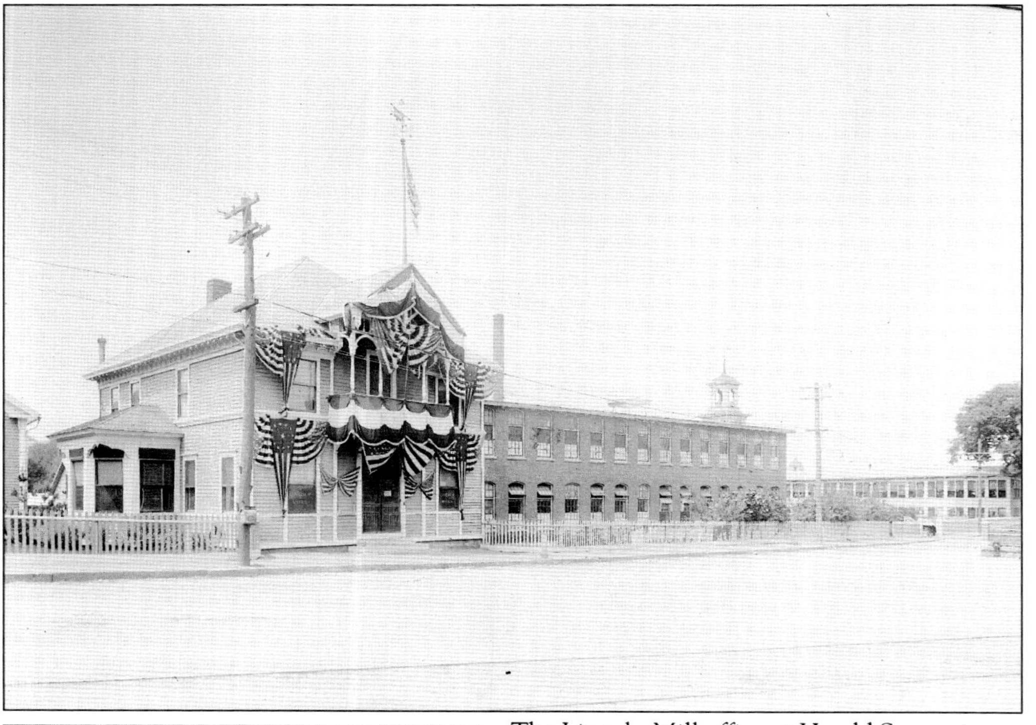

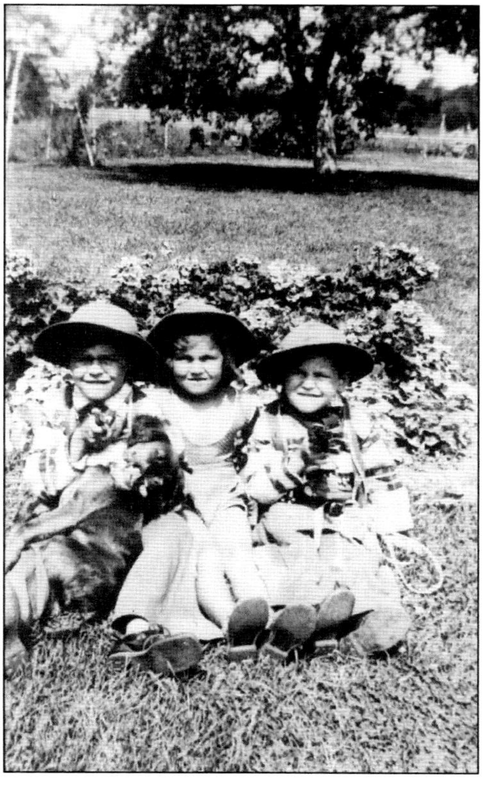

The Lincoln Mill office at Herald Square in Pascoag was decorated for the first Old Home Day in 1915. The *Pascoag Herald and Burrillville Gazette* newspaper was printed upstairs over the mill office. The last edition was printed in 1917.

George, Del, and Al Zifchock and their pets were photographed on Church Street in Bridgeton around 1935. Our dad, Joseph G. Zifchock, ran the Delmo Press in Pascoag.

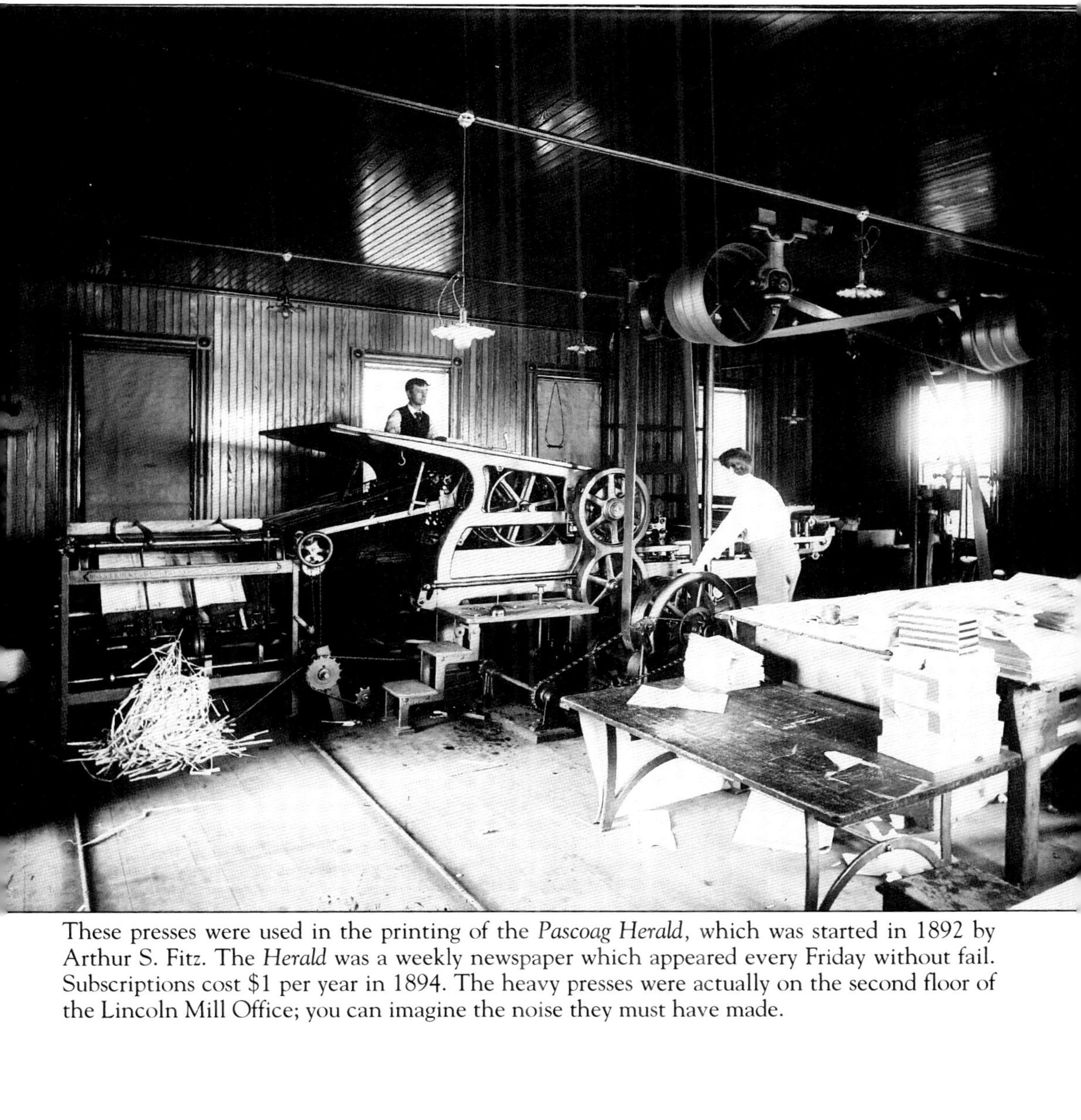

These presses were used in the printing of the *Pascoag Herald*, which was started in 1892 by Arthur S. Fitz. The *Herald* was a weekly newspaper which appeared every Friday without fail. Subscriptions cost $1 per year in 1894. The heavy presses were actually on the second floor of the Lincoln Mill Office; you can imagine the noise they must have made.

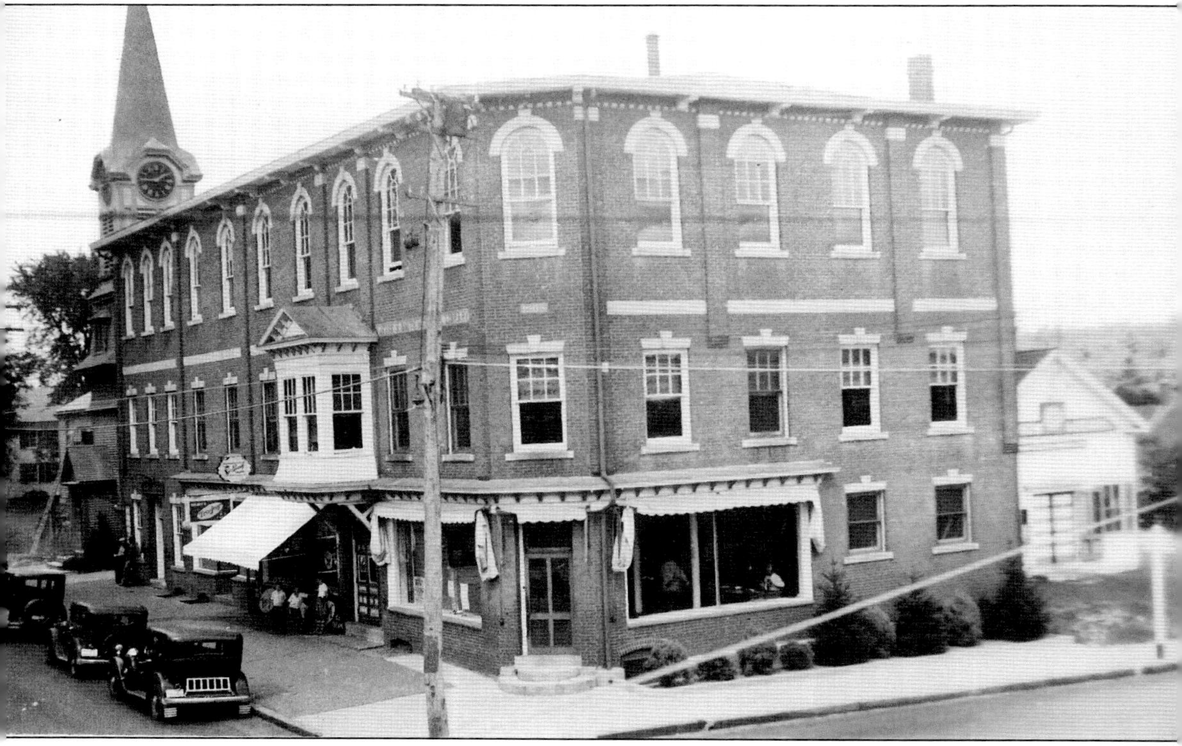

The old Jesse M. Smith Memorial Library was located in Harrisville. The first two floors contained businesses, the town hall, the courthouse, and a very small library. The third floor was used as an assembly hall, and there was a bowling alley in the basement. The Jesse M. Smith Memorial Library was built in 1900 and replaced by the new library and other buildings by Mr. Levy in 1934. This picture had to be taken just before it was razed because the First Universalist Church next door was just beginning renovations.

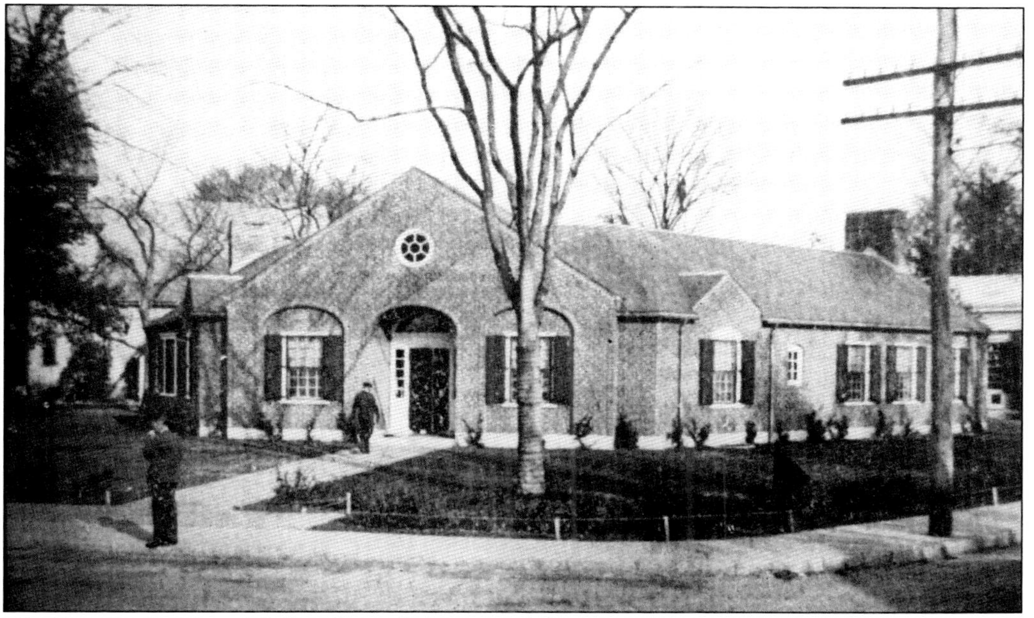

The Burrillville Town Hall is shown here at its dedication ceremonies on June 3, 1934. Austin T. Levy gave the town building, the assembly, the courthouse, and the library buildings to the Town of Burrillville to replace the Jesse Smith Memorial Building.

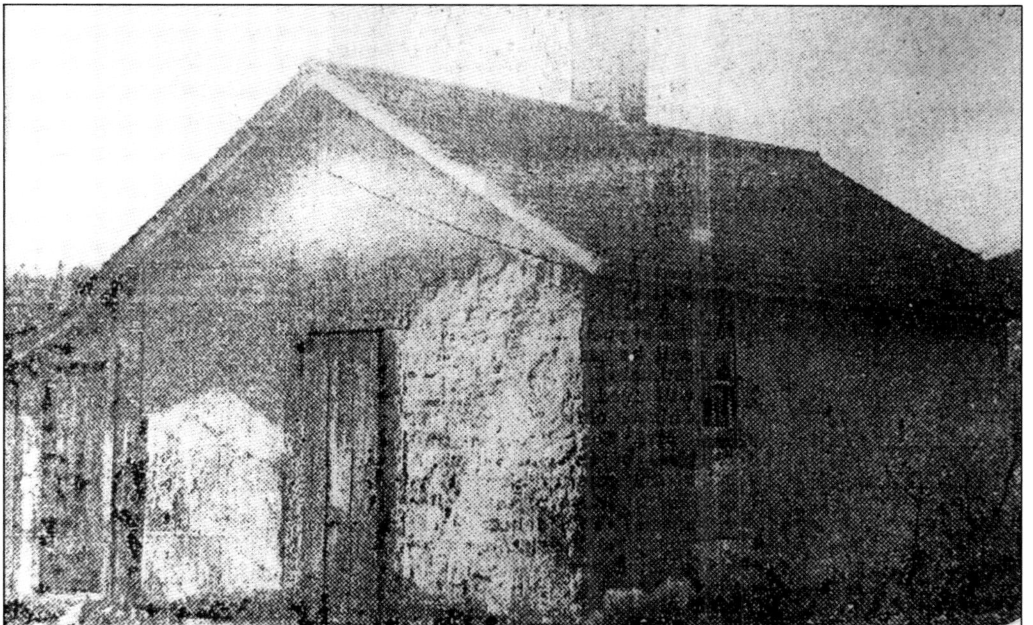

The old town jail in Harrisville was located across the tracks from the railroad station. In 1888, Officer Oliver Inman arrested a large family of itinerants, including twelve people (ranging in age from a baby to an elderly person), two bears, three monkeys, two dogs, and a horse and wagon. He placed most of them in this jail.

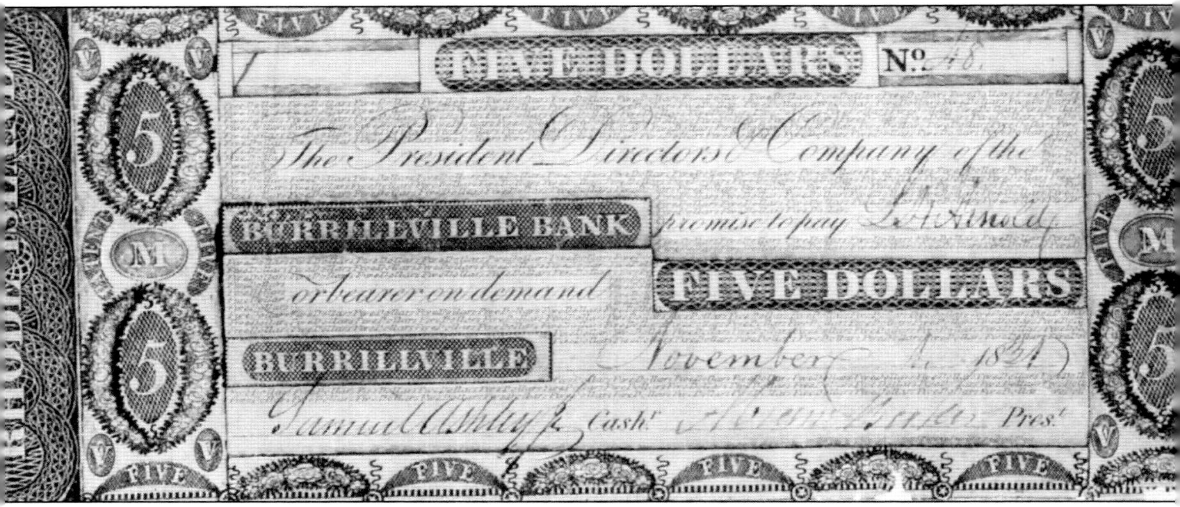

This 1831 $5 bill was printed for the Burrillville Bank, which started near the "Eddy Cooper Place" near the present village of Mapleville. Built after 1818, it continued under Abram Baker until 1831, when John W. Aborn and John L. Clark were successively chosen as presidents. Their failure to meet certain notes from the Suffolk County Bank of Boston compelled the closing of the Burrillville Bank. Previous to that, in 1815, a charter was obtained from the General Assembly for the Burrillville Agricultural and Manufacturers Bank, which was to be established in the "Smith Neighborhood" in the vicinity of Tarkiln and Oak Valley. John Slater was asked to become the president, but he declined unless the bank was located in Slatersville. Thus, the first bank in this section of Rhode Island was funded with Burrillville money.

Two

Mills and Workers

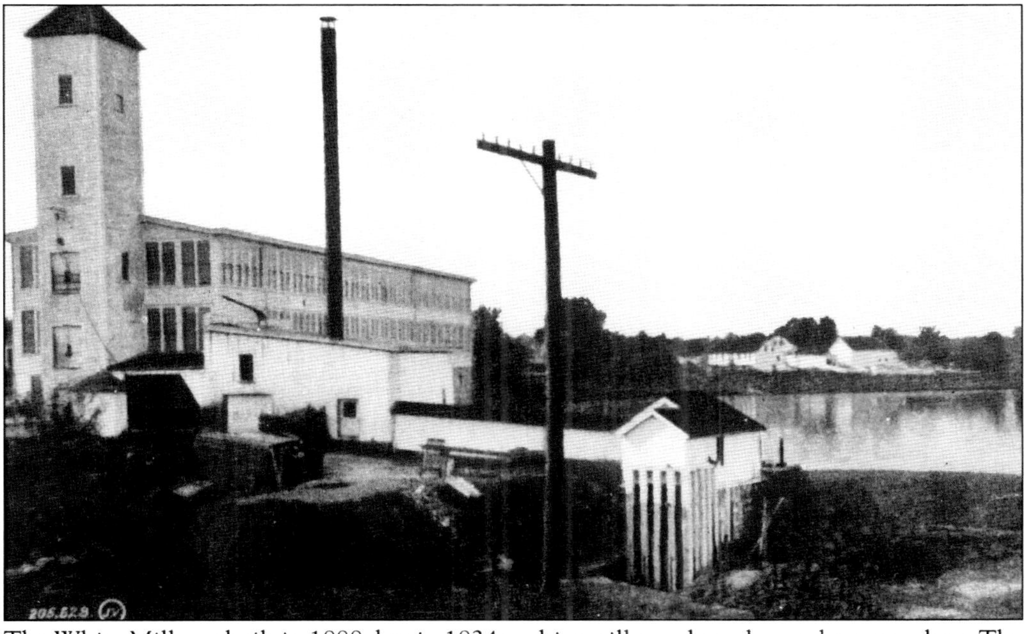

The White Mill was built in 1888, but in 1834 a white mill stood on almost the same place. The area was also known as Huntsville, then Turkeyville, and finally Bridgeton (so named because the post office was located between two bridges at Hopkins Machine Works).

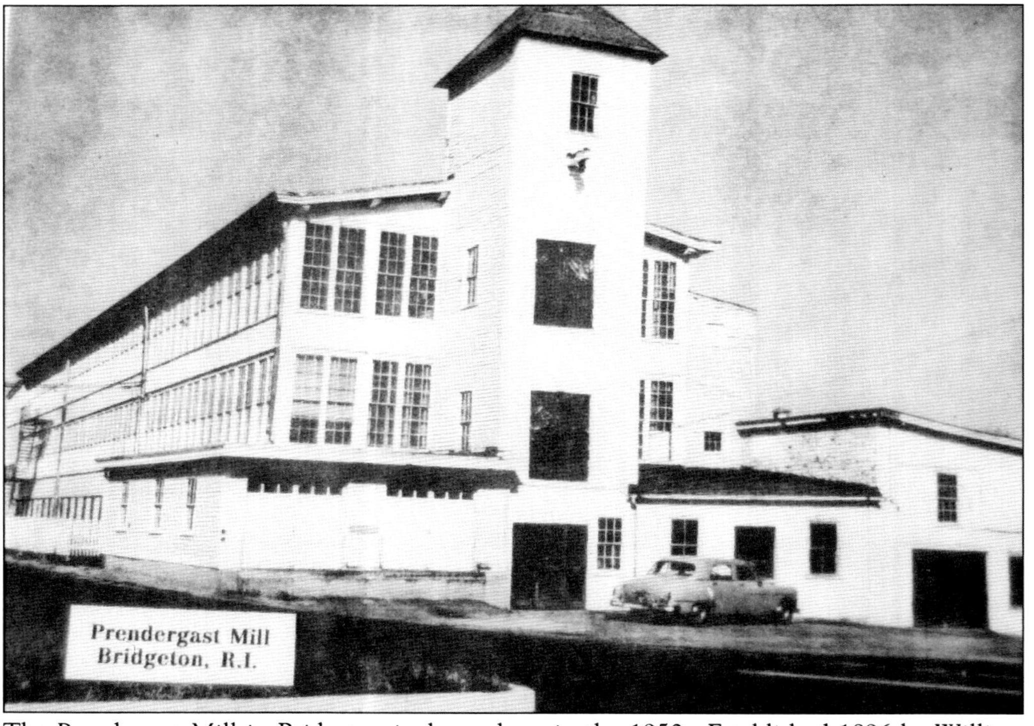

The Prendergast Mill in Bridgeton is shown here in the 1950s. Established 1896 by William H. Prendergast, it employed about 160 workers making fancy worsteds. The mill was destroyed by fire in 1969. In October 1993 the present White Mill Park was dedicated by the Town of Burrillville.

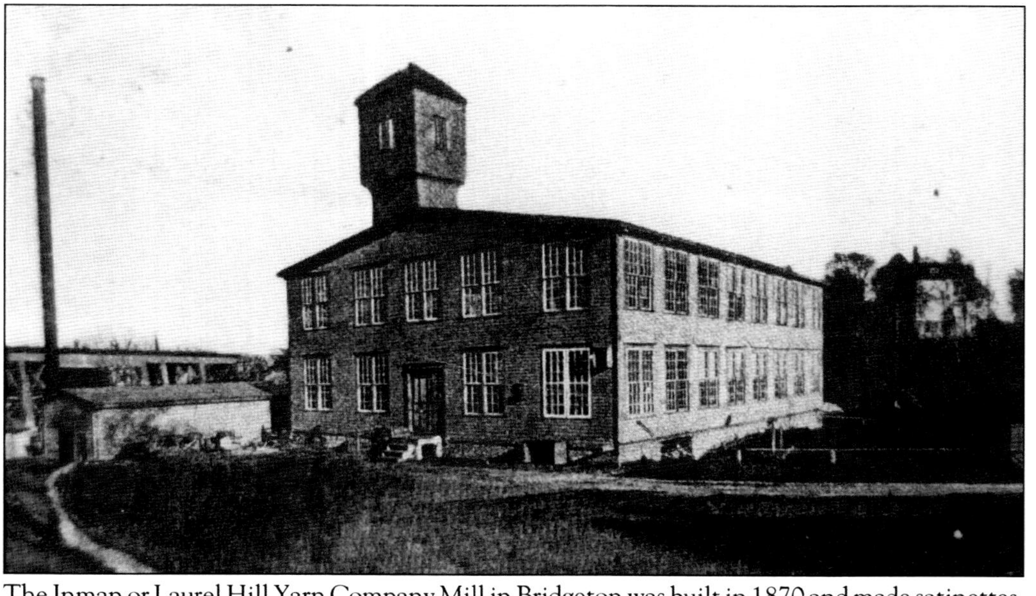

The Inman or Laurel Hill Yarn Company Mill in Bridgeton was built in 1870 and made satinettes. This 1893 building manufactured shoddy and woolen yarn. The first mill was constructed here in January 1803. The railroad bridge is in the background.

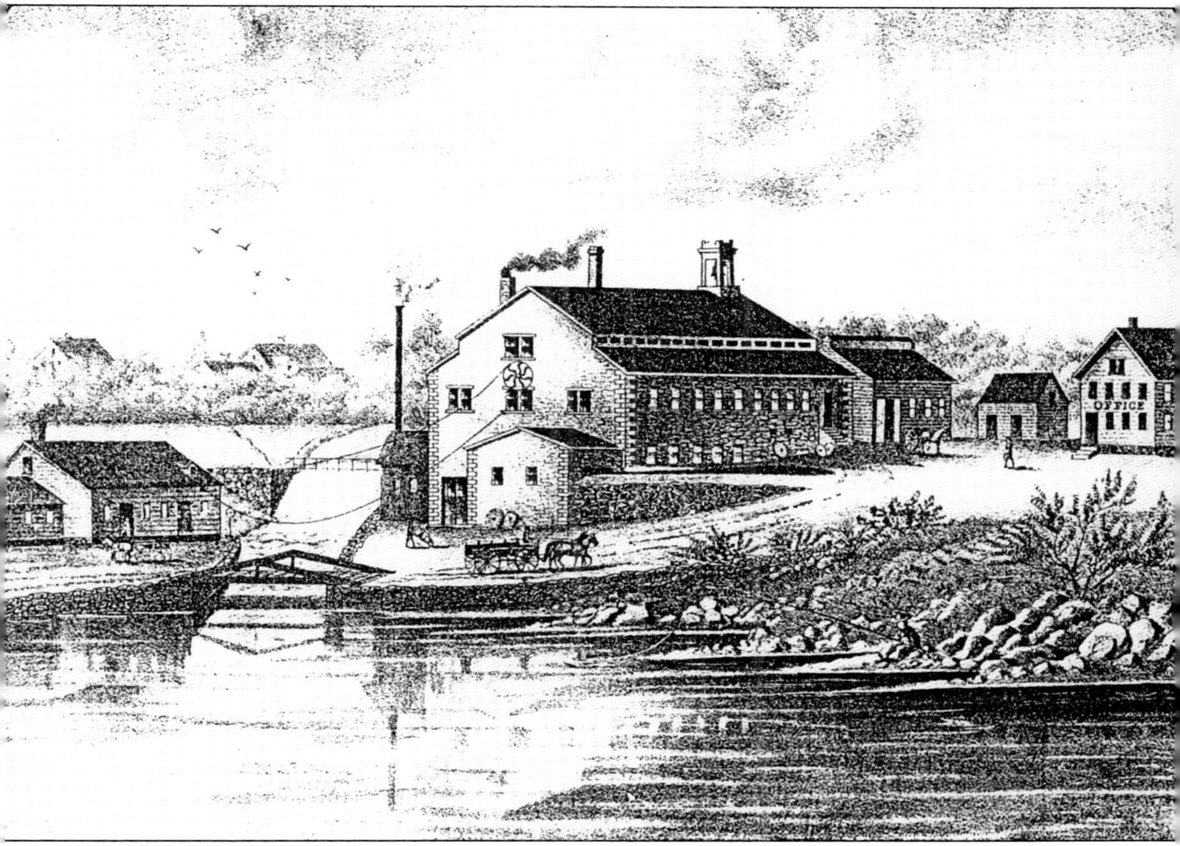

Hopkins Machine Works in Bridgeton started in 1831 and manufactured spindles and all types of machinery for the woolen manufacturers. Mr. Hopkins held many patents for the machines used in processing wool at that time, including the patent for the "Acme Spindle."

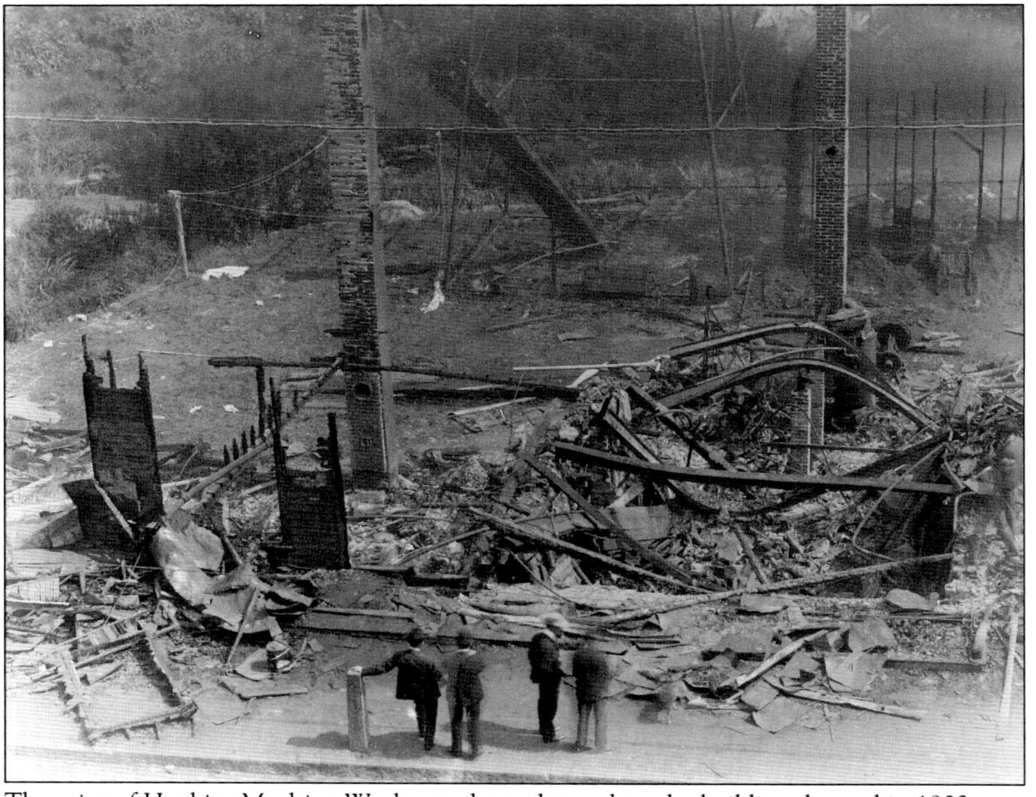

The ruins of Hopkins Machine Works are shown here when the buildings burned in 1903.

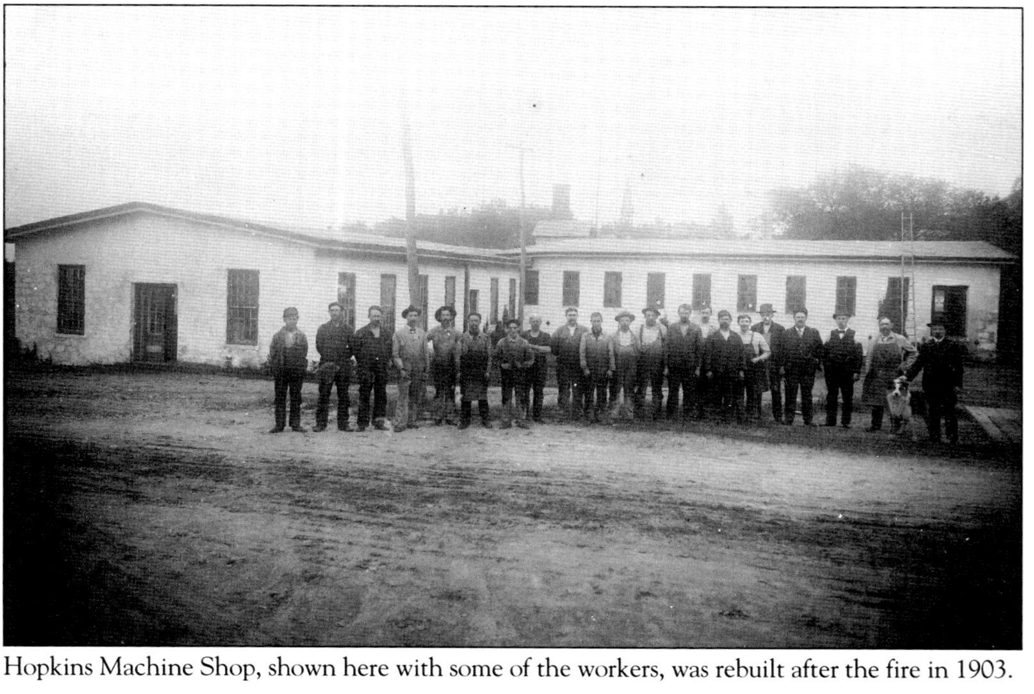

Hopkins Machine Shop, shown here with some of the workers, was rebuilt after the fire in 1903.

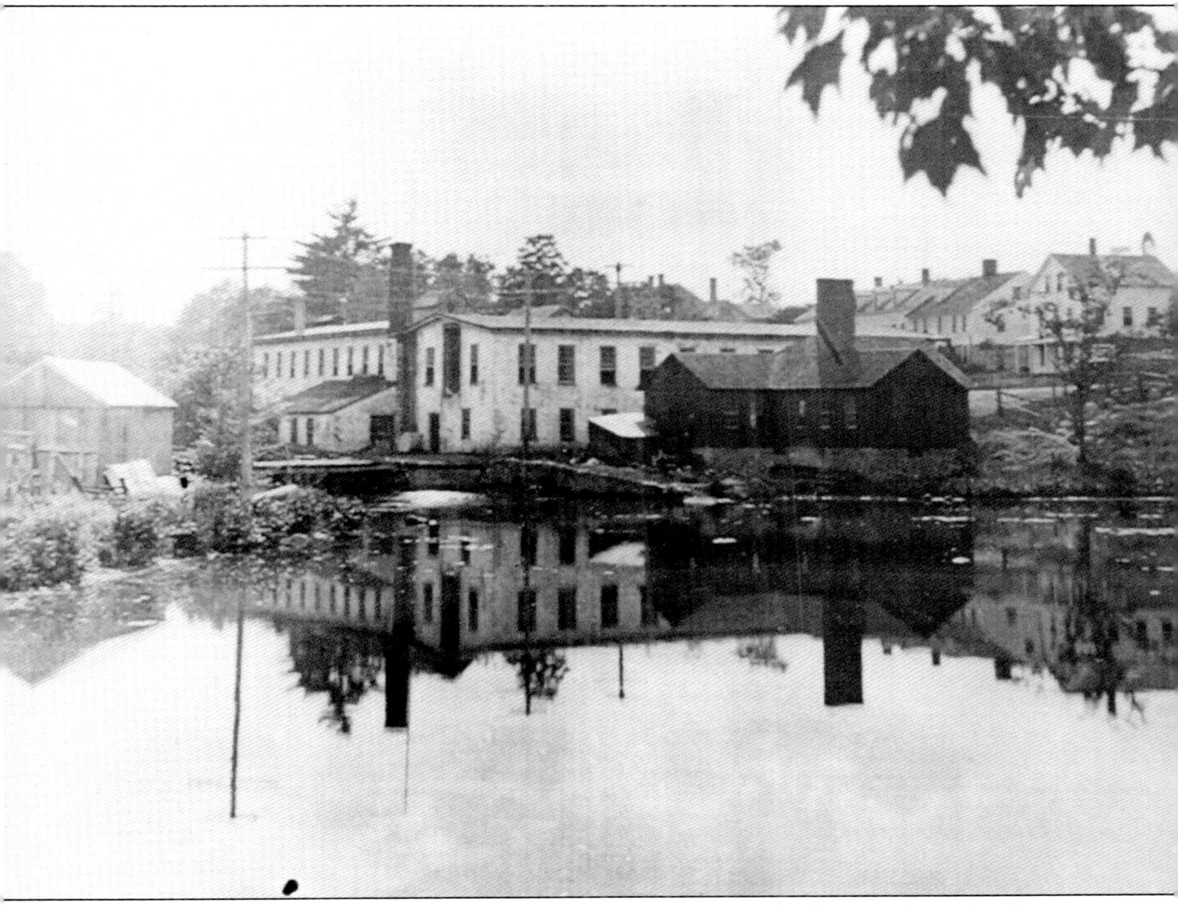

The Clear River Woolen mill on Grove Street in Pascoag was built around 1886, where it stood until it burned to the ground in March 1982. As early as 1793, there was a forge here. Kentucky jeans were manufactured in 1844, then fancy cassimeres, and in 1865 woolen goods were created here with the building of the stone mill.

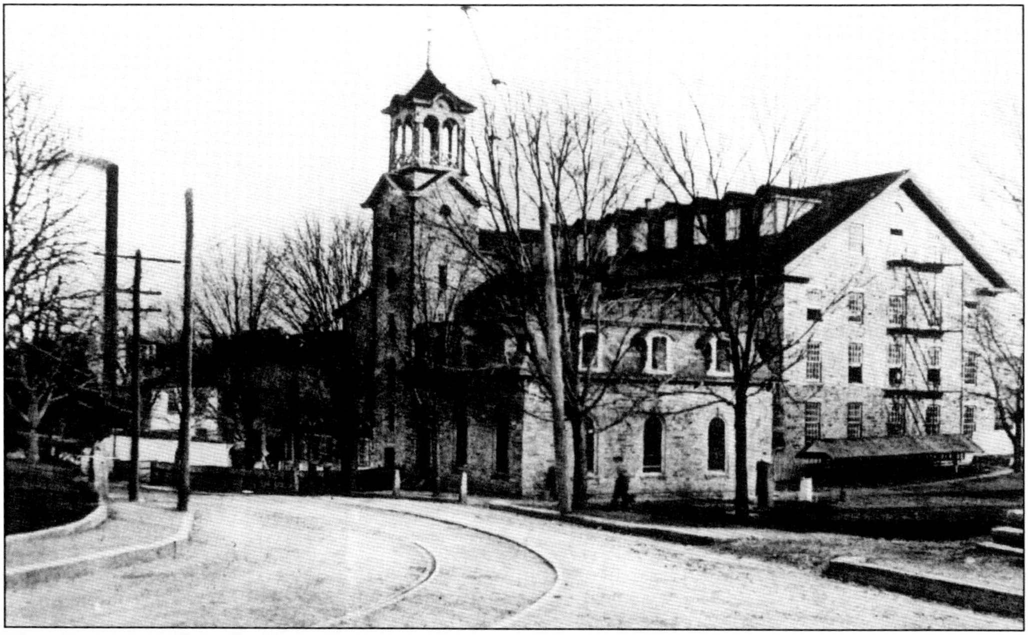

The Granite Mill and office, shown with the trolley tracks coming from Church Street visible, was destroyed by arsonists in May 1981. Plans had been made to renovate the mill into apartments for the elderly.

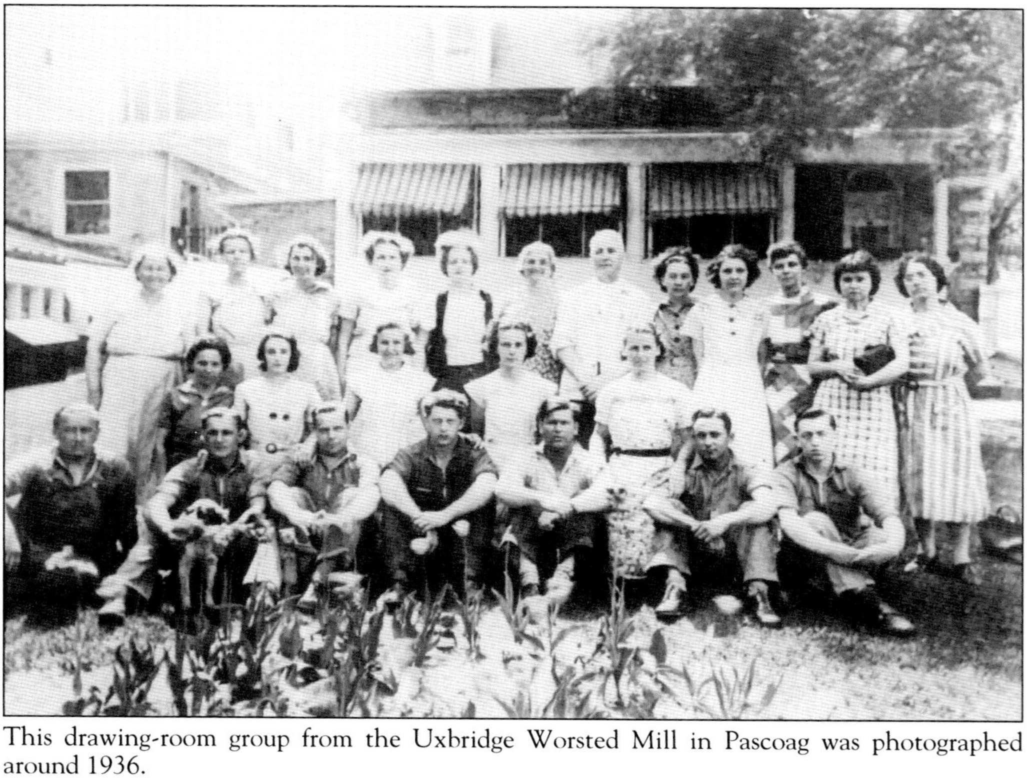

This drawing-room group from the Uxbridge Worsted Mill in Pascoag was photographed around 1936.

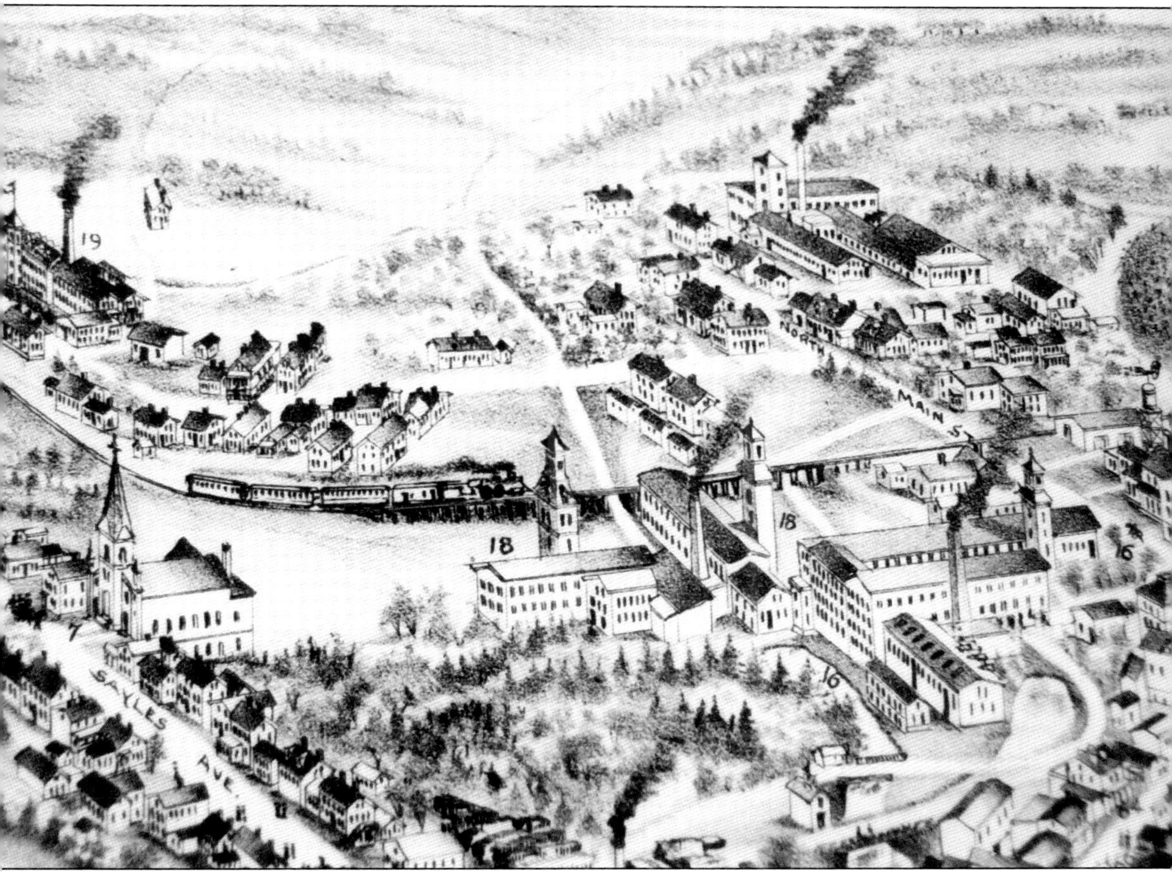

An overview of the Anchor, Lincoln, and Premier Mills from the 1895 *Pascoag Herald* map. The railroad train is passing over the trestle near the Anchor Mill at North Main Street in Pascoag. On the upper right is the Magner Brothers Mill. St. Joseph's Church on Sayles Avenue is on the lower left.

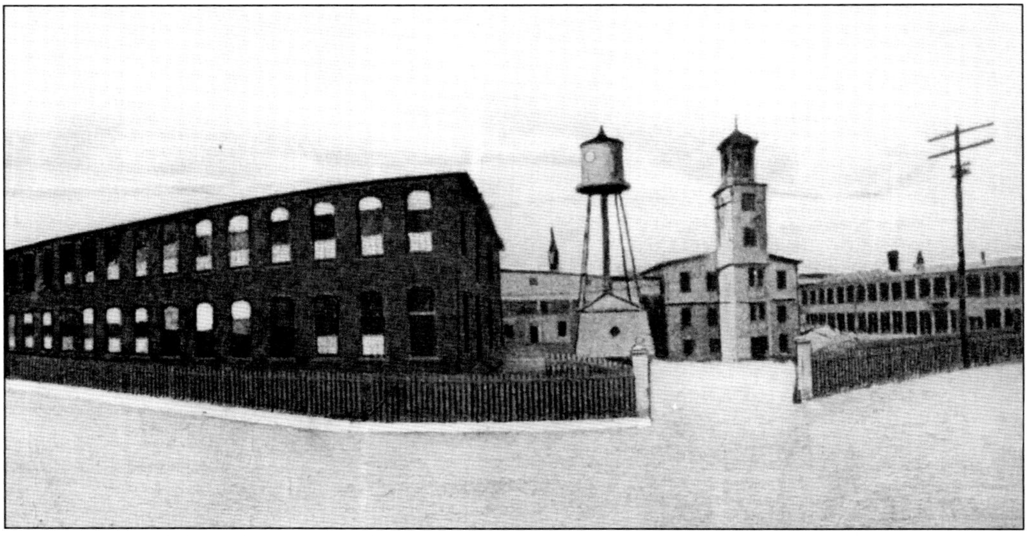

The Lincoln Mill was located at Herald Square in Pascoag. A cotton-spinning mill started here before 1807. In 1815, the Pas-cogue Cotton Spinning Factory operated at the site of the Lincoln Mill. In 1966 both properties were sold at auction for $5,000 and subsequently demolished.

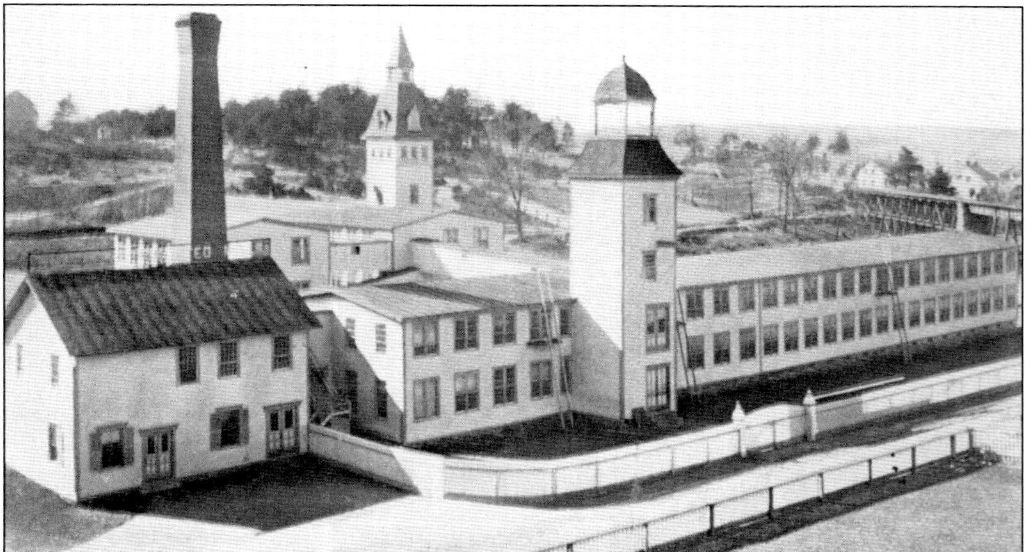

The Anchor Mills were located in Pascoag. A scythe factory was on this site in 1832, then a cotton mill, and later a woolen mill. The large mill was constructed in 1887 employing 124 workers. By 1895, 5,000 yards of woolen goods were shipped from here a week.

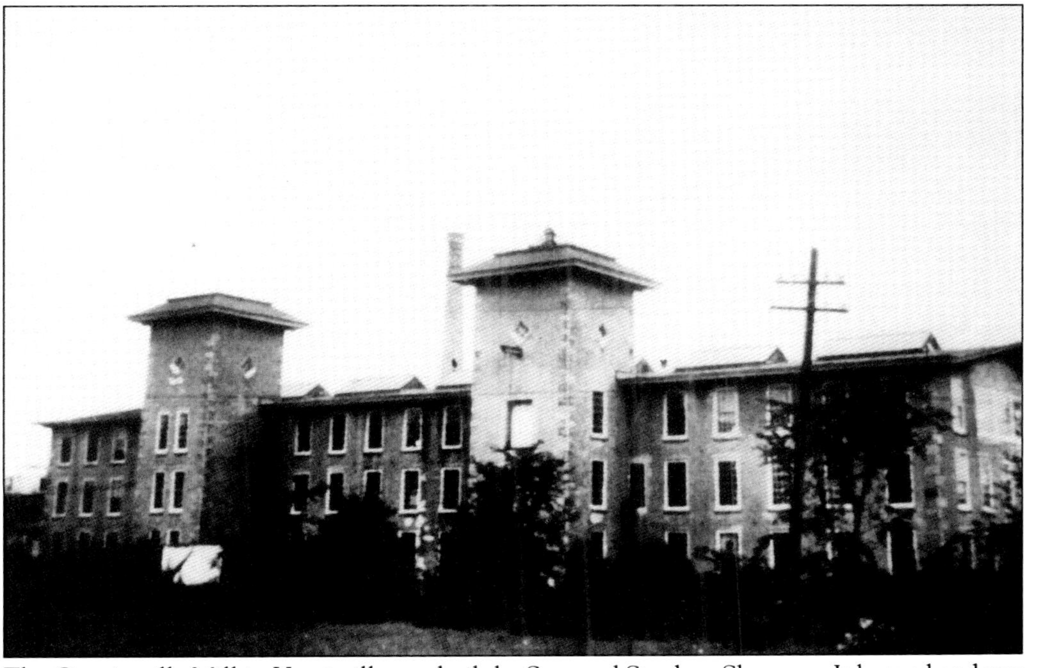

The Graniteville Mill in Harrisville was built by Syra and Stephen Sherman. It burned and was rebuilt in 1882, with sufficient housing to accommodate the workers. Later used for storage by Stillwater, it was taken down for safety reasons in the 1980s.

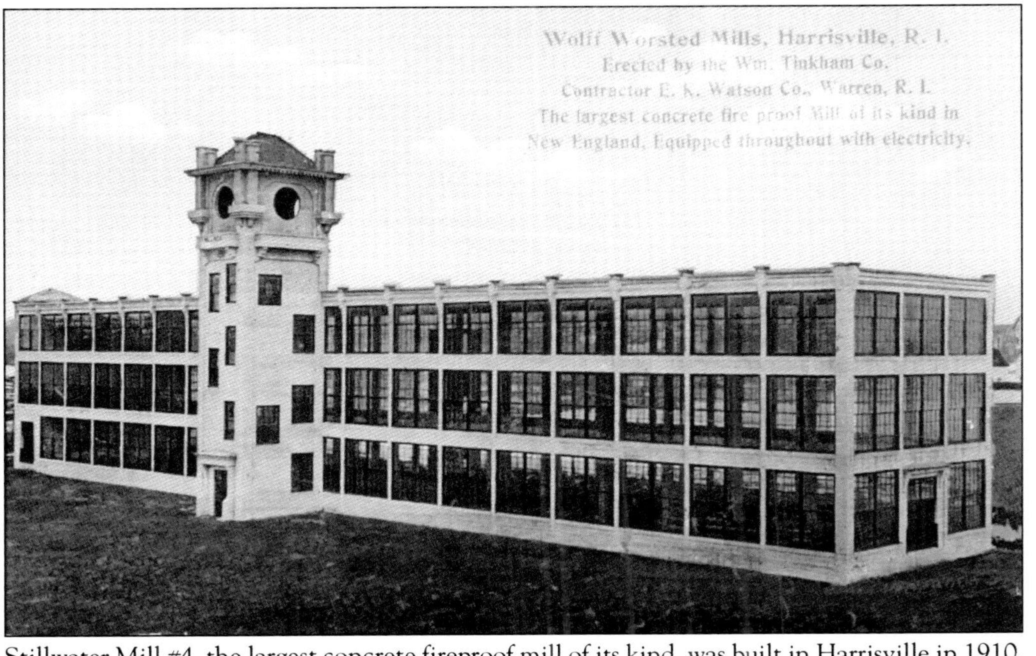

Stillwater Mill #4, the largest concrete fireproof mill of its kind, was built in Harrisville in 1910. Two hundred railroad boxcars of cement were used to construct it. It is one of the few mill buildings still standing in Burrillville.

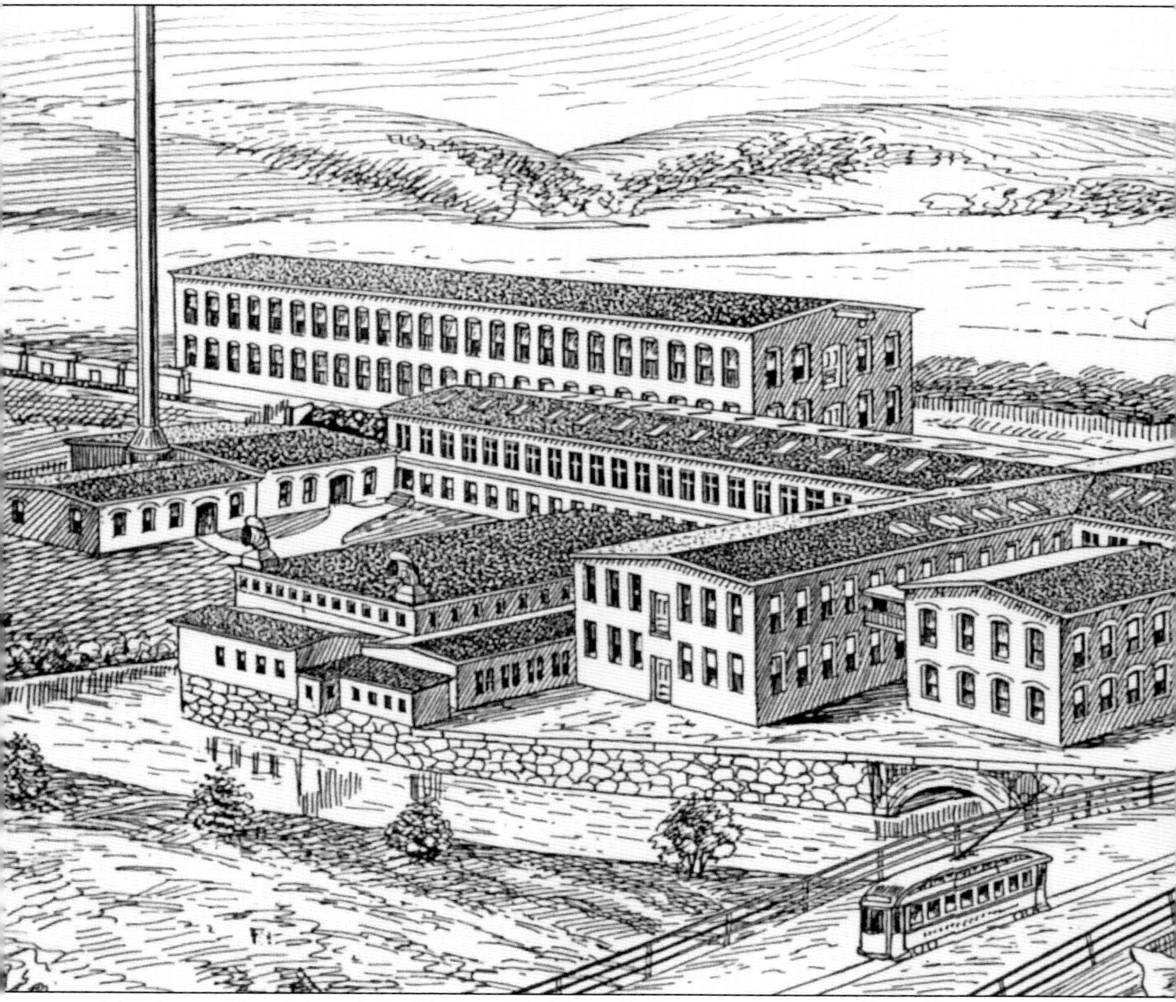

This is an old etching of the William Tinkham & Company's Harrisville mill. During the first part of the 1800s the locality was known as Rhodesville, named after Captain William Rhodes, who owned considerable land and other property in the village. He acquired his wealth as the commander of a privateer during the Revolutionary War by capturing English vessels on their way to the West Indies laden with sugar and molasses. He had a saw and grist mill as well as a

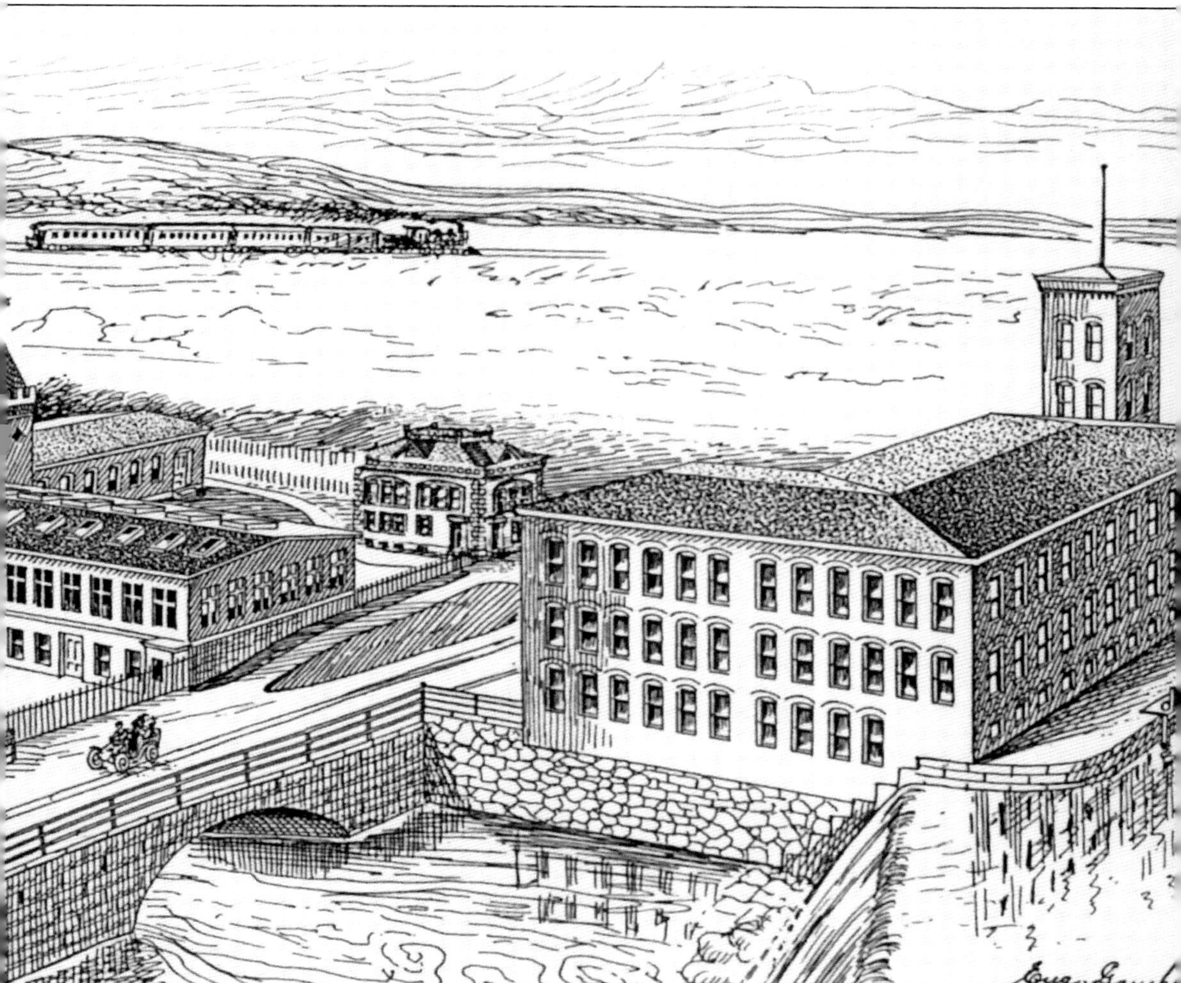

general store on the mill site, and built a large house for a residence. Andrew Harris purchased Mr. Rhodes' assets and started shops for the manufacture of spindles and flyers, built a cotton mill about 1820, and continued to operate the saw and grist mills already on the mill privilege. Harris died in 1844 and Steere and Tinkham purchased the mill property in 1856.

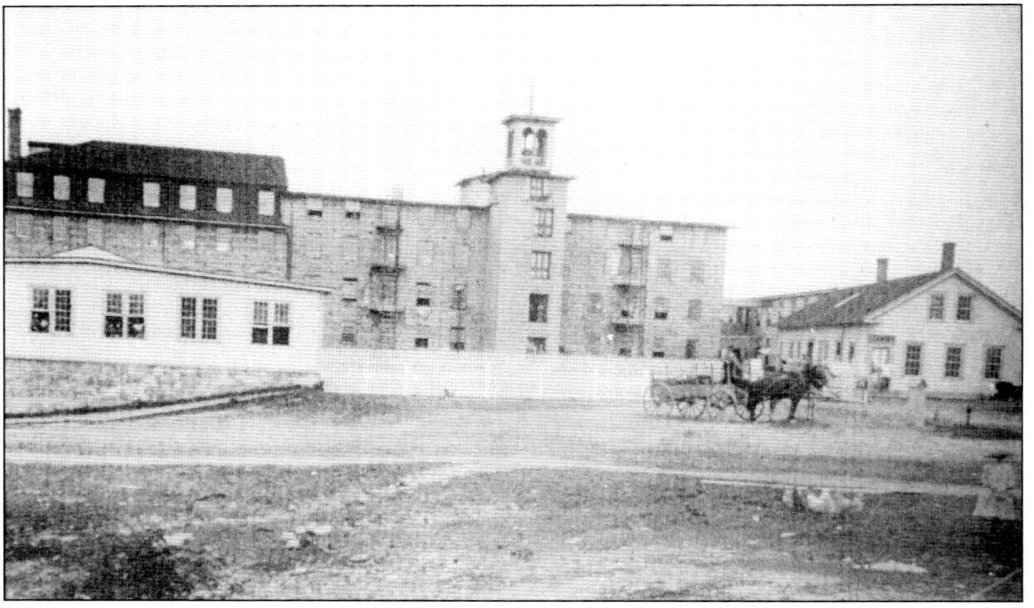

Five buildings of the Tinkham Mills in Harrisville were on this site by 1893 for the manufacture of fancy worsted cloth. Mr. Tinkham's son Ernest leased the business in 1912 to the Stillwater Worsted Company.

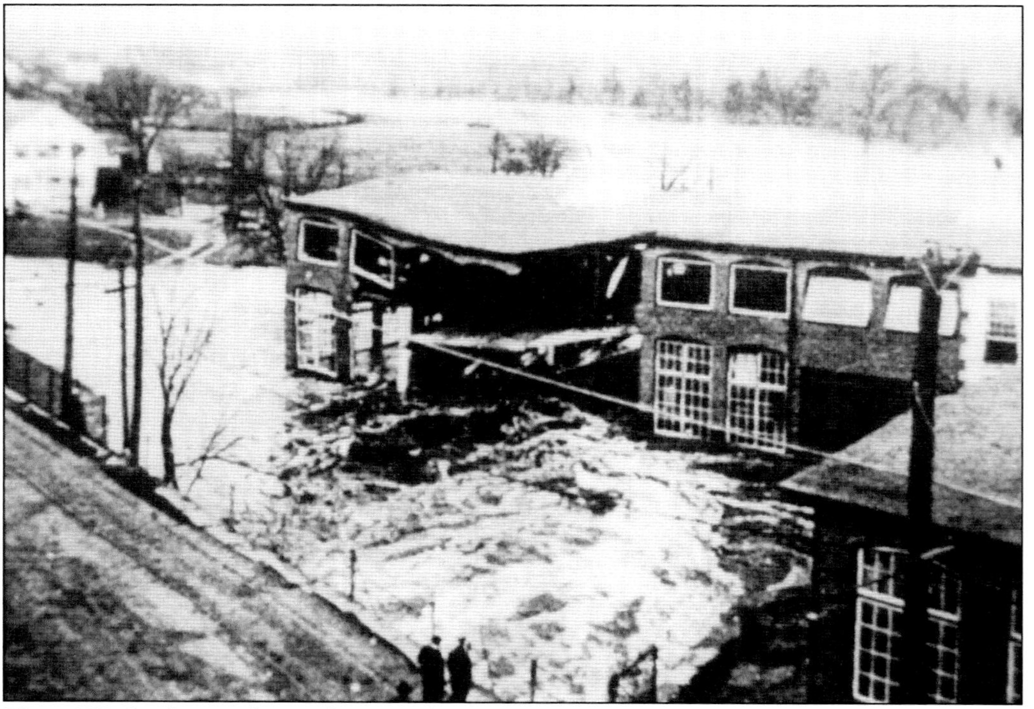

The 1927 flood caused a washout at the Stillwater Mills. Keyes Bailey was in this building rescuing materials and left just before it collapsed into the Clear River.

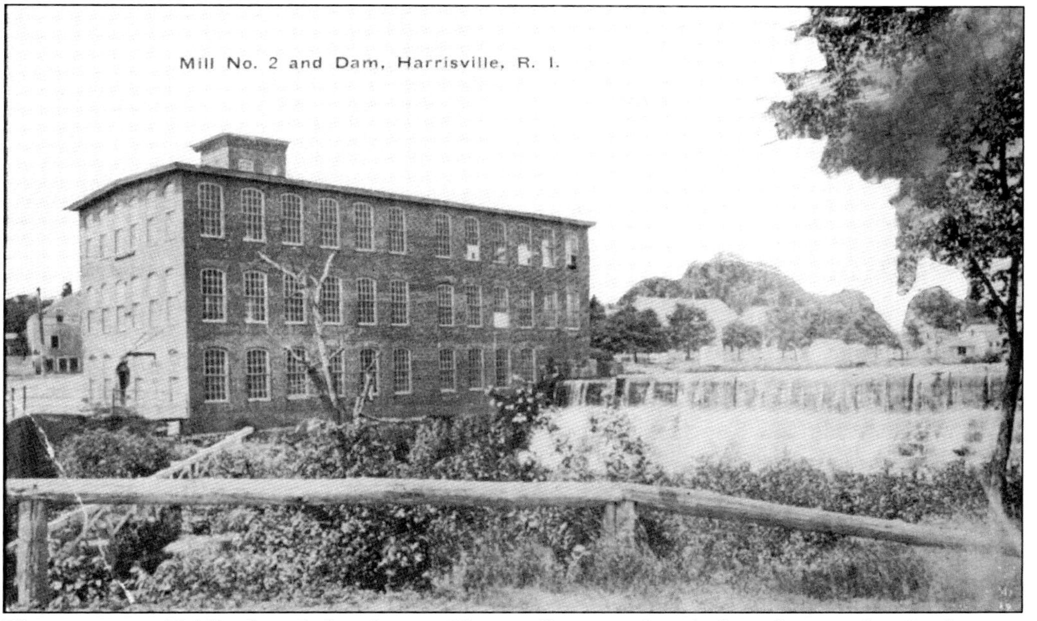

This picture of Mill #2 and the dam at Harrisville was taken before the wooden bridge was replaced by the Stone Arch Bridge.

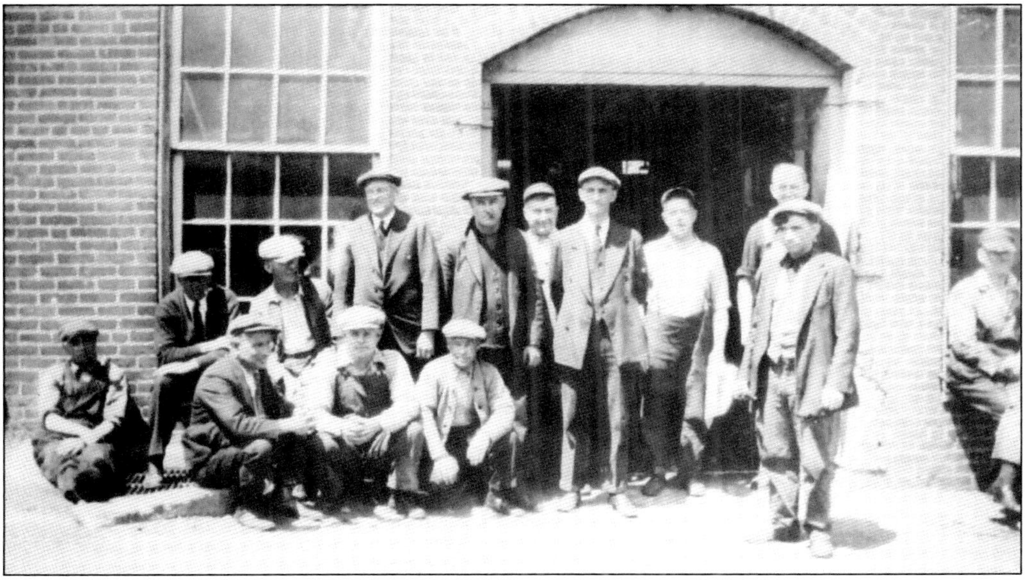

A group of mechanics from Mill #2 in Harrisville were photographed in 1928. From left to right are: (front row) Edward Bailey, John Steere, and Adelbert Angell; (back row) James Shaw, John Wetherbee, James Seath, J. Gordon Dozier, Frank Shippee, Archie Brown, George Lovell, Manton Browne, Charles Tourtellotte, and Julian Kesteloot.

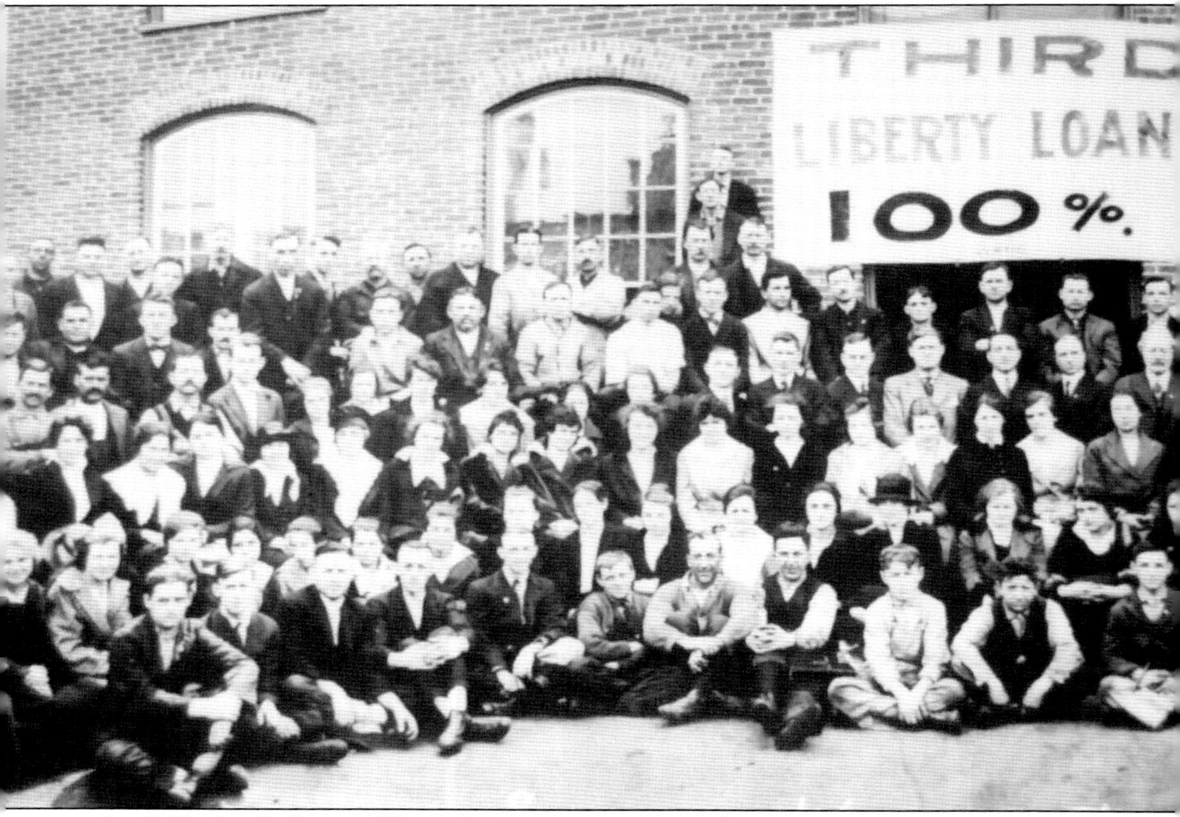

In 1918 the Stillwater Worsted Co., Inc. in Harrisville celebrated the employees 100% participation in the drive for Liberty Bonds to support America's efforts in World War I. Burrillville mills contributed blankets and uniform cloth to soldiers in the Civil War, World War I, and World War II. By 1855 there were twenty-two woolen establishments and two cotton factories in Burrillville. As the mills grew, so did the villages around them. In several instances, mill owners built homes for their employees and company stores to serve them. Local

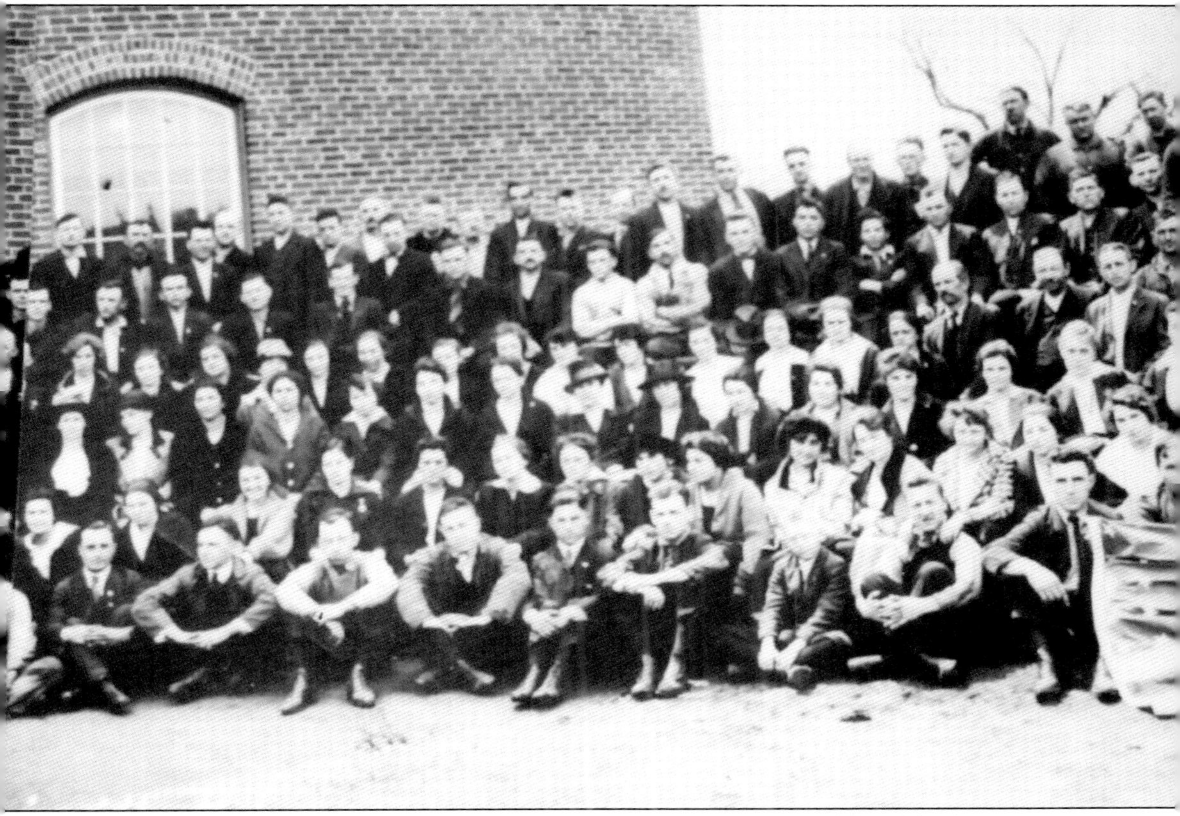

farmers were the first workers, then the Irish came, and toward the middle of the last century, French Canadian workers were prominent in the local mills. All were assimilated into the village populations and continued with pride in their accomplishments to make Burrillville what it was—a booming mill town.

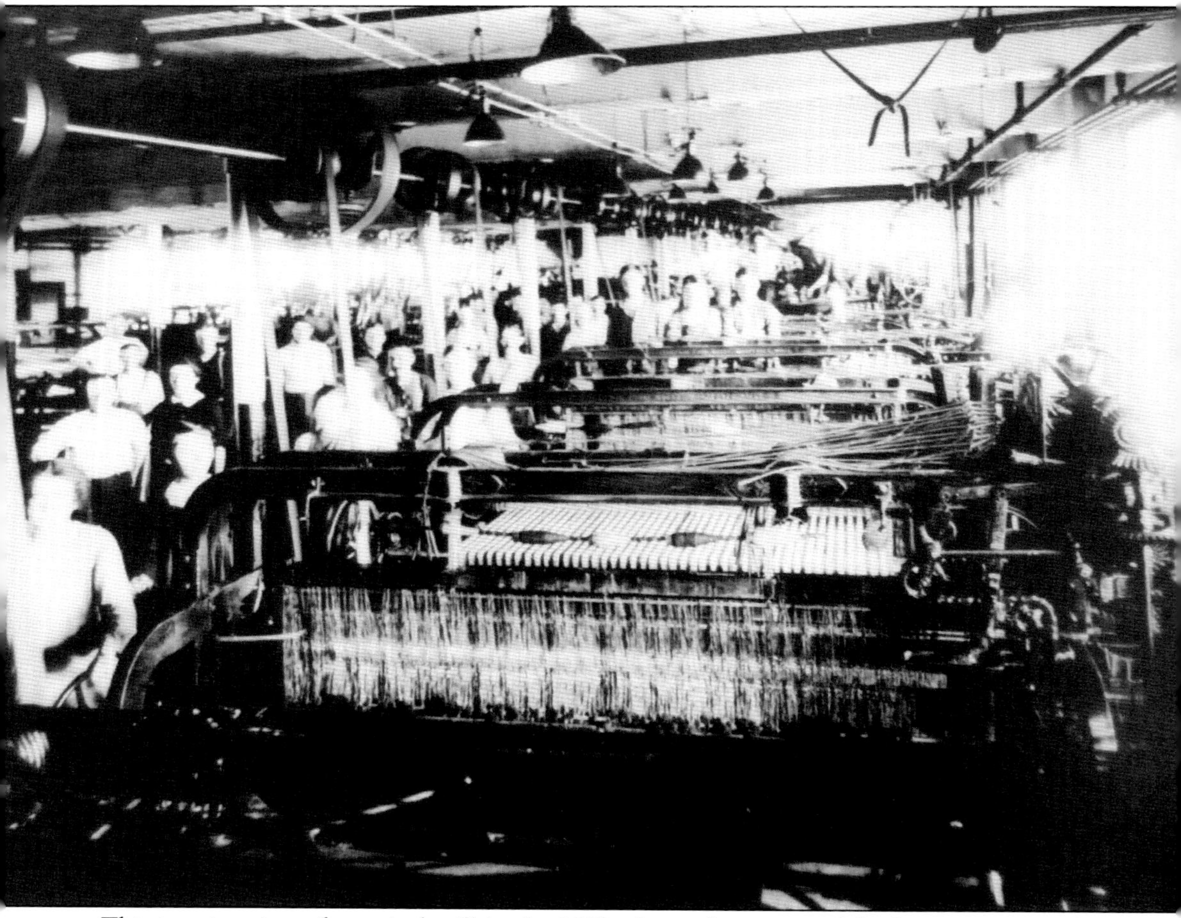

This interior view of a typical mill in the 1920s shows the extent of the looms. In 1895 there were 15 mills in operation, using 772 various kinds of looms, making Burrillville one of the most active mill towns in the state.

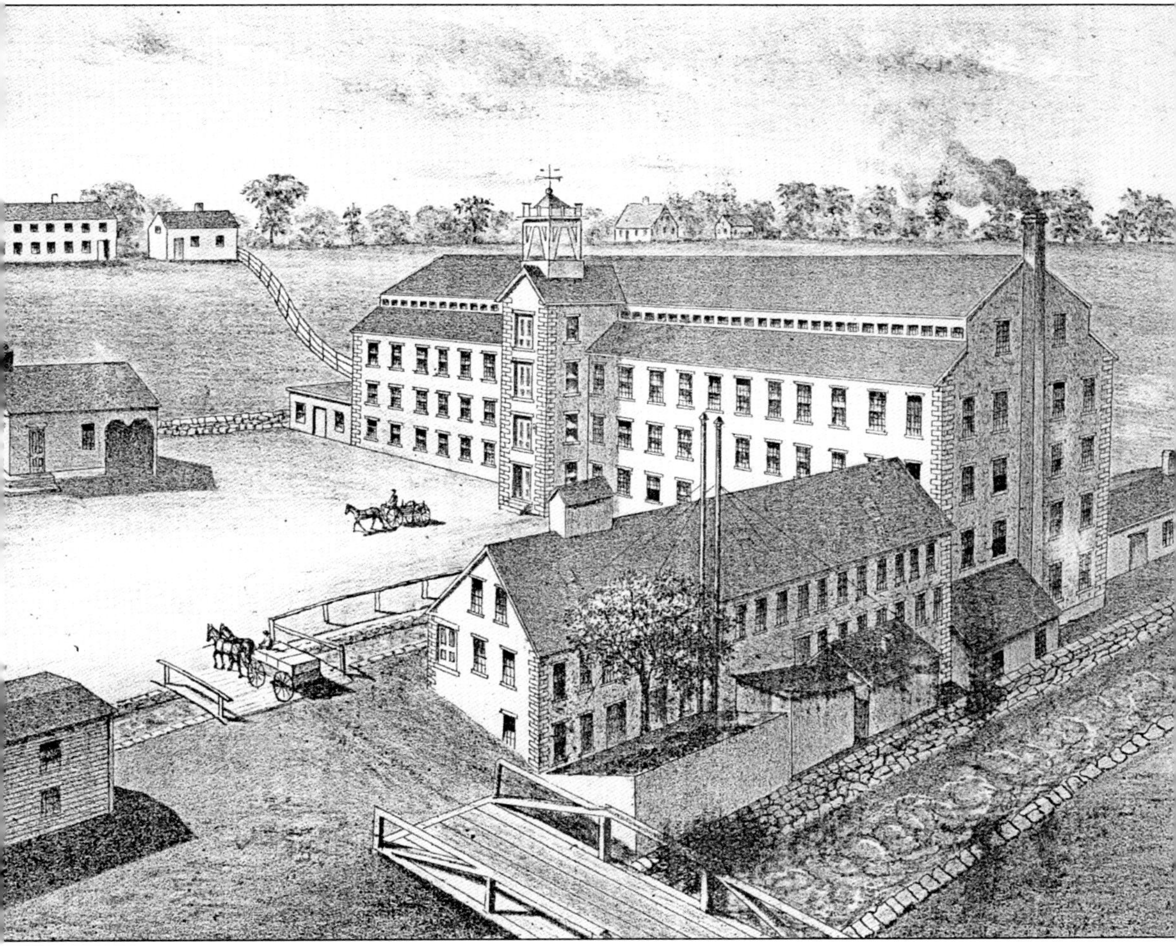

The original water privilege in the area of the Glendale Mill (shown here) went from Jirah Ballou to Arnold Smith in 1785. The dam was built along with a saw mill, corn mill, and other water works. A cotton mill began operating in 1841, and in 1853 woolens were manufactured here. William Orrell purchased the mill in 1889 and completely rebuilt it. In 1895 it contained 9 sets of cards, 42 looms, and 2,500 spindles, and 150 people were employed manufacturing 25,000 yards of cloth a month.

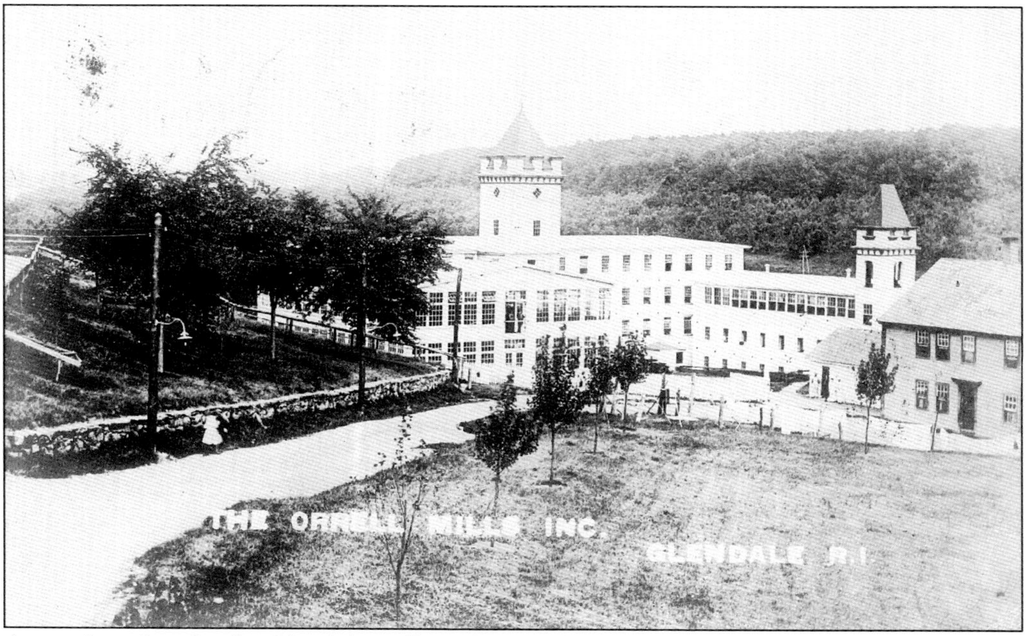

Austin Levy bought the Glendale Mill site from William Orrell in 1934. He sold it to Brisbane Fabrics, Inc. in 1960.

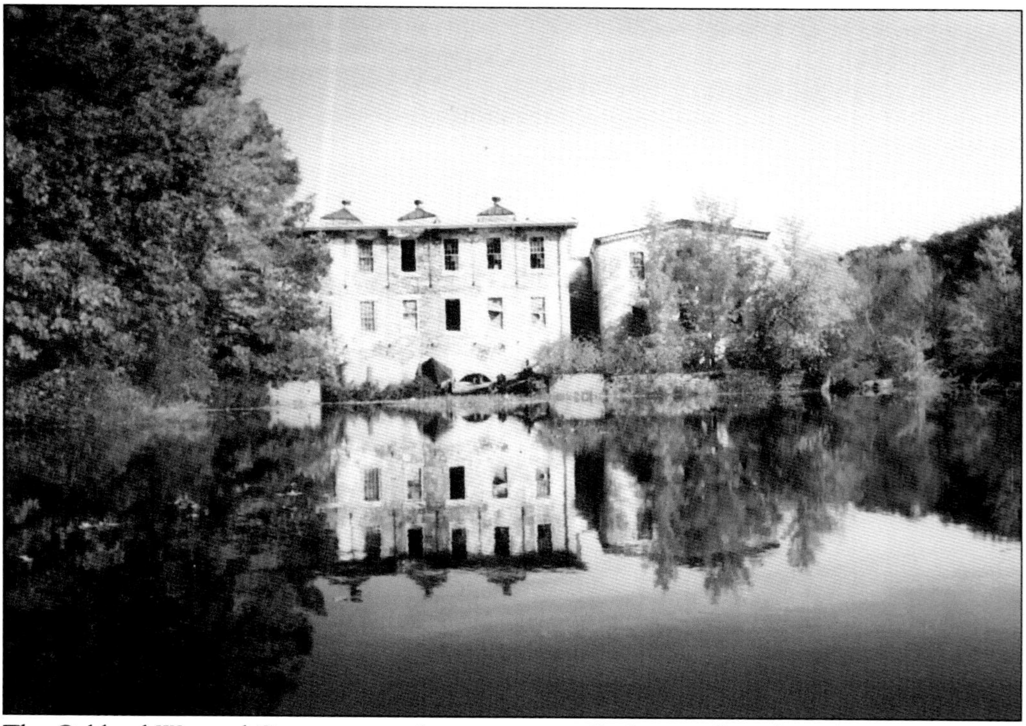

The Oakland Worsted Company was first a cotton mill, then a silk mill, and finally a woolen mill. The dam was built in 1848 and the first mill in 1850. The Clear River joins the Chepachet River here and forms the Branch, which, in turn, meets the Blackstone.

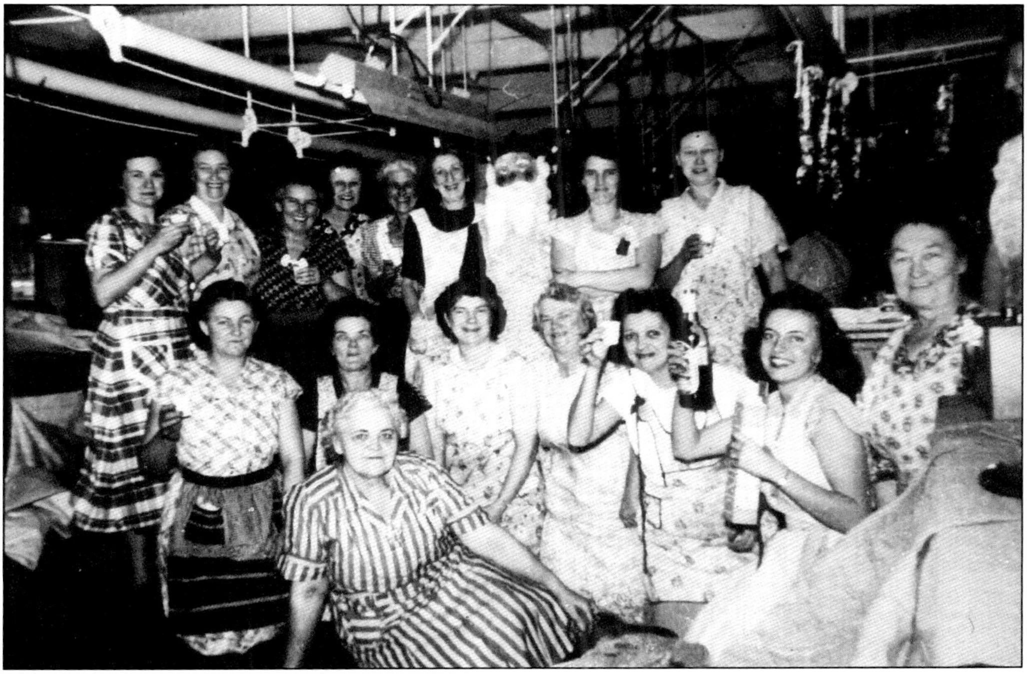

These Oakland Mill workers were photographed in 1949. In 1987 the whole of Oakland Village received the distinction of being put on the National Register of Historic Places because of its visual conception of a typical mill village. From the 1890s onward, Oakland has changed very little in its appearance.

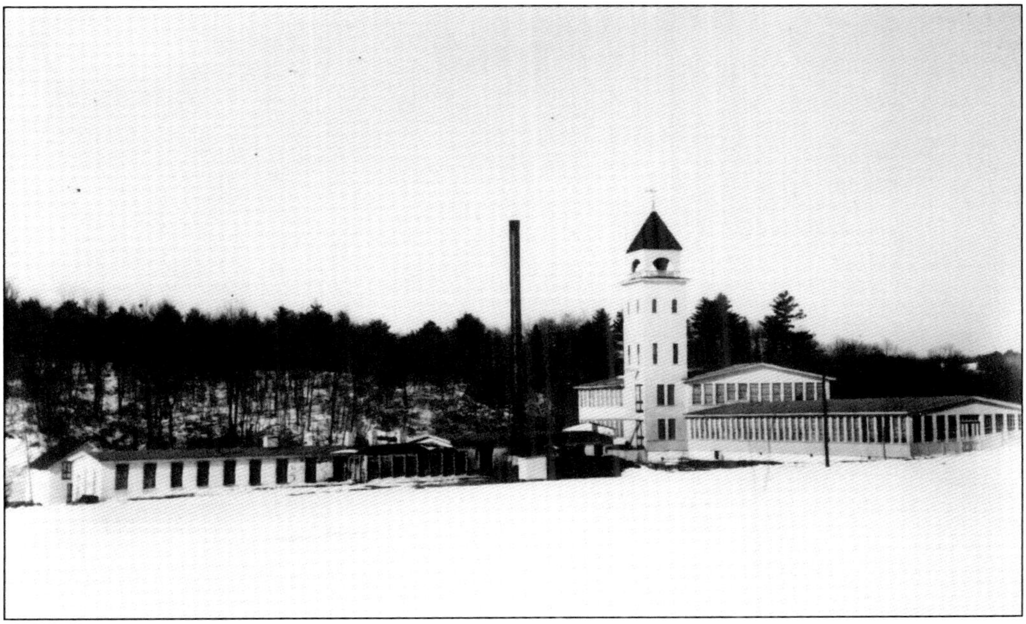

In 1824, water power was used to manufacture scythes on this site. During the Civil War, the Mohegan Mill (shown here) made Army cloth at the rate of 3,000 yards a week. In 1892 the mill burned but was rebuilt, and the Wanskuck Co. ran it from 1898 until it closed in 1954.

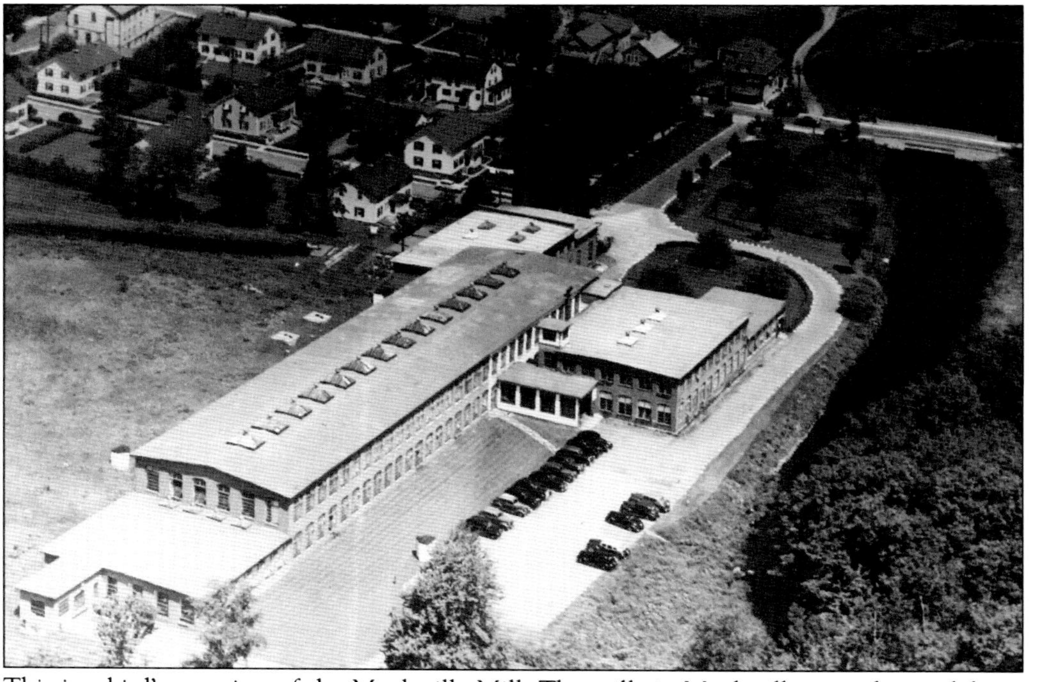

This is a bird's-eye view of the Mapleville Mill. The mills in Mapleville manufactured fancy woolens in 1857. In 1867, James Legg acquired the mills and built the large addition around 1871. In 1895 both mills combined produced 4,000 yards of fancy cassimeres and cheviots per week.

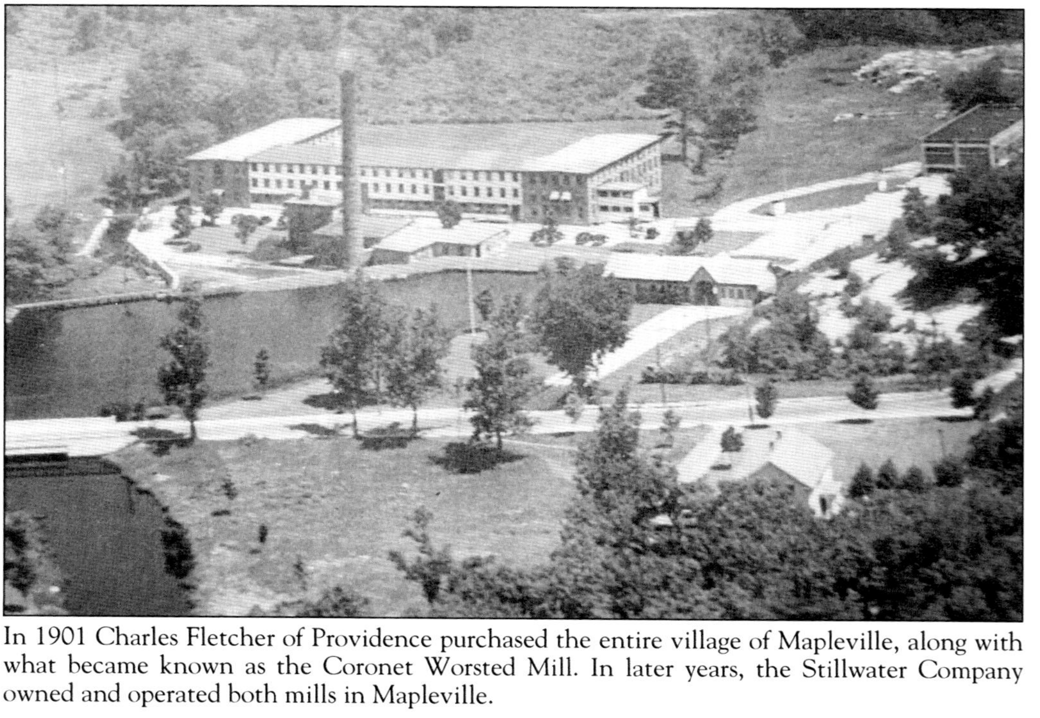

In 1901 Charles Fletcher of Providence purchased the entire village of Mapleville, along with what became known as the Coronet Worsted Mill. In later years, the Stillwater Company owned and operated both mills in Mapleville.

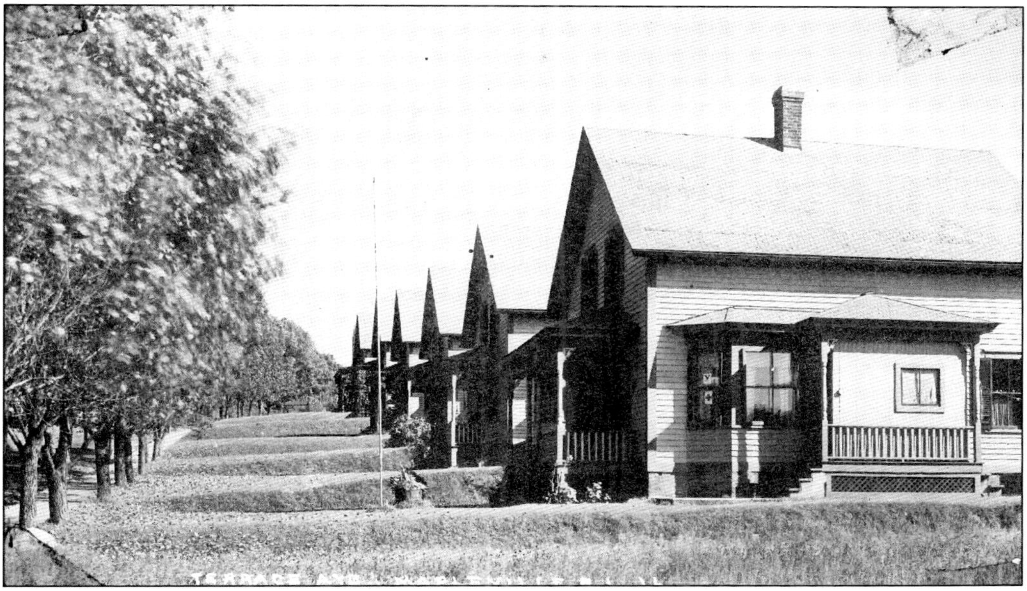

Fletcher built many of the houses in this view looking up Cottage Street, Mapleville. He had fifty-four tenements built for the workers around 1910.

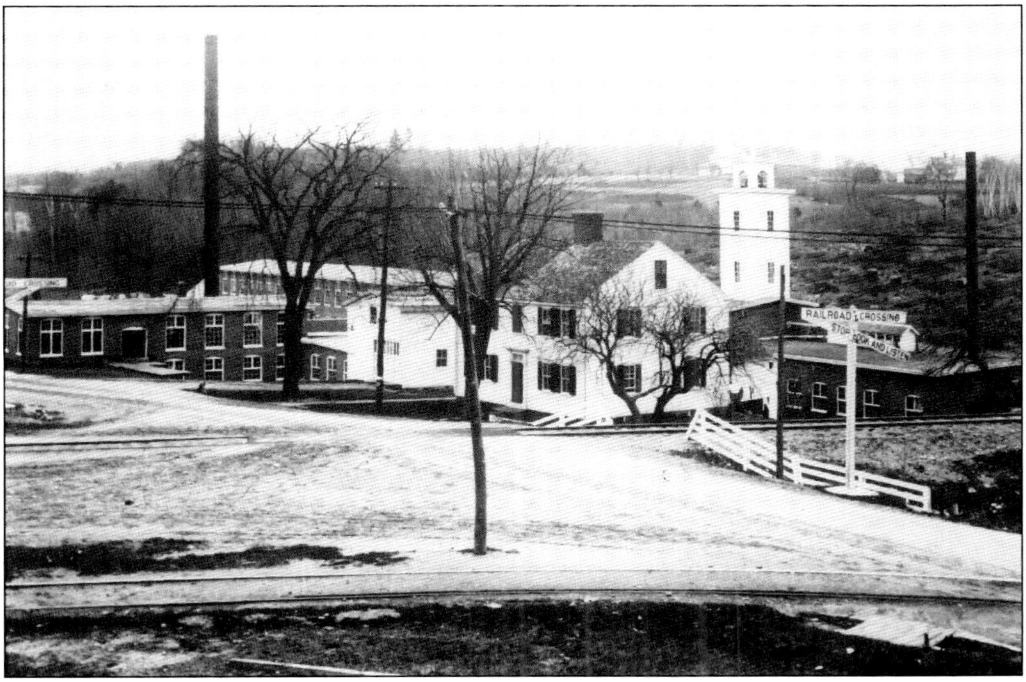

The first industry was founded by Leonard Nason in 1825, who bought and cleared the land, built a dam, trench, and race, erected a dwelling house, and put up a small mill for the manufacture of axes and hoes. By 1850, one thousand chopping axes and hoes a day were manufactured. The Nasonville Mill (shown here) was destroyed by fire in 1881 but was immediately rebuilt. Joshua Perkins manufactured cassimeres here, and Levy later ran it and sold out in 1959.

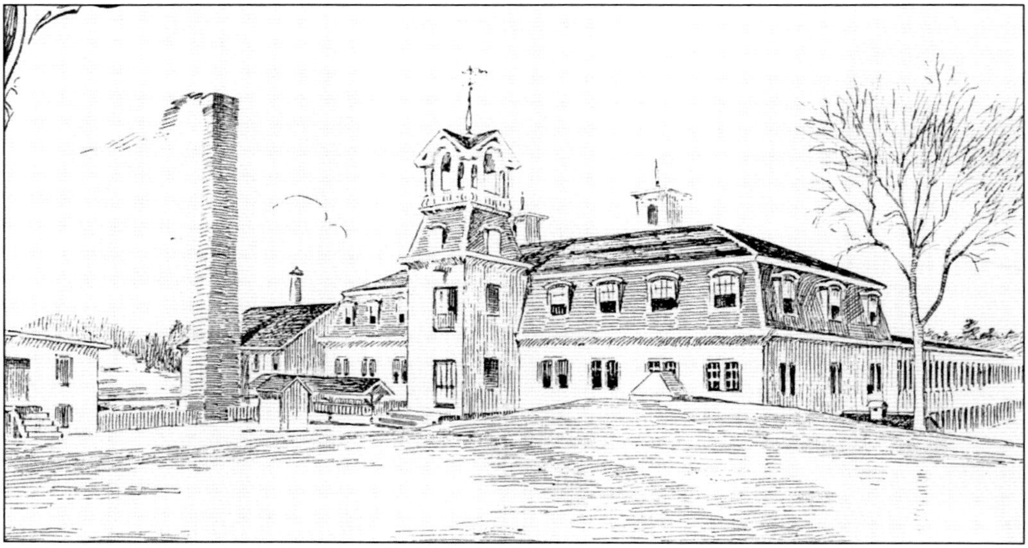

This 1895 etching of the Oak Valley Mill shows four mills, a tannery, a grist mill, and a saw mill in the Oak Valley-Tarkiln area. In 1810 a cotton mill was erected, and in 1856 a woolen mill was built near the Tarkiln Station. The Girard Woolen Company in Tarkiln ceased operations in 1935.

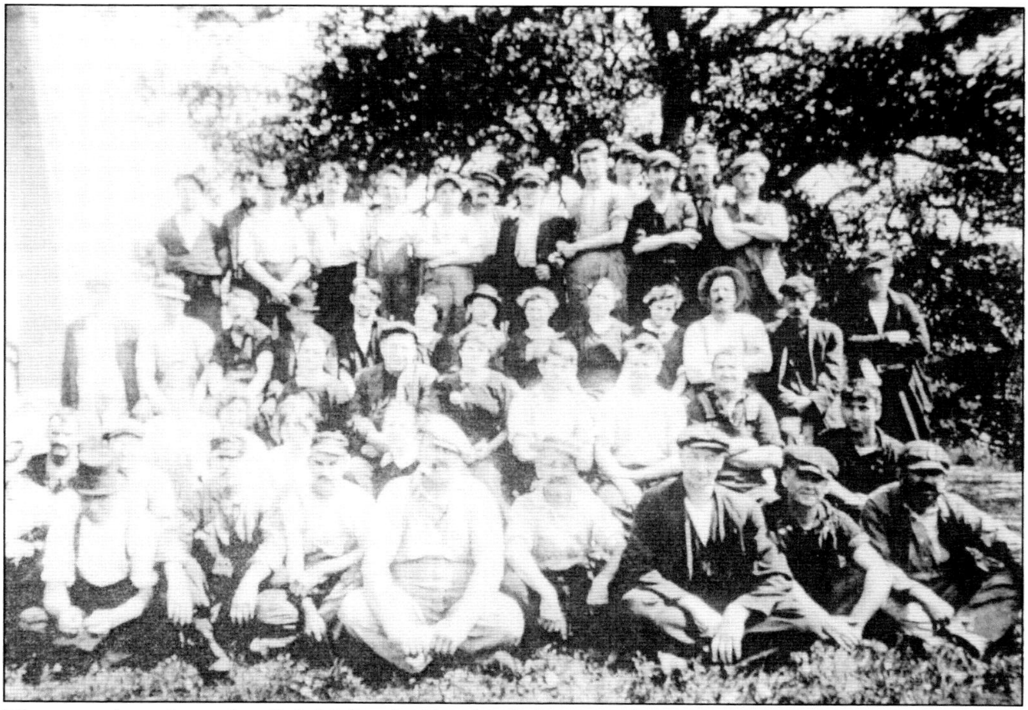

These workers from the Oak Valley Mill in Tarkiln were photographed in the early 1930s.

Three

Horses, Buggies, and More

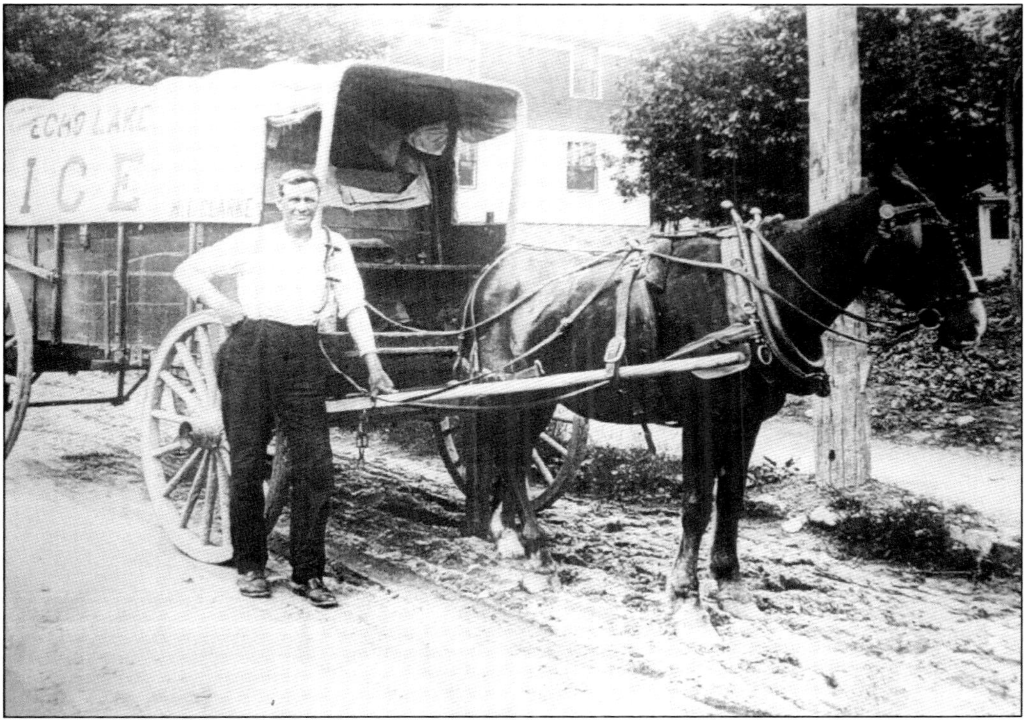

Homer Clarke delivered ice locally in his Ice Wagon for many years before selling out to Henry Jarvis, who continued the tradition.

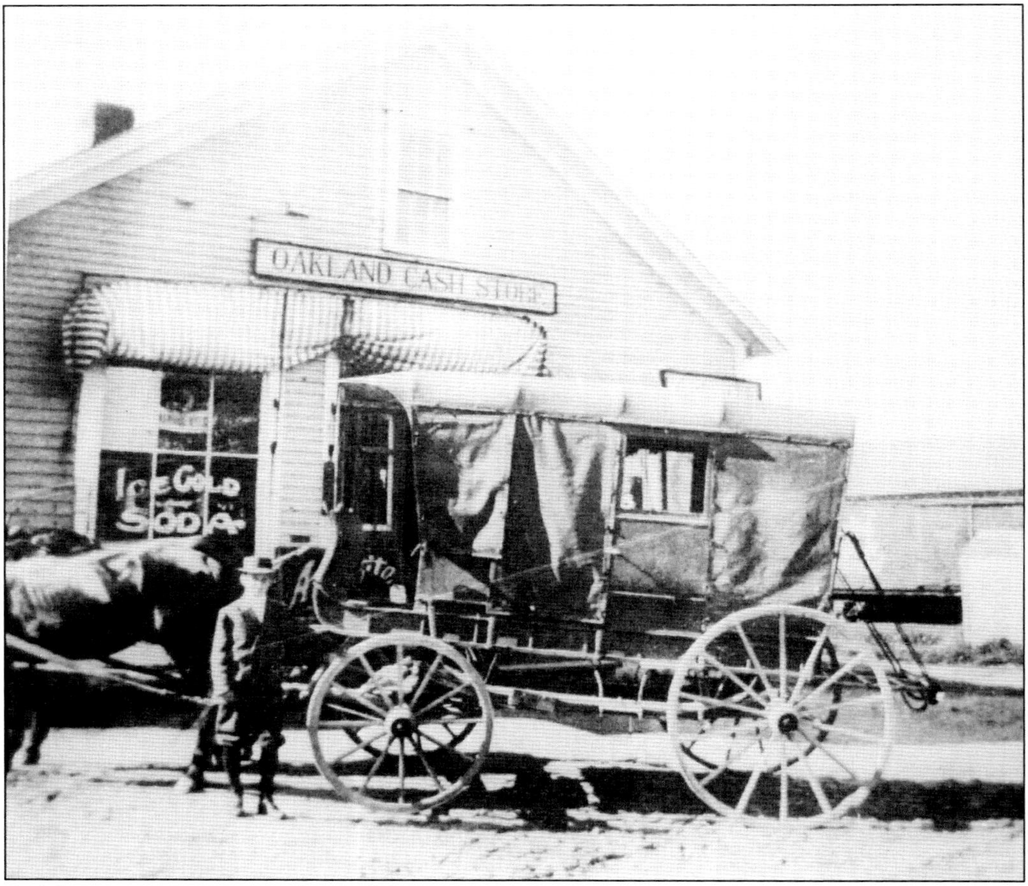

A delivery wagon waits in front of the Oakland Cash Store. This store was typical of the many small stores scattered throughout Burrillville in that it sold just about everything.

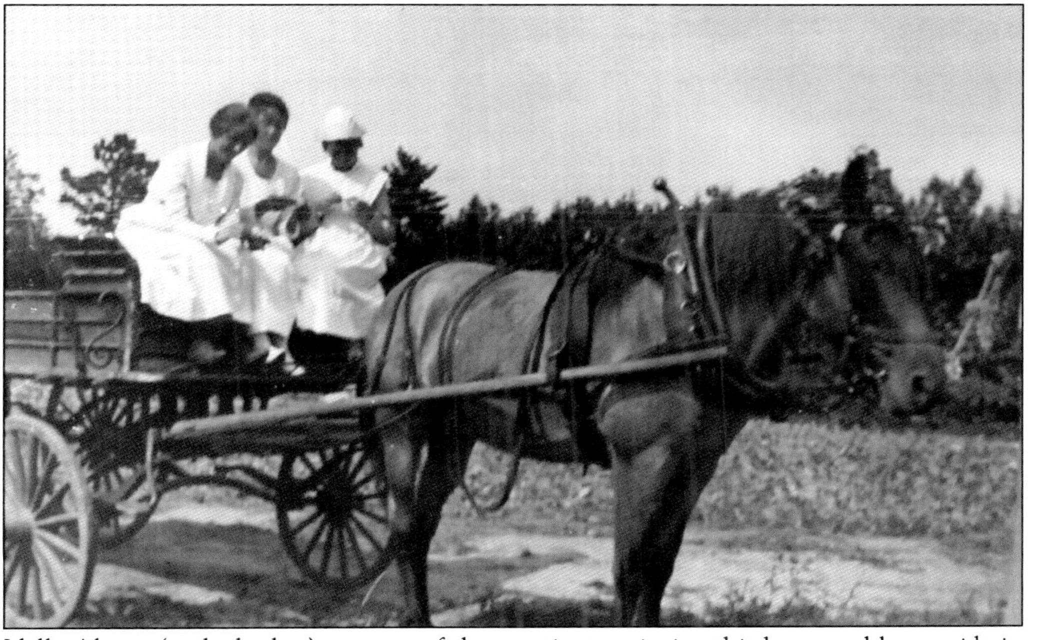

Idella Almon (with the hat) was one of three patients enjoying this horse and buggy ride in 1916. Patients at Wallum Lake had much more freedom in those days.

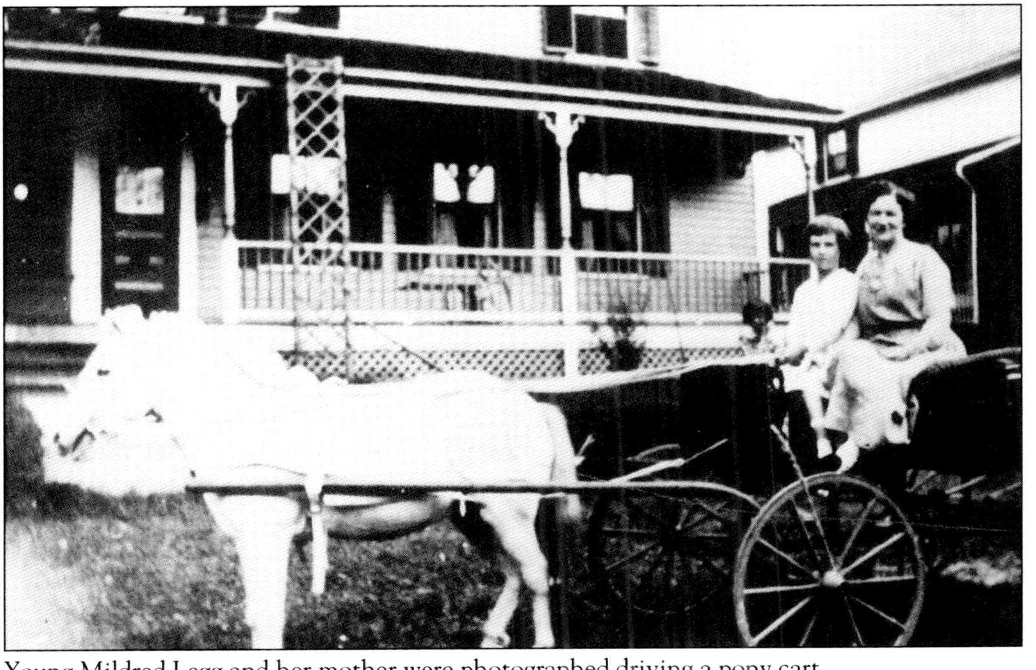

Young Mildred Legg and her mother were photographed driving a pony cart.

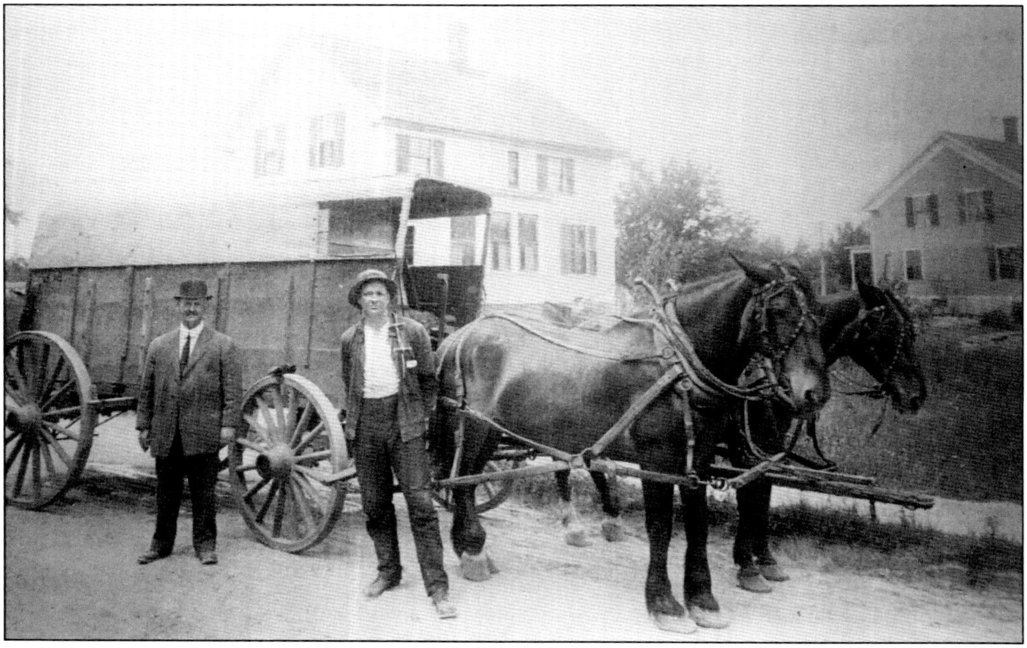

Milton Sherman recalled peddling meat and vegetables from a wagon for a local store from 7 am until 2 pm. His route was down the length of Church Street in Pascoag, up Broad Street, through Eagle Peak, and back to Bridgeton. Clarke's Delivery Wagon is shown here.

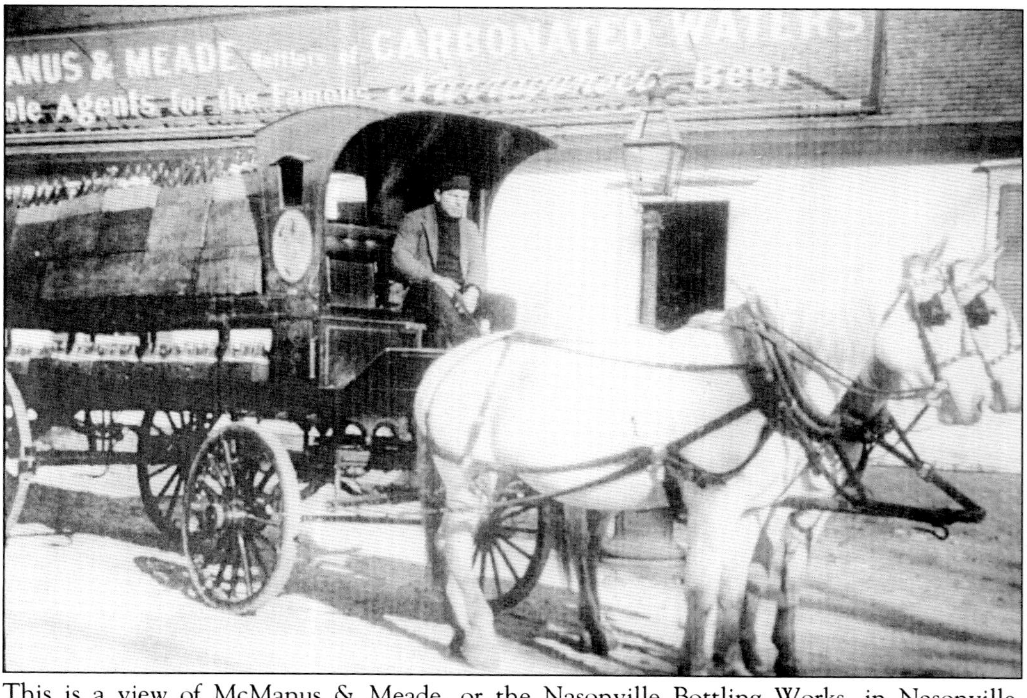

This is a view of McManus & Meade, or the Nasonville Bottling Works, in Nasonville. Soda was manufactured here until 1924 with the water supplied from a spring in back of the Western Hotel.

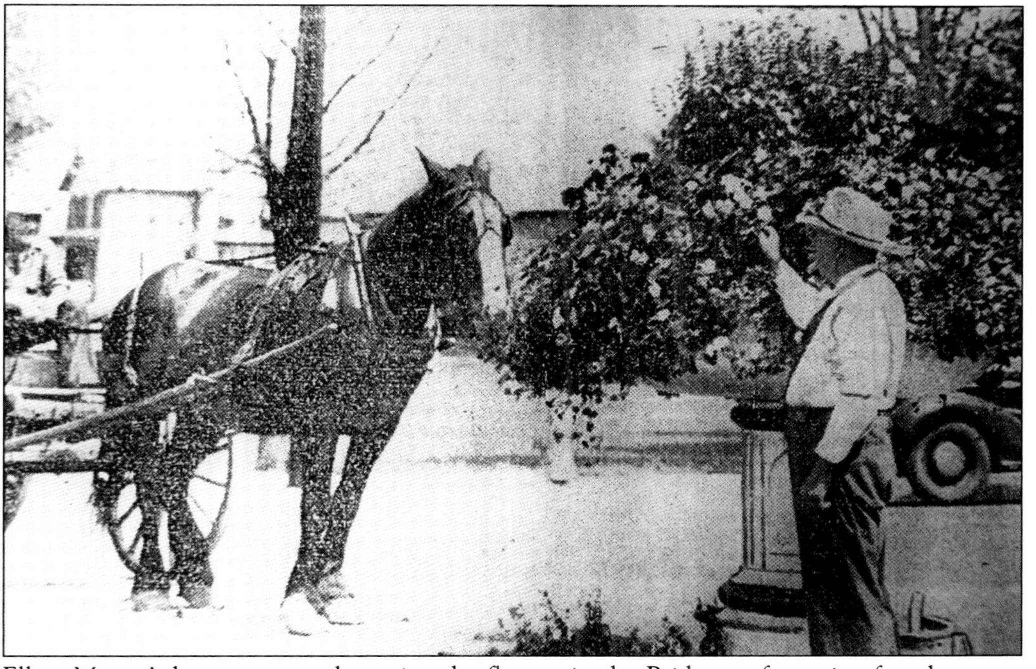

Ellery Mowry's horse was caught eating the flowers in the Bridgeton fountain after the water was replaced by foliage. Looking on is the local barber, George Wilcox. The fountain was built in 1897 with water supplied from the White Mill.

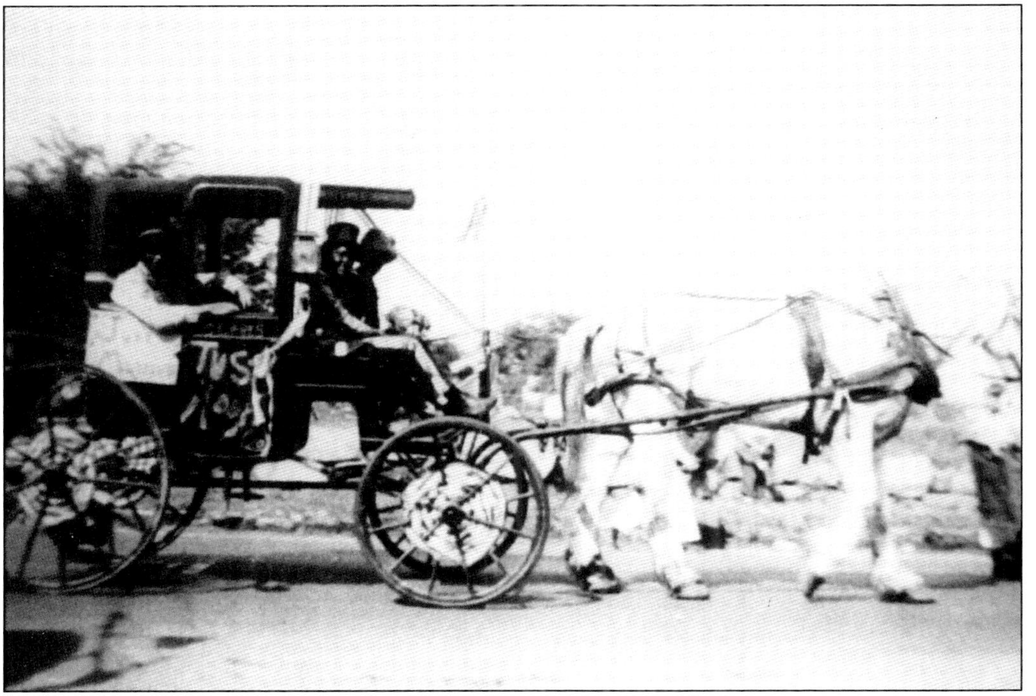

This was one of the many floats with a humorous twist in the Burrillville Tercentennial Parade.

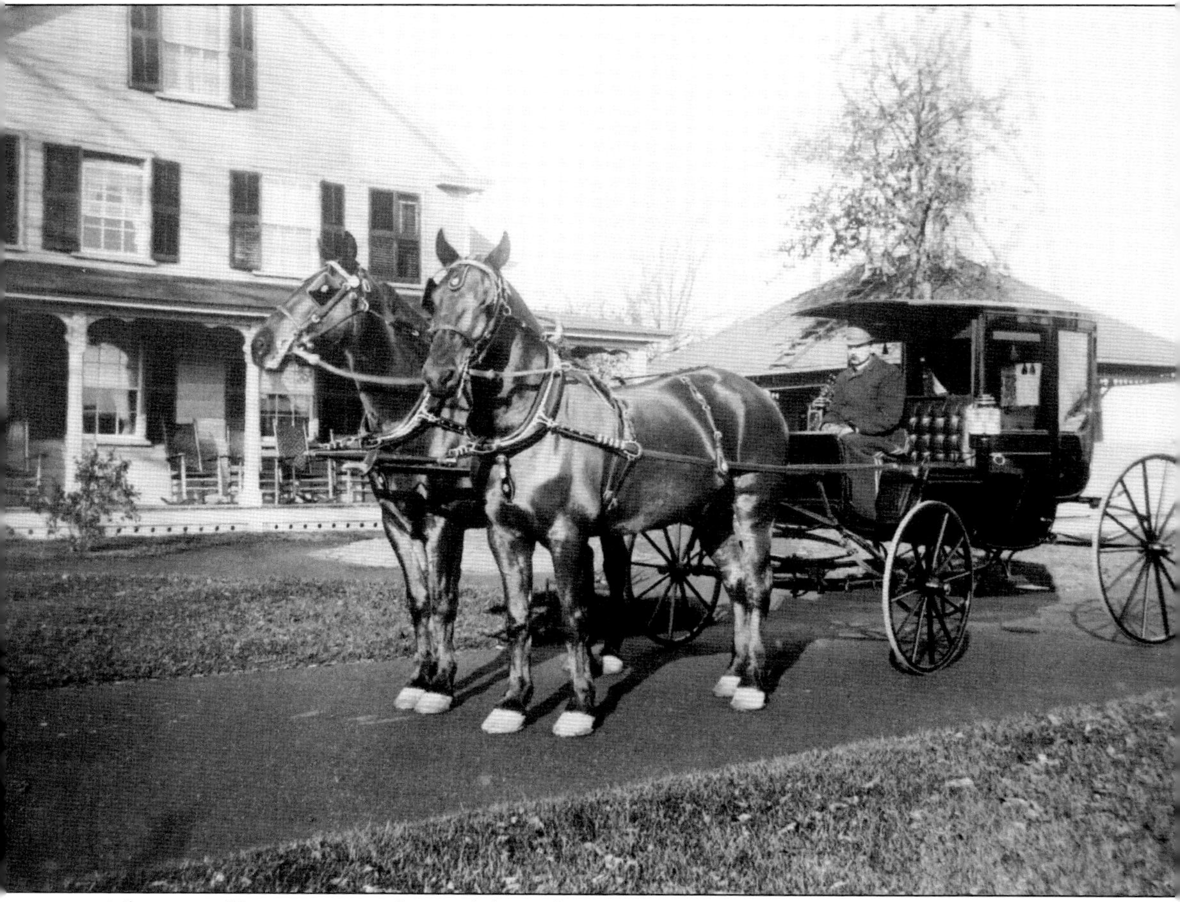

A horse and buggy wait in front of the Fiske Homestead at Herald Square in Pascoag in 1894. James Fiske owned the Sheffield Worsted Mills, later known as the Anchor Mills. The unknown driver was the chauffeur for Mr. Fiske. Bradford Court housing for the elderly is currently located on this site.

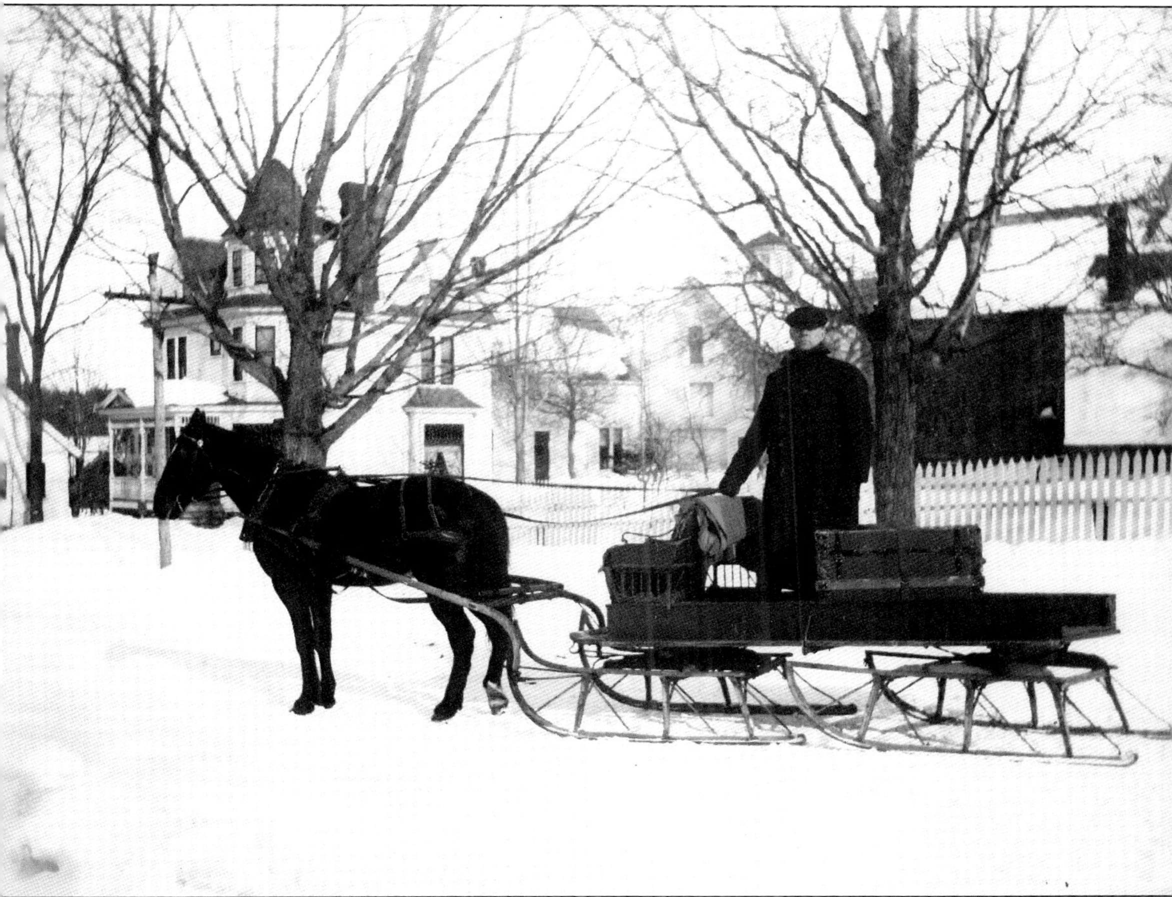

A horse and sled on Laurel Hill were photographed in the snow in the early 1900s. In 1888 one of the heaviest snowstorms ever hit with major force. Even the trains became helpless, and an engine got stuck in a snow bank near the Oakland Station.

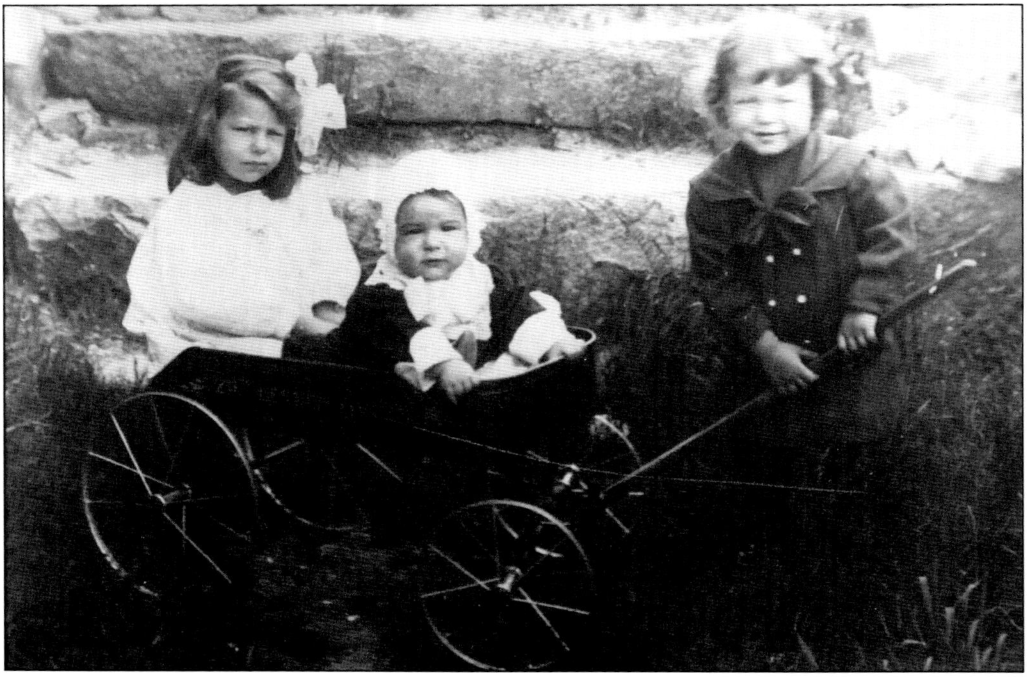

Rose, Leo and Oscar Robillard were photographed while playing on South Main Street in Pascoag around 1907.

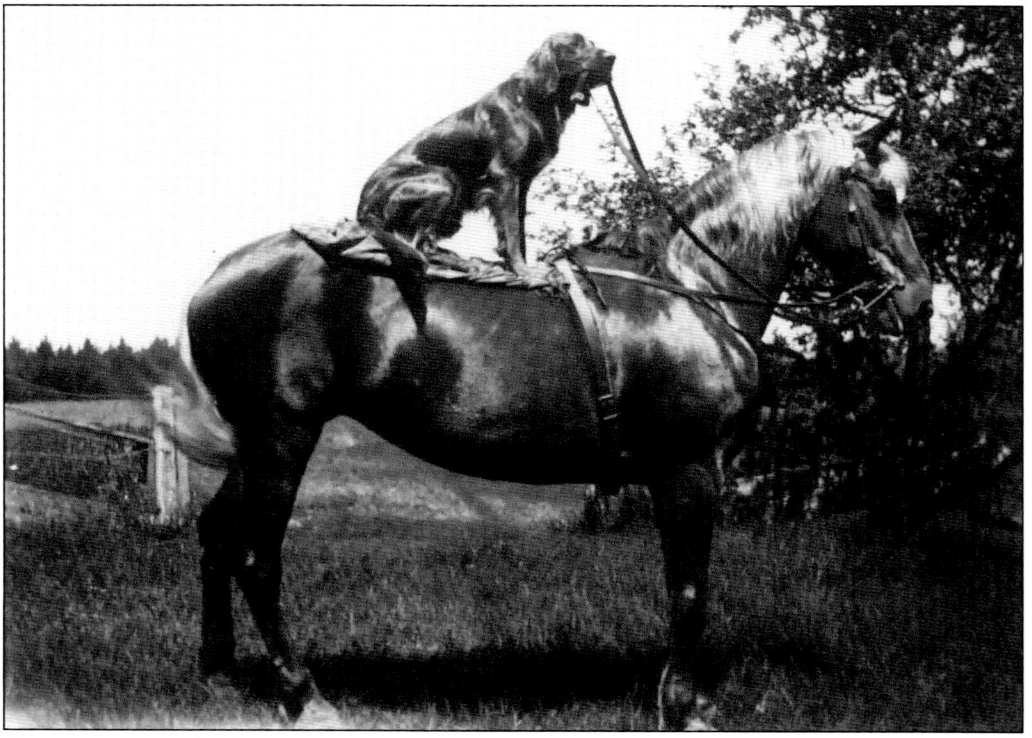

"Romeo on Horseback" is the title of this glass slide, dated around 1900.

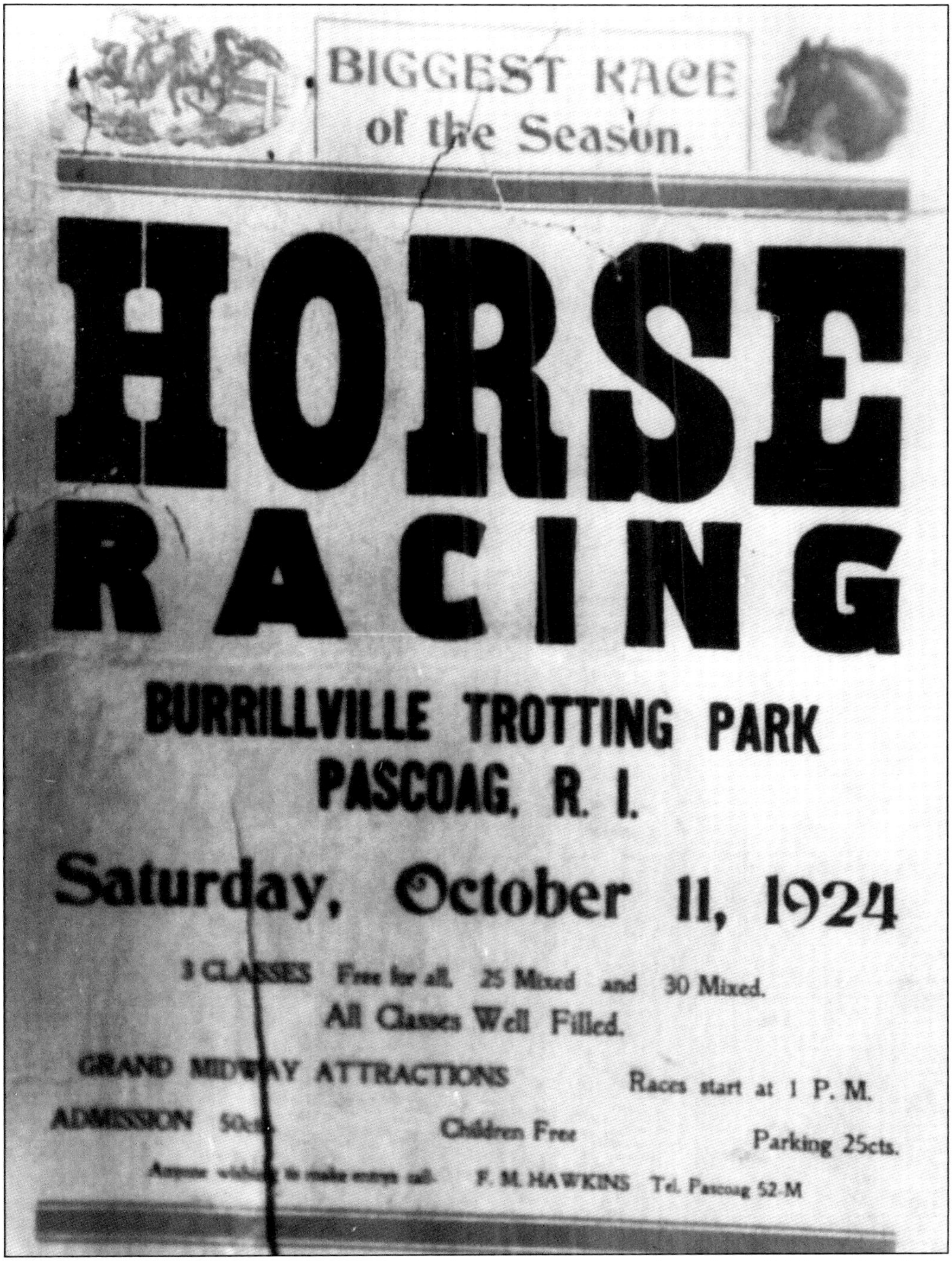

Printed by the Delmo Press of Pascoag, this horse racing poster dates from 1924. A *Burrillville Gazette* story from 1885 stated that the "old" half mile track at the Burrillville Trotting Park between Pascoag and Chepachet was due to be renovated and reopened. The local mill owners and doctors who owned horses raced their buggies from the top of Sayles Avenue at Laurel Hill Avenue straight down to Fountain Square in Pascoag.

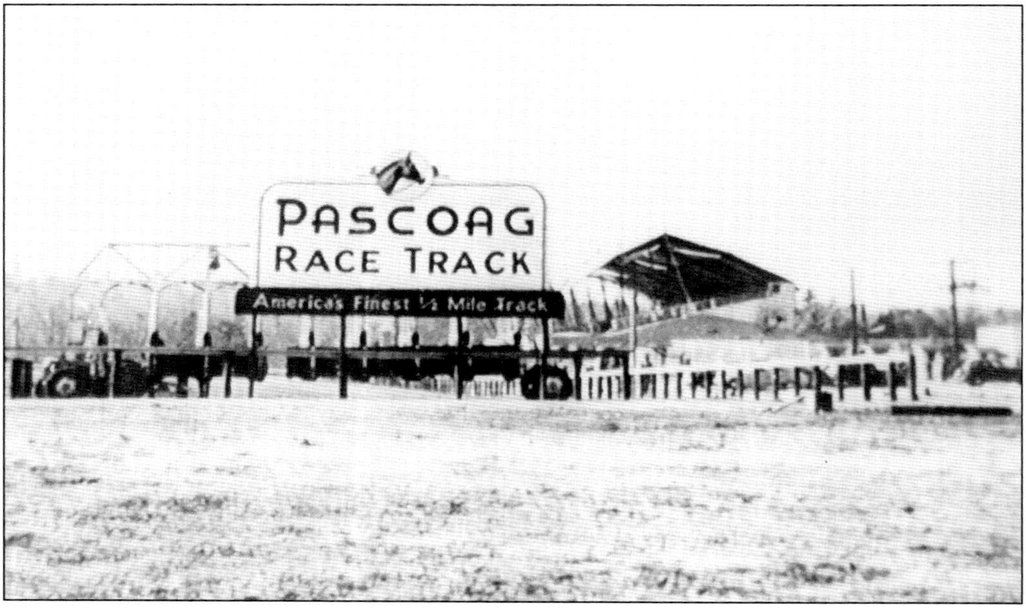

The Pascoag Race Track, "America's Finest One-half Mile Track," was photographed in 1941. During its halcyon days the track was famous around the country among the racing circuit.

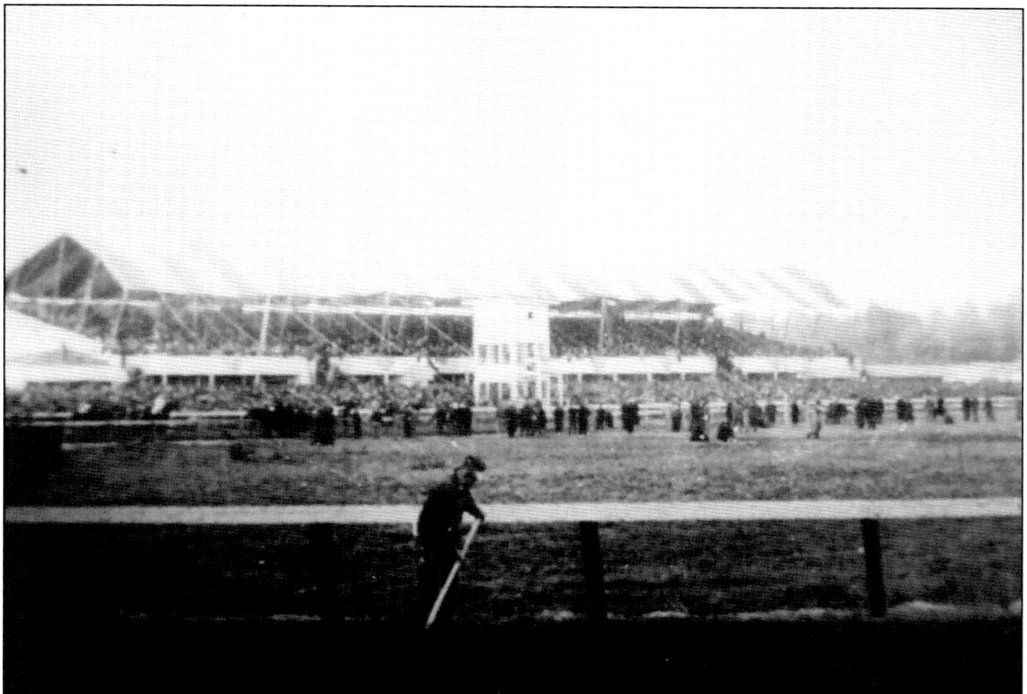

The grandstand at Pascoag Park is shown here in 1941 with its temporary roof. It was torn down in 1952.

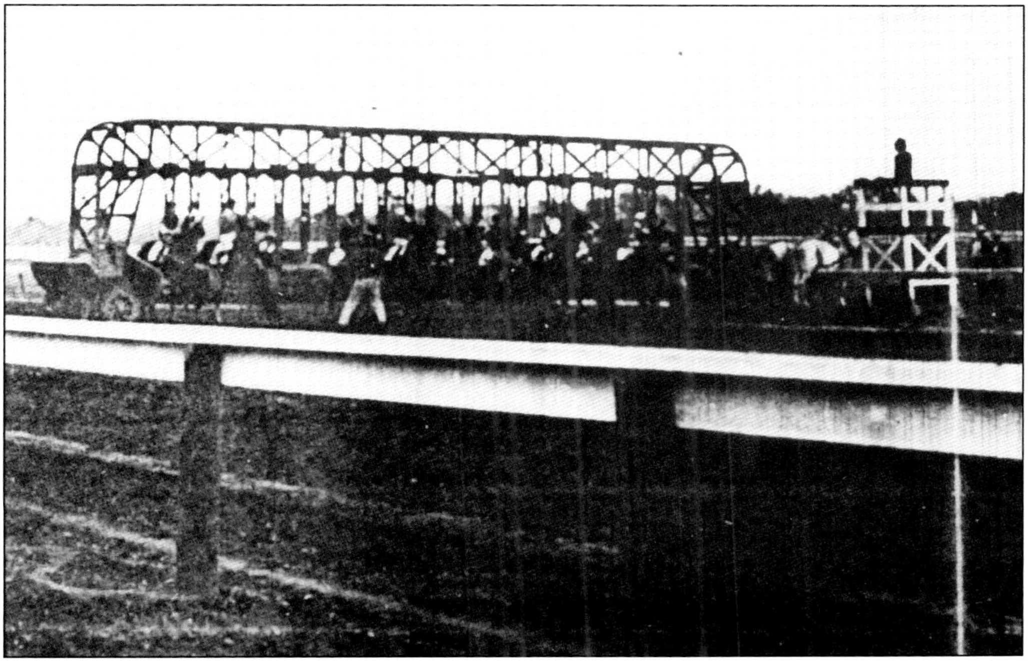

In 1941, the Burrillville Driving Club sold their interest to the Burrillville Racing Association which, in September of that year, built the grandstand to accommodate 5,000 spectators. The racing license was transferred to Lincoln Downs in 1946.

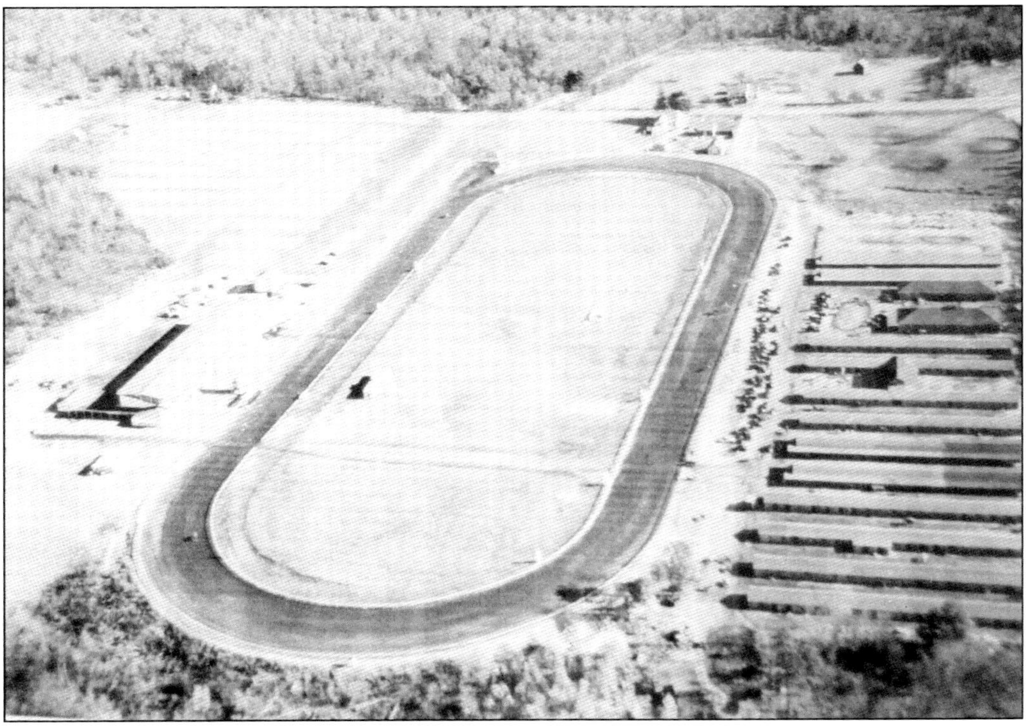

This view shows the Pascoag Race Track Oval.

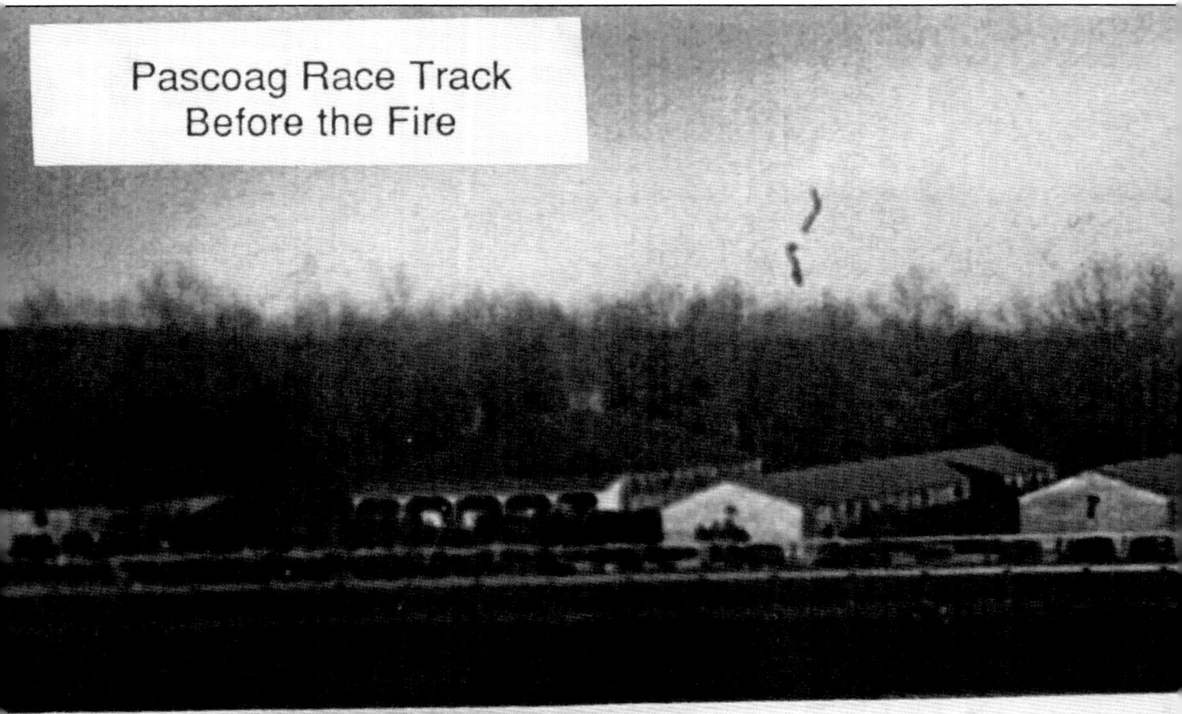

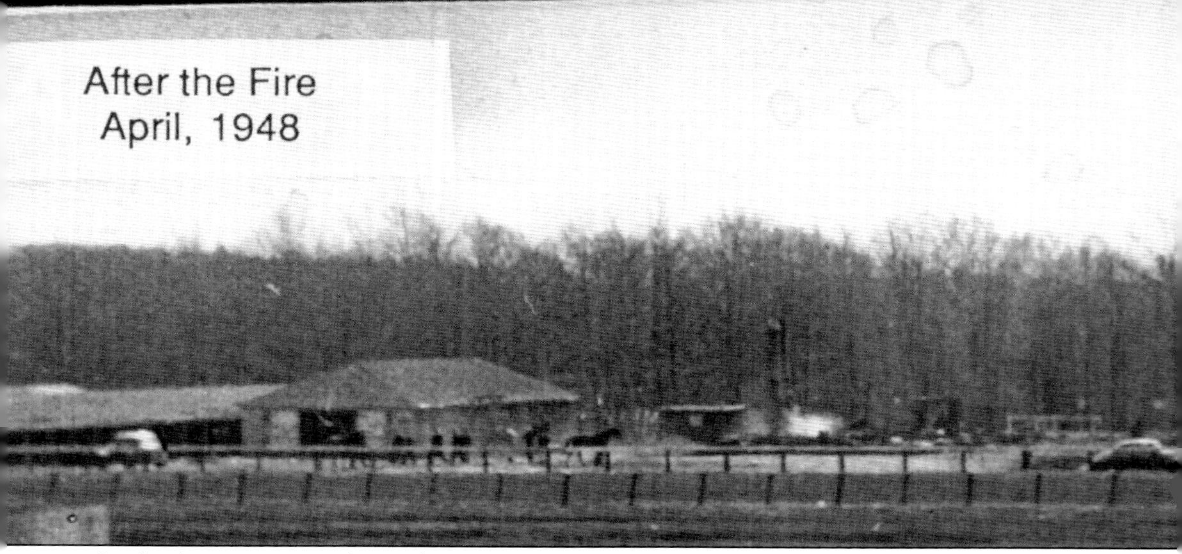

In the disastrous 1948 fire at the Pascoag Track approximately one hundred horses escaped and ran for their lives. A groom died, as did thirty-three horses that were housed here for the Lincoln Track. A short history follows: on March 18, 1896, the Burrillville Trotting Association sold the land for $100 to Alice J. Law. However, they reserved the rights at any and all times to use and repair the race track on said premises for racing purposes. The Burrillville Driving Club was formed in 1924 and in 1934 permits were given by the Town to reinstitute legal betting on the races at the Oval. Between 1938 and 1940, auto races were also held here, both with

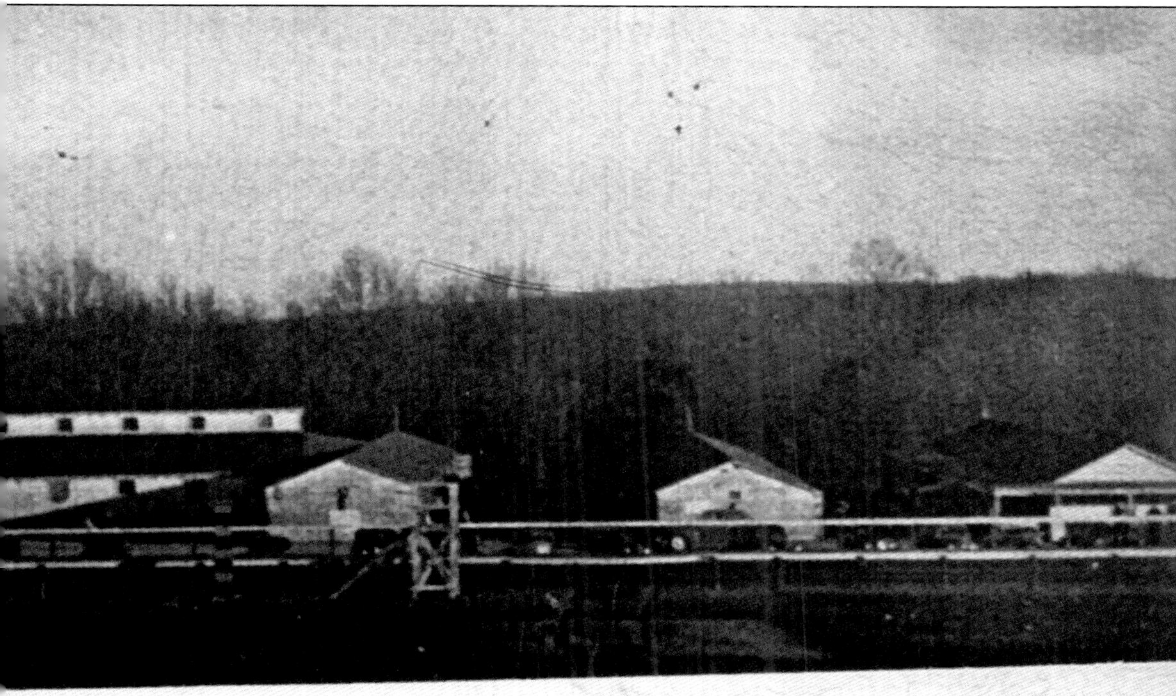

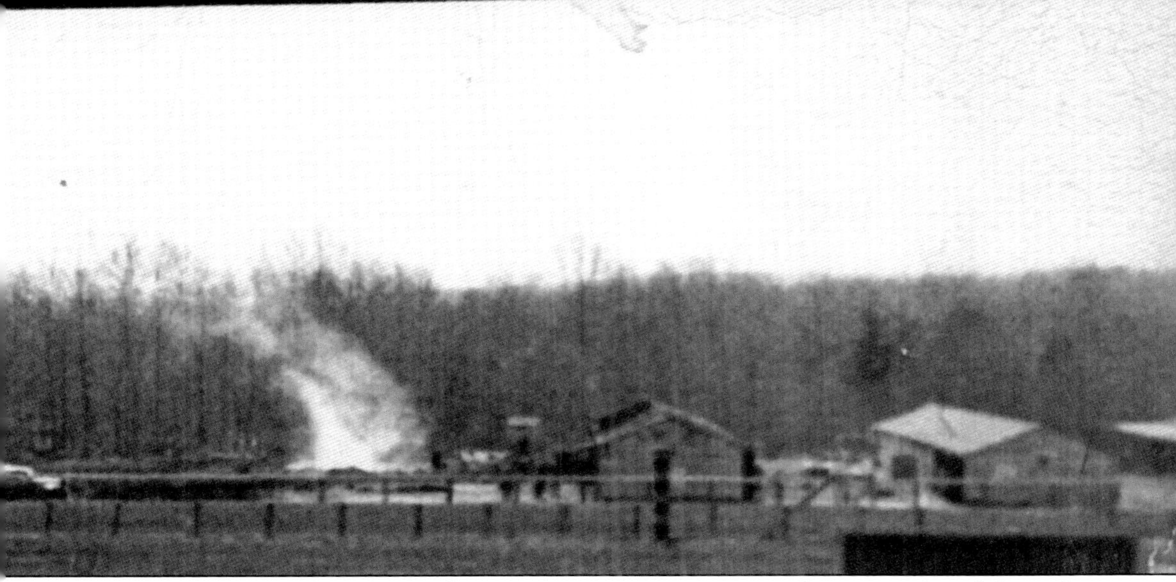

regular racing cars and midgets. The 35.8-acre Pascoag Race Track was purchased from the Maude H. Smith Knapp estate by the Burrillville Industrial Foundation for $18,000 in April 1964. Previously, they had purchased a 15-acre plot for the purpose of opening the Burrillville Industrial Park, which is now located on the site.

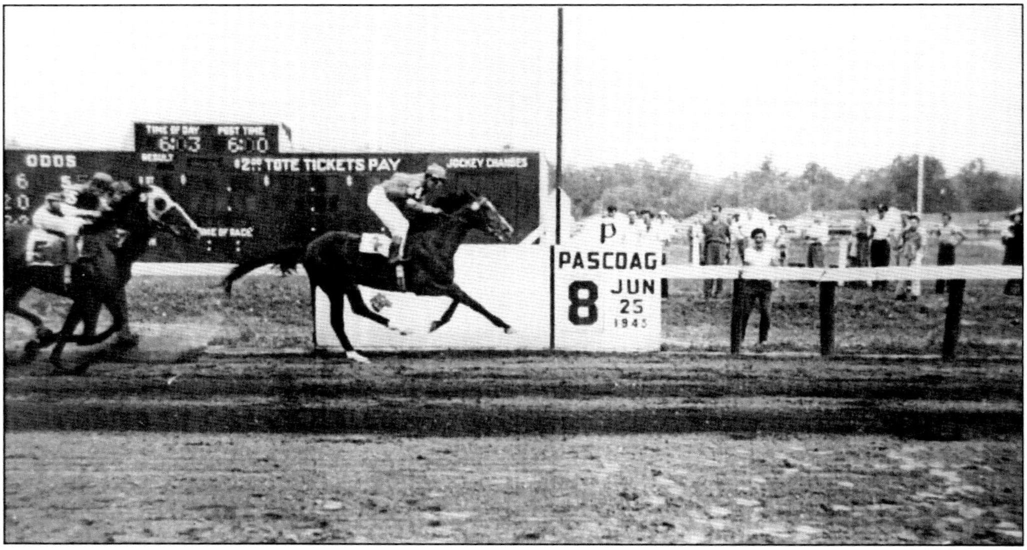

Master Key came in first on June 25, 1945, with P. Connolly as the winning jockey.

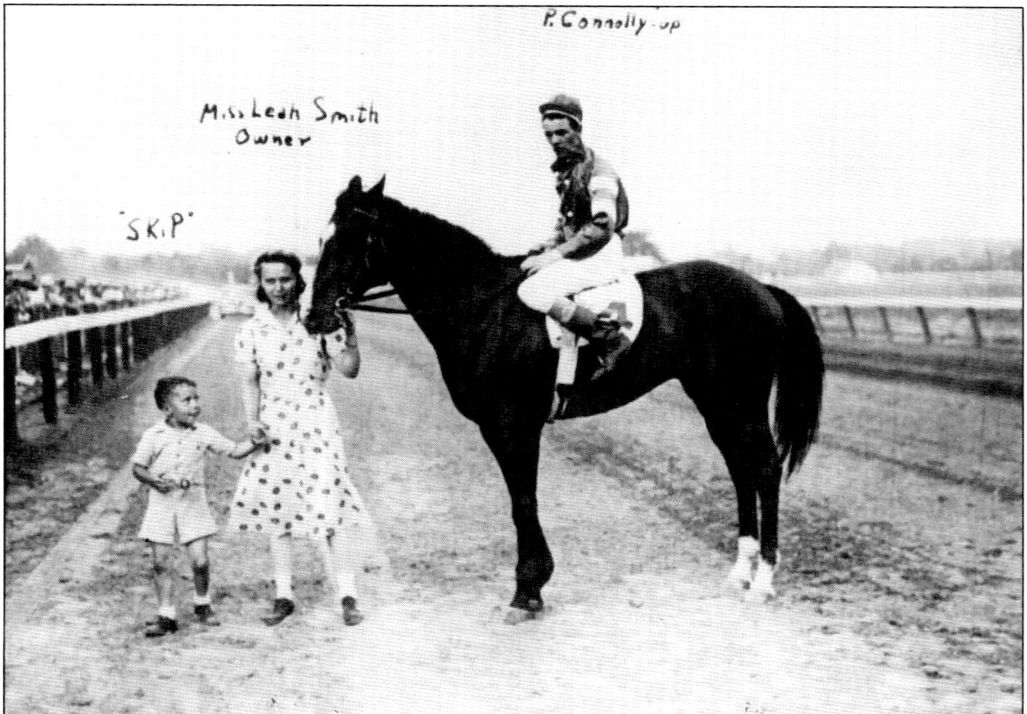

The proud owner Miss Leah Smith and her friend "Skip" congratulate the winner of the eighth race.

Four

Automobiles and Trucks

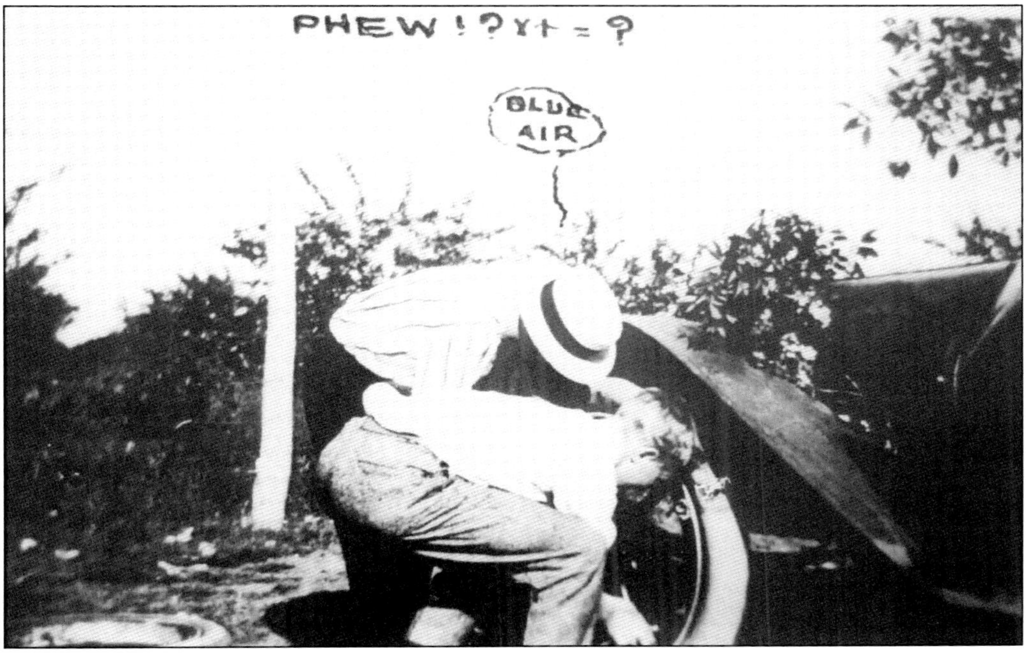

Changing the solid rubber tires on those old cars was not much fun.

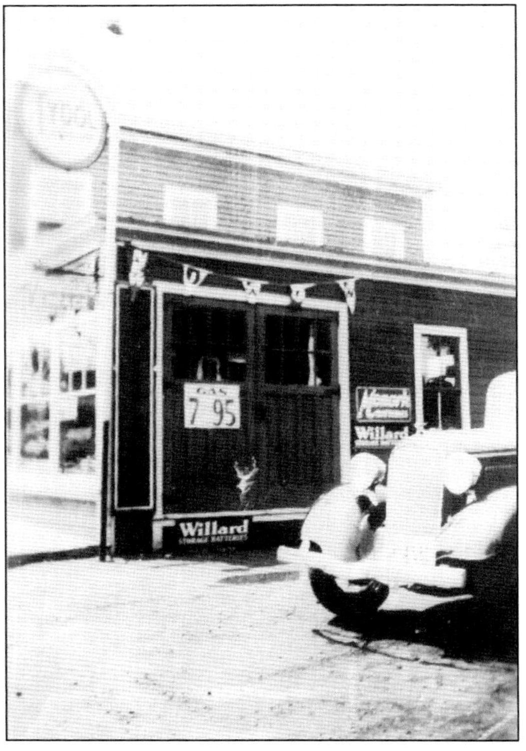

The right-hand end of Maher's Ice Cream Parlor is where Trinque's Garage in Mapleville started in business.

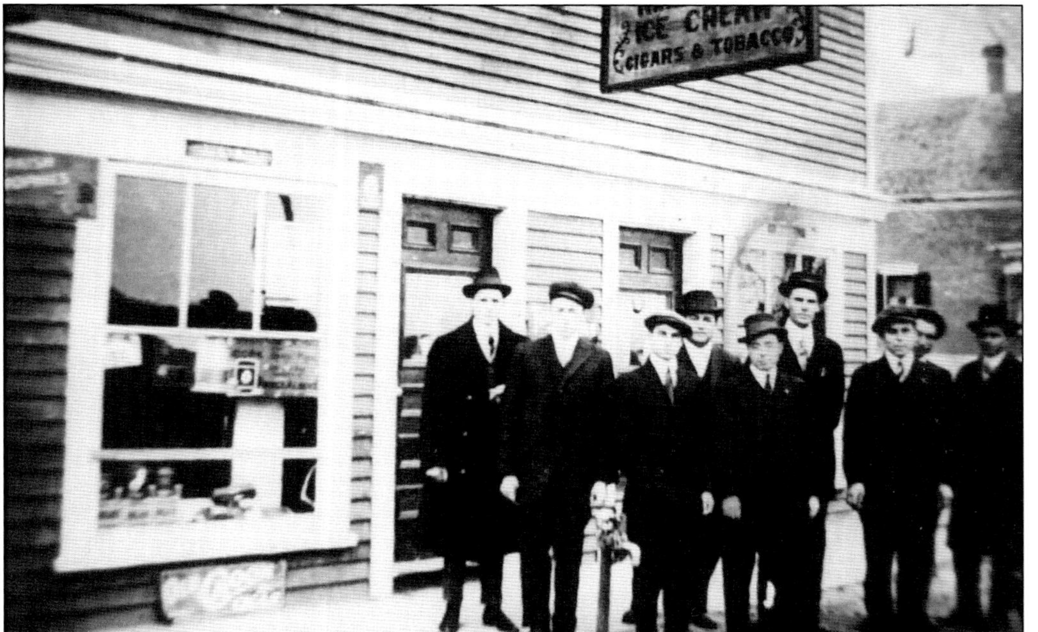

The pipe in front of the gentlemen on the left was the early gas pump used for fueling automobiles in front of Maher's Ice Cream Parlor and Trinque's Garage.

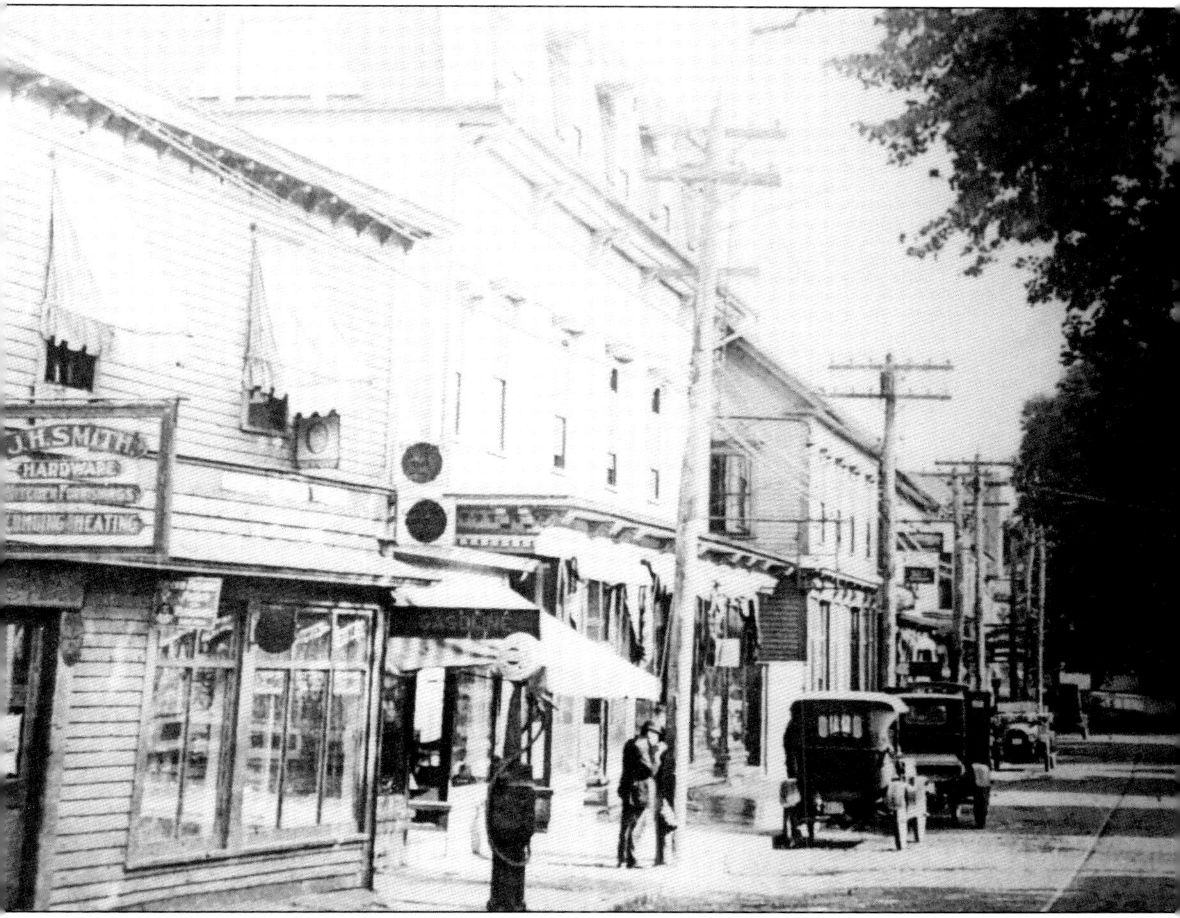

This 1915 photograph of Main Street, Pascoag, shows Smith Hardware on the left. Note that the gas pump was located on the street in front of the store for greater convenience. The *Pascoag Herald* from 1887 states that James H. Smith started in business in 1879. Business was so good that he kept expanding and at that time sold stoves, crockery, hardware, glass, tin and wooden ware, skates, library lamps, and everything else with prices clear down to hardpan. Mr. Smith erected the first streetlight in town, fueled by kerosene. The building still stands and is occupied by Chum's Hardware Store.

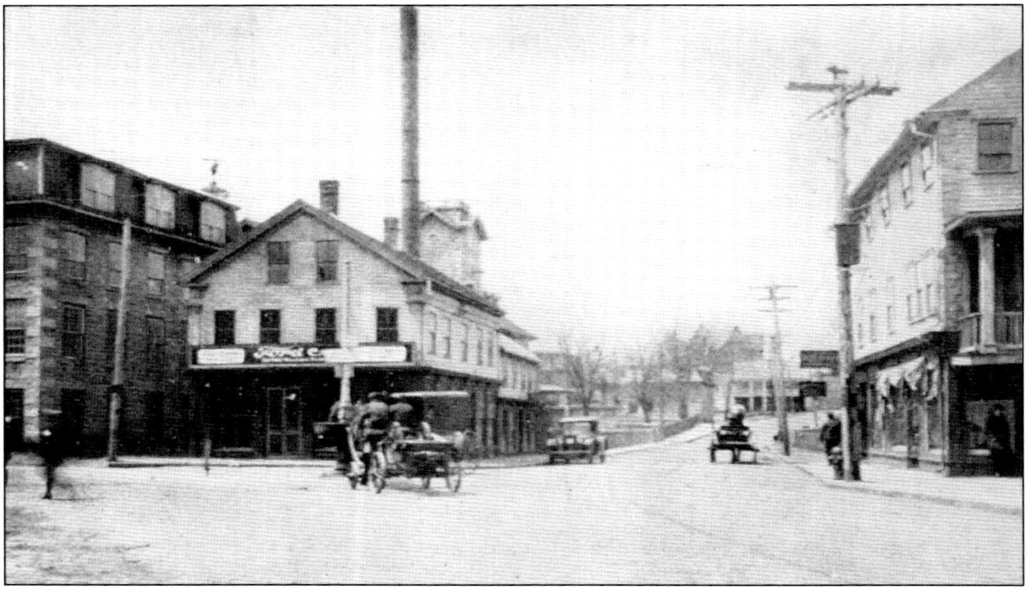

Fountain Square in Pascoag was photographed around the 1920s with buggies and autos sharing the roads. A Ford dealership can be seen on the corner next to the Granite Mill.

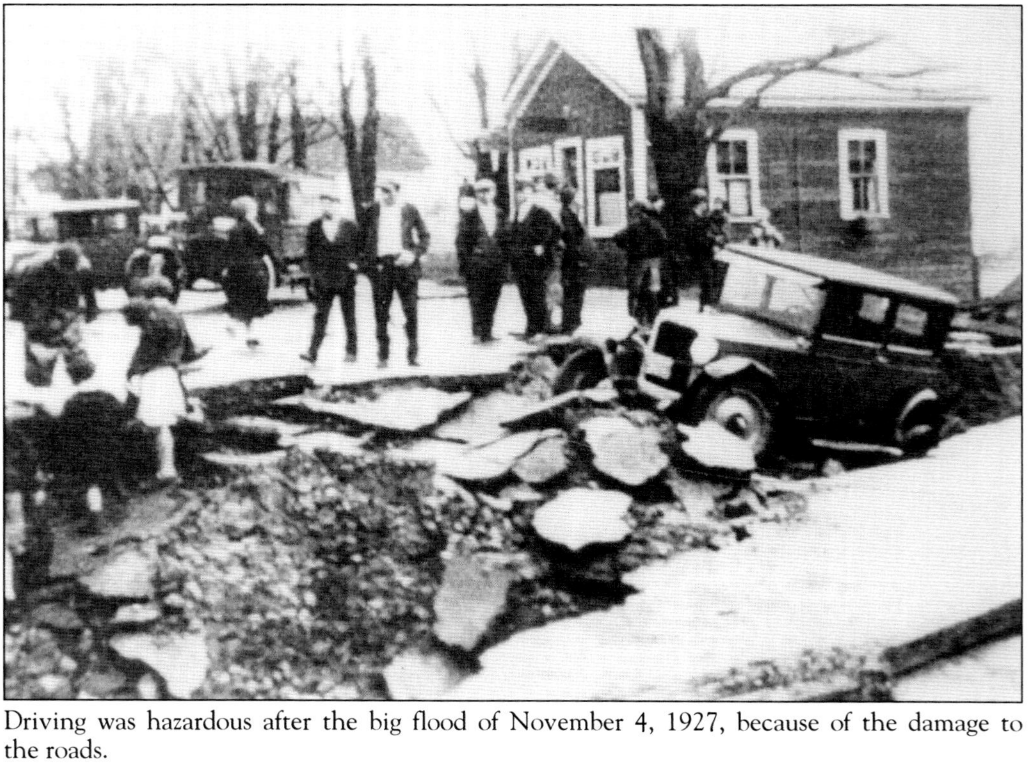

Driving was hazardous after the big flood of November 4, 1927, because of the damage to the roads.

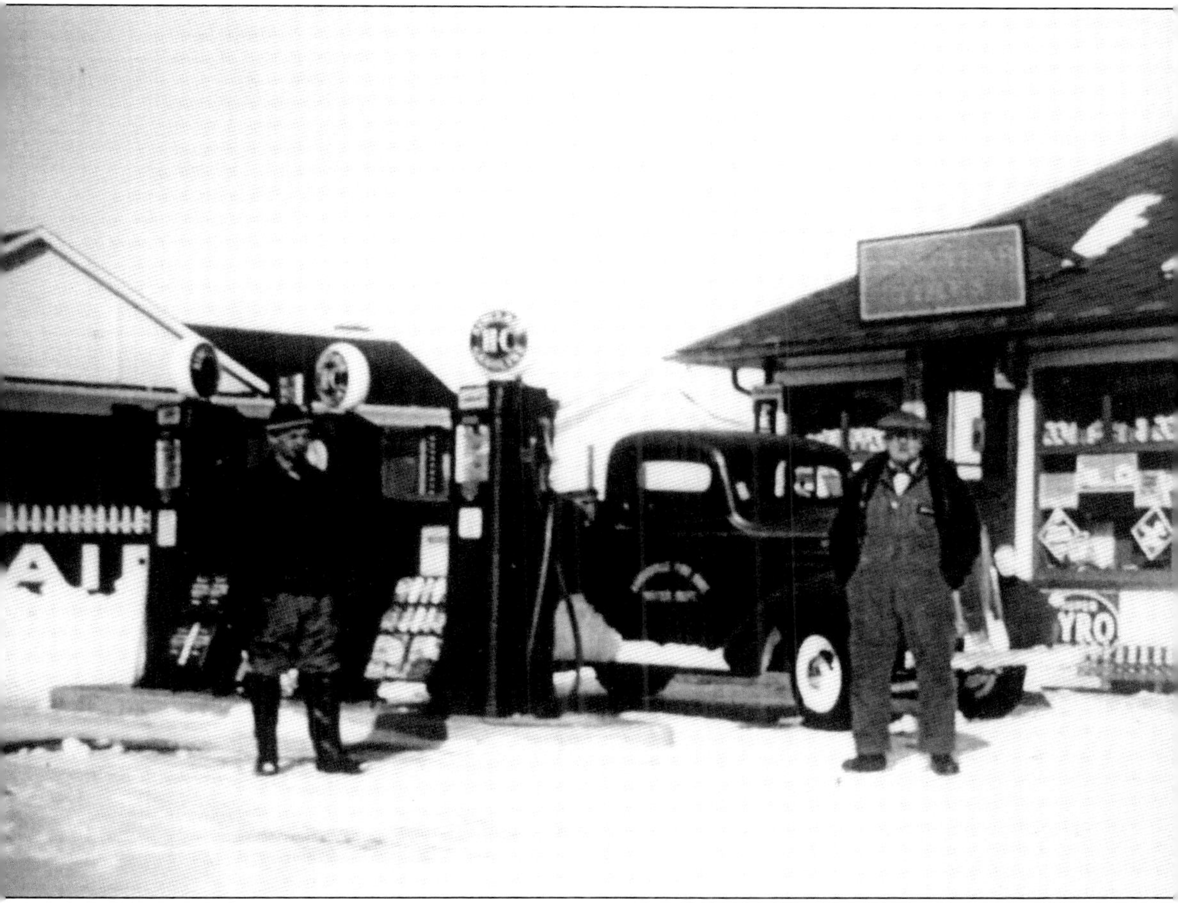

The Chapel Street Garage is shown here with a Harrisville Fire District Water Department truck at the pumps. The two gentlemen are unidentified. Dr. Ashton's home is on the left. He was a prominent local doctor who delivered hundreds of babies over the years. In 1968 his house was demolished and an eleven-building, seventy-six-unit complex was built at Walling's Field in the back. It was called Ashton Court in his memory.

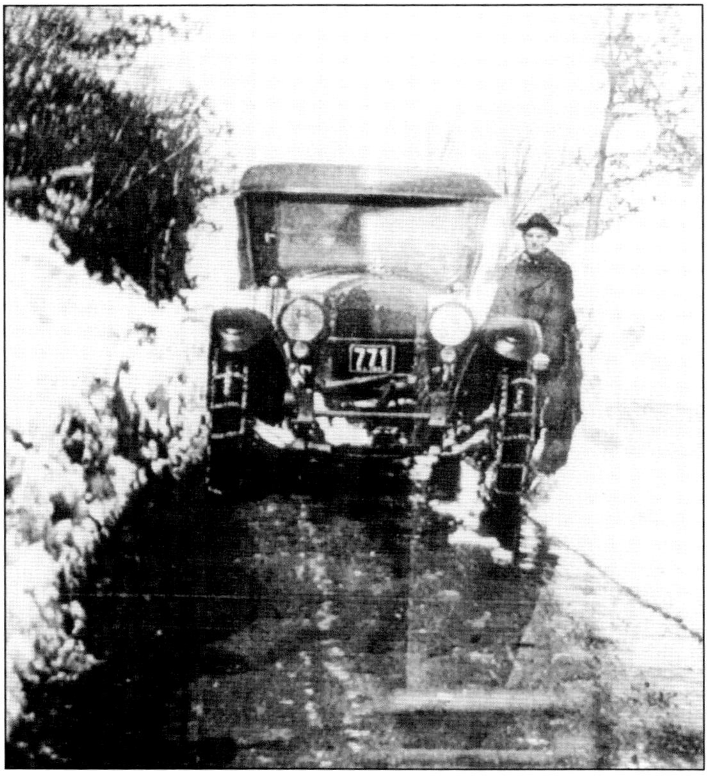

Jack Stratford, chauffeur, was photographed with Austin T. Levy's 12-cylinder Packard on Steere Farm Road in Harrisville after the blizzard of March 14, 1924.

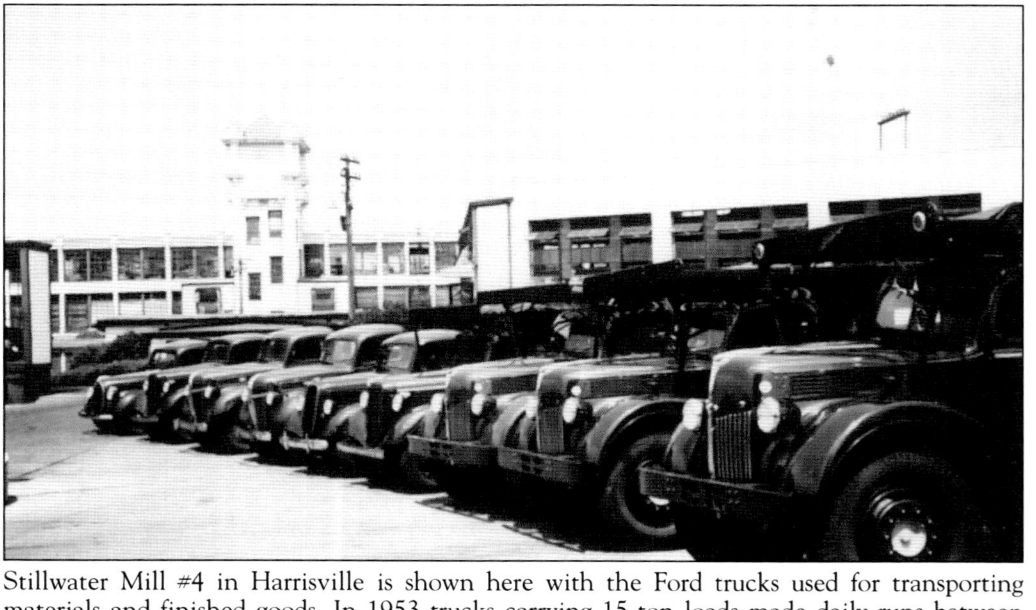

Stillwater Mill #4 in Harrisville is shown here with the Ford trucks used for transporting materials and finished goods. In 1953 trucks carrying 15-ton loads made daily runs between Uxbridge, Massachusetts, and New York City in four-and-a-half hours. In 1920 it took fifteen-and-a-half hours for the 5-ton Pierce Arrow trucks.

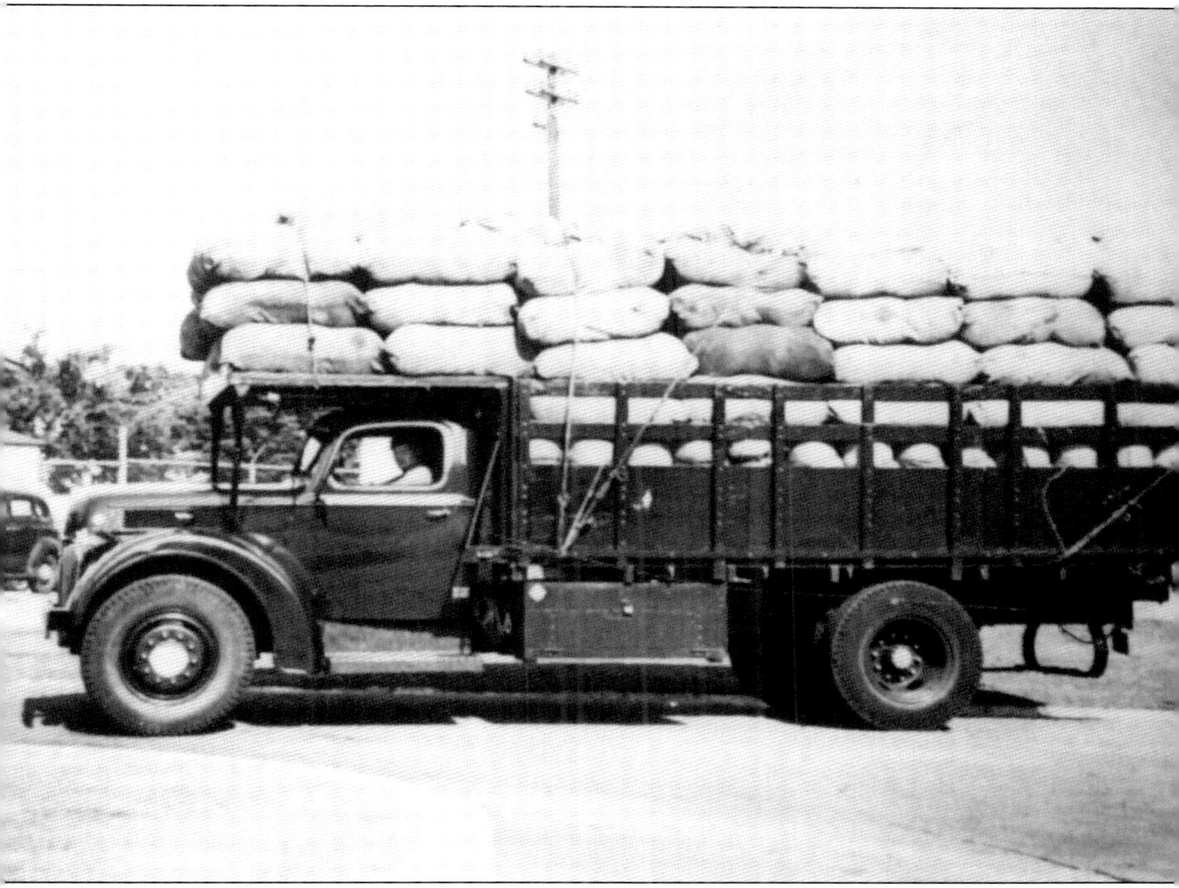

This Stillwater truck is loaded with warps and filling for delivery to the different mills owned by the Stillwater Company. Milton Sherman, a driver for Stillwater for thirty-two years, is in the cab.

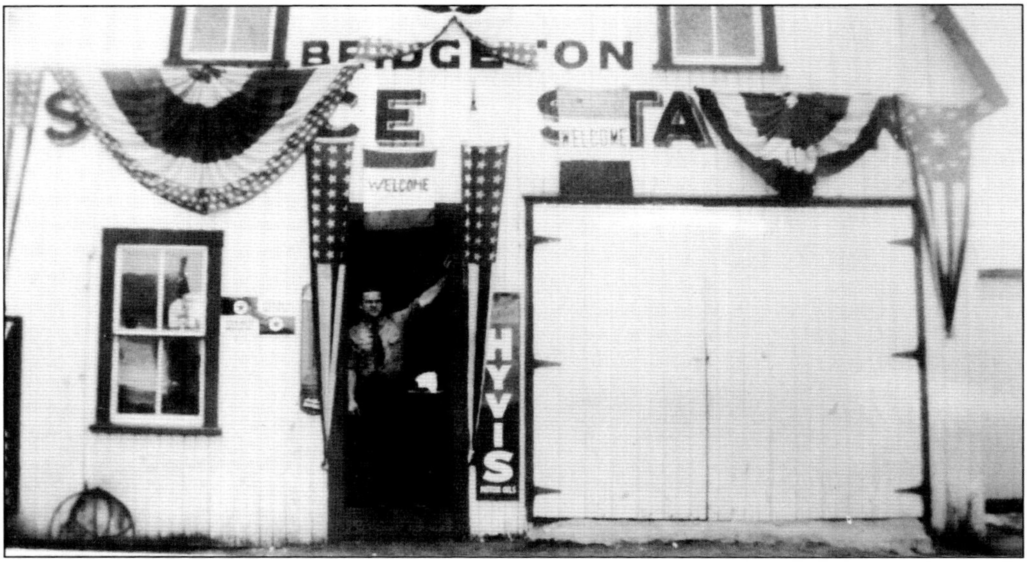

Tom Blessington's garage on Church Street was decorated for Rhode Island's Tercentennial in 1936. The building was later moved down Church Street and used as a service station and then as an antique shop.

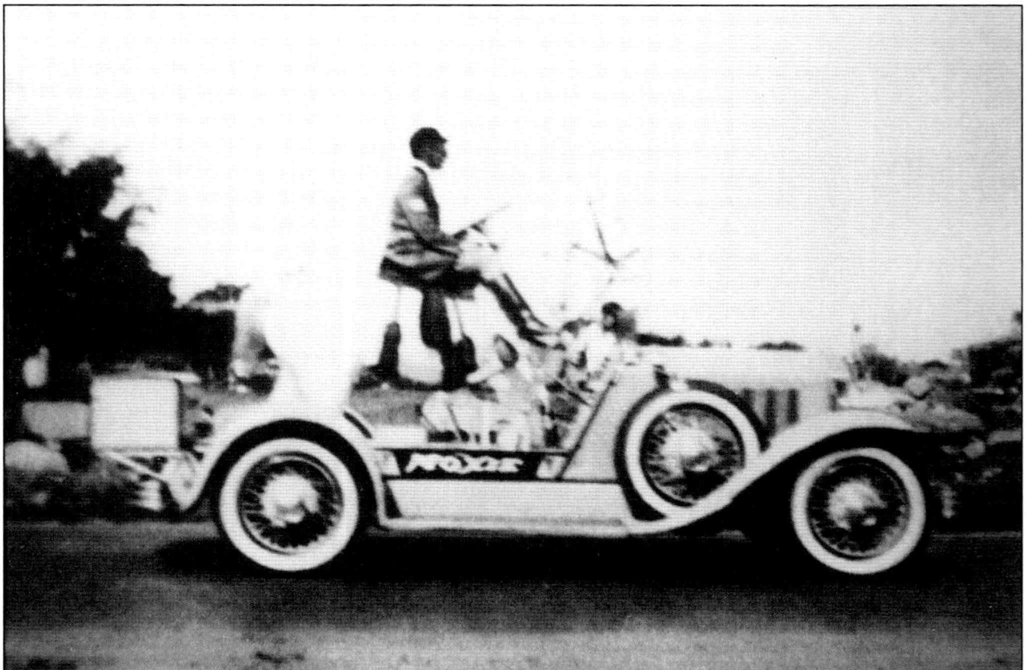

This photograph of the 1936 Tercentennial Parade raises a question: is the horse driving the car or is the man doing it?

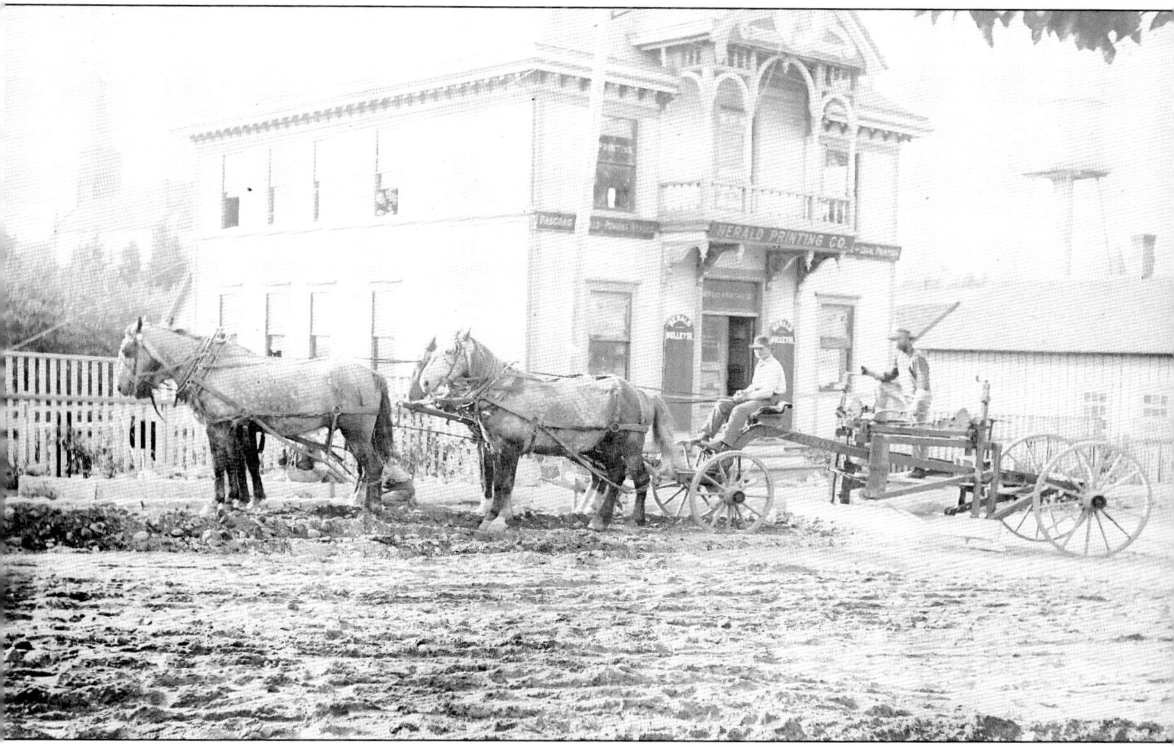

The first town-owned road grader was photographed in the 1890s in front of the *Pascoag Herald* building. It was used to smooth the gravel which was applied to the roads to keep the mud down.

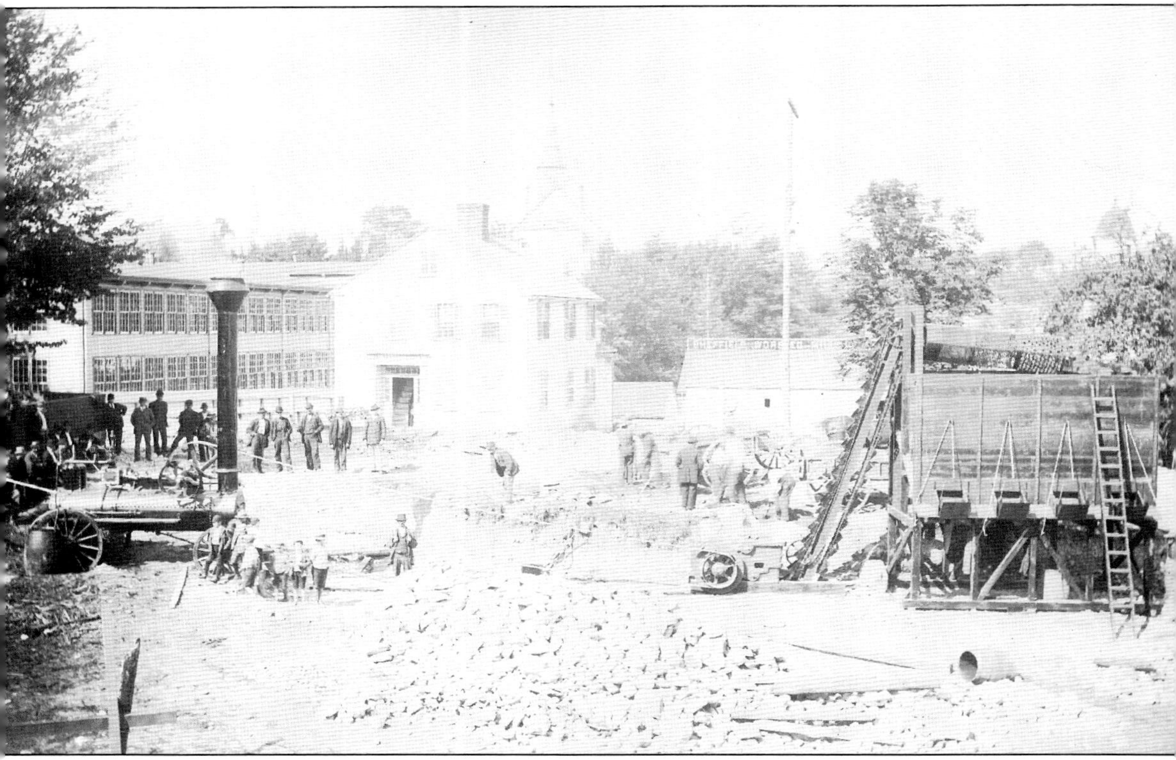

The first stone crusher in Burrillville was located at the Fiske (Sheffield) Mill at Herald Square in the early 1890s. It was used to make the gravel used on the local roads. The house in this photograph was moved so the mill could be built out to the street.

Five

Trains and Trolleys

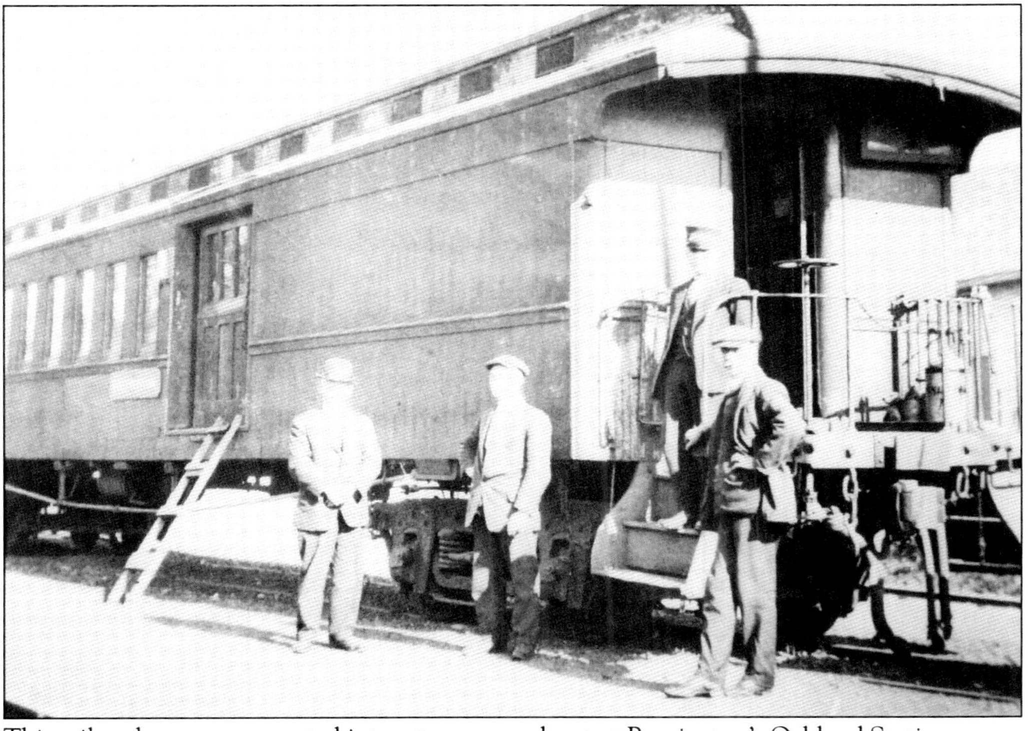

This railroad car was converted into a temporary depot at Remington's Oakland Station.

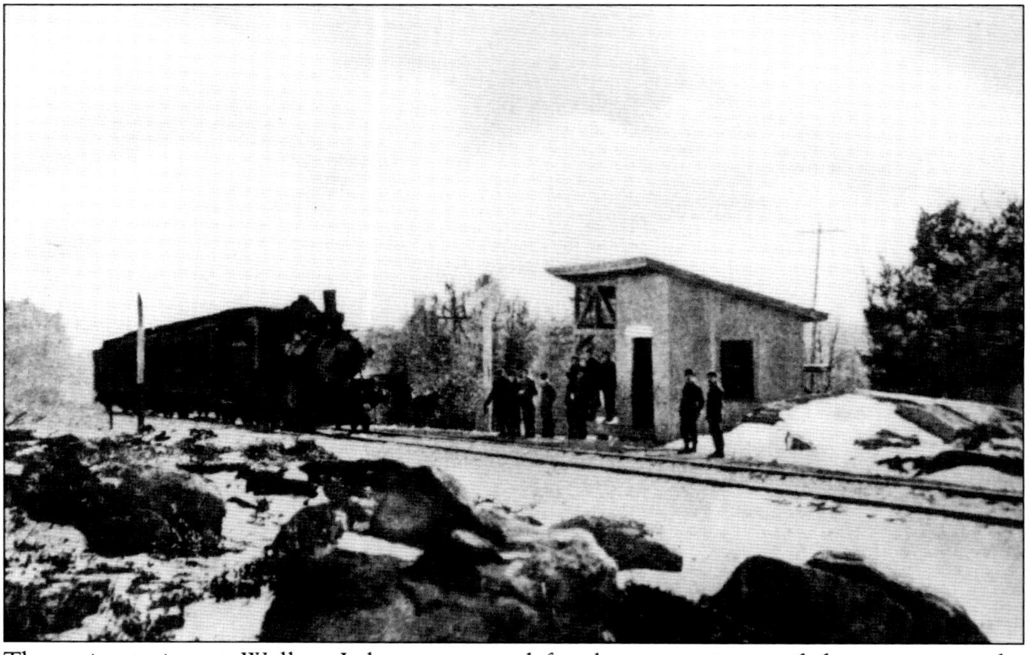

The train station at Wallum Lake was opened for the convenience of those going to the Sanatorium. The Providence and Springfield Railroad extended the line past the lake in 1891. A wagon met the train and picked up the passengers for the short ride to their new home.

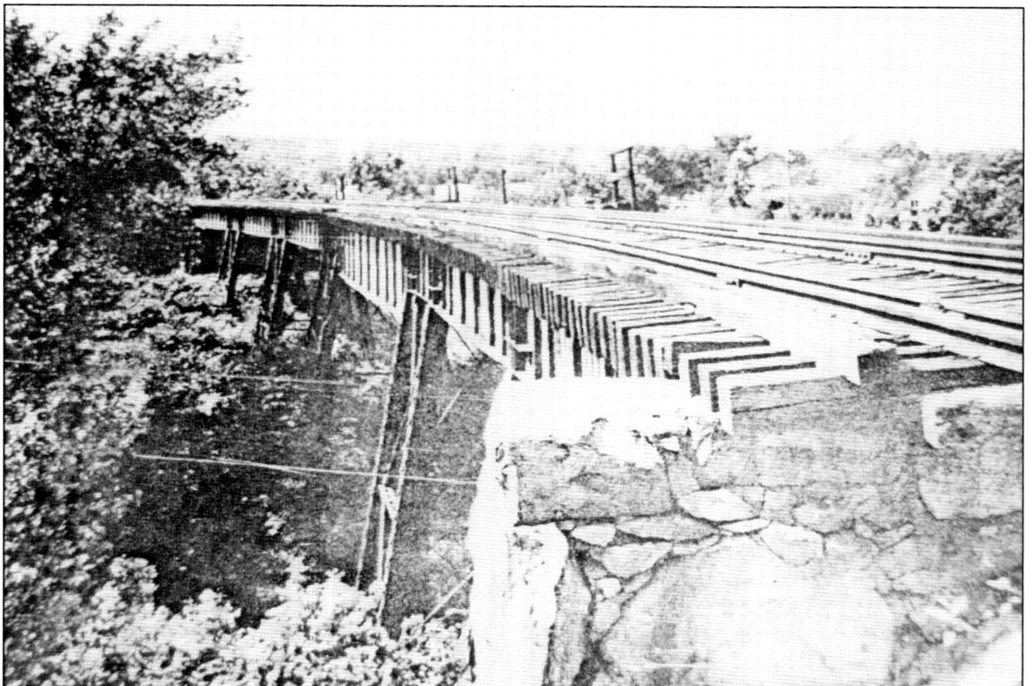

The longest curved iron bridge in Rhode Island at that time was across this ravine over Laurel Ridge in the Bridgeton section of Burrillville.

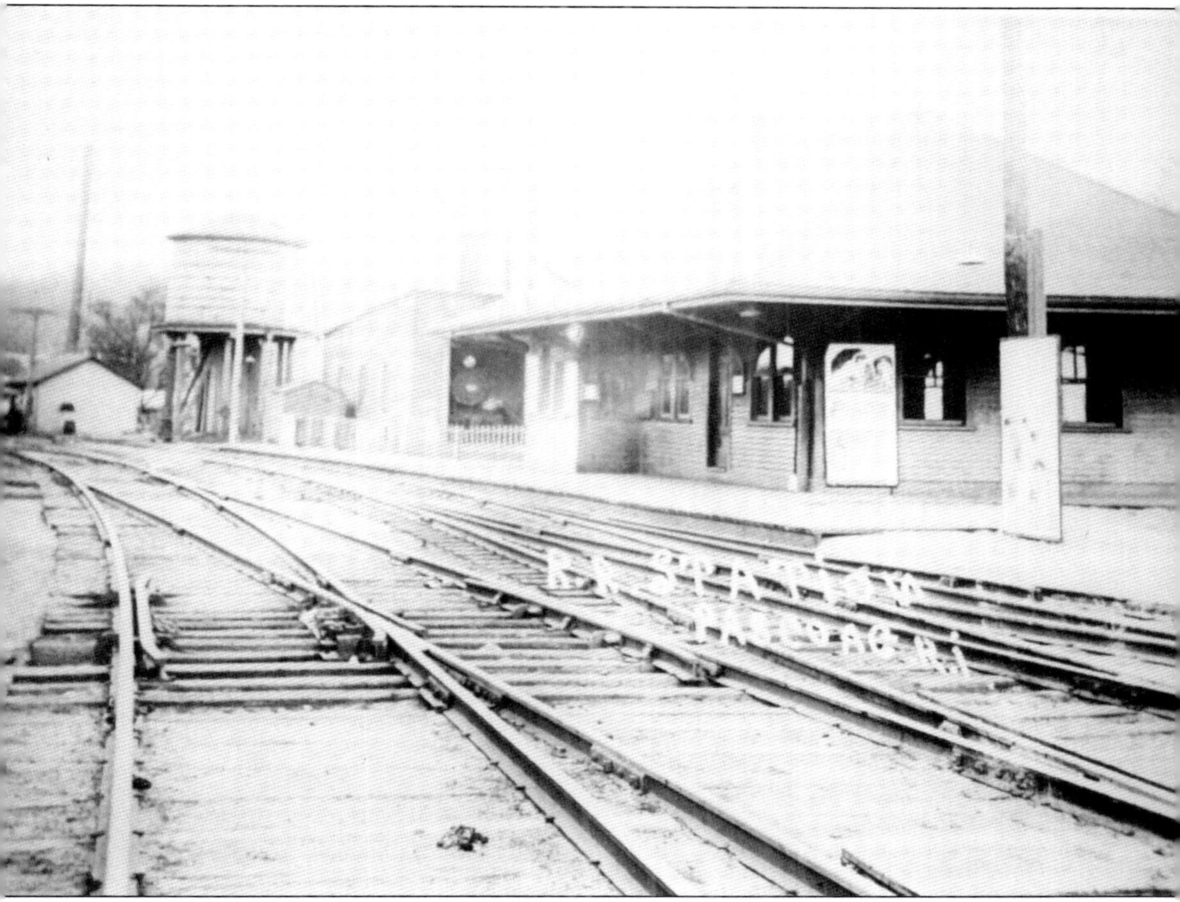

The railroad came to Burrillville through the efforts of mill owners William Tinkham of Harrisville and Albert Sayles of Pascoag. The Providence and Springfield Railroad opened for traffic to Pascoag in August 1873, before the Pascoag Station was built.

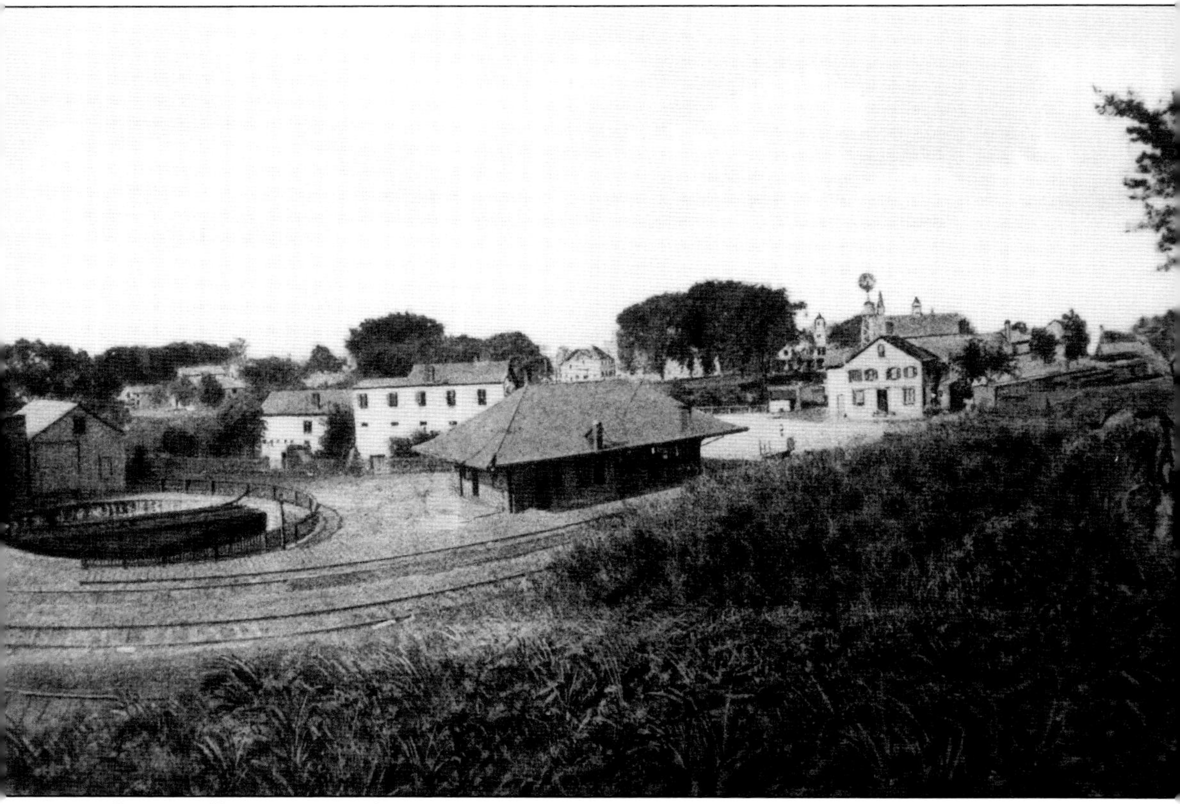

This roundhouse was used to turn trains at the Pascoag Station. The station was completed in January 1874. In the beginning, there were only two passenger trains each way daily for the convenience of those working in Providence.

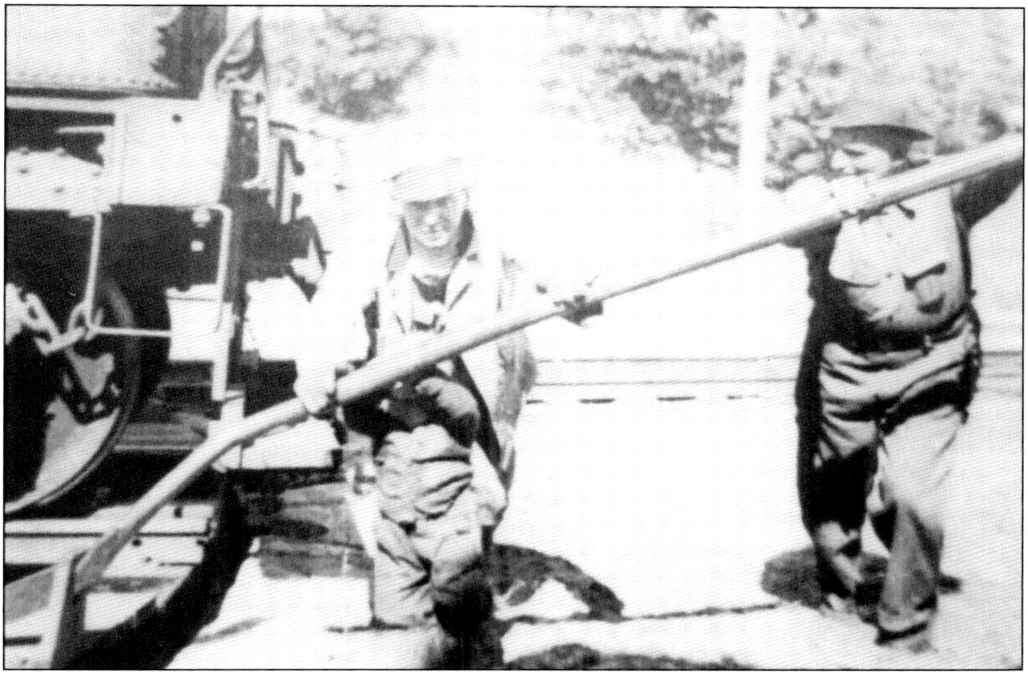

Many of the local youths enjoyed helping turn the train. Skip and his dad are shown here, with the other man unidentified.

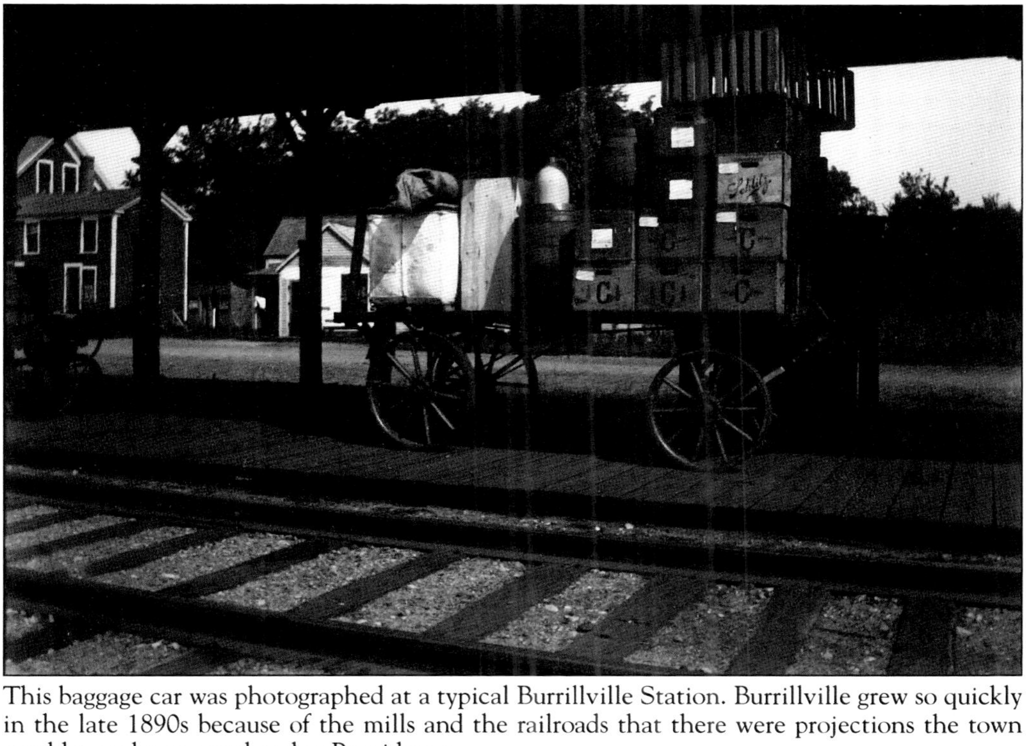

This baggage car was photographed at a typical Burrillville Station. Burrillville grew so quickly in the late 1890s because of the mills and the railroads that there were projections the town would soon be as populated as Providence.

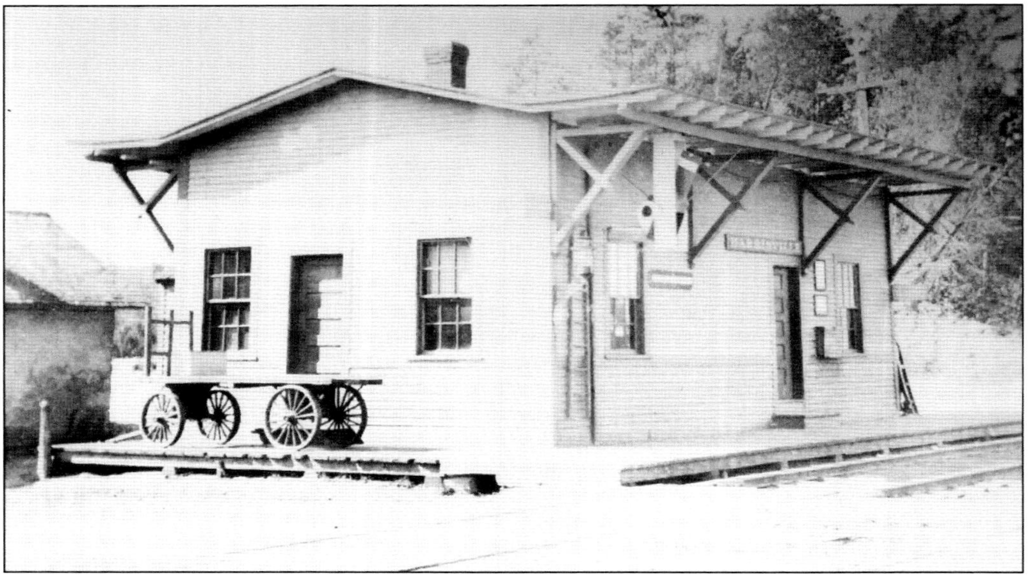

This view shows the Harrisville Station on the Springfield and Providence branch of the New York and New England Railroad.

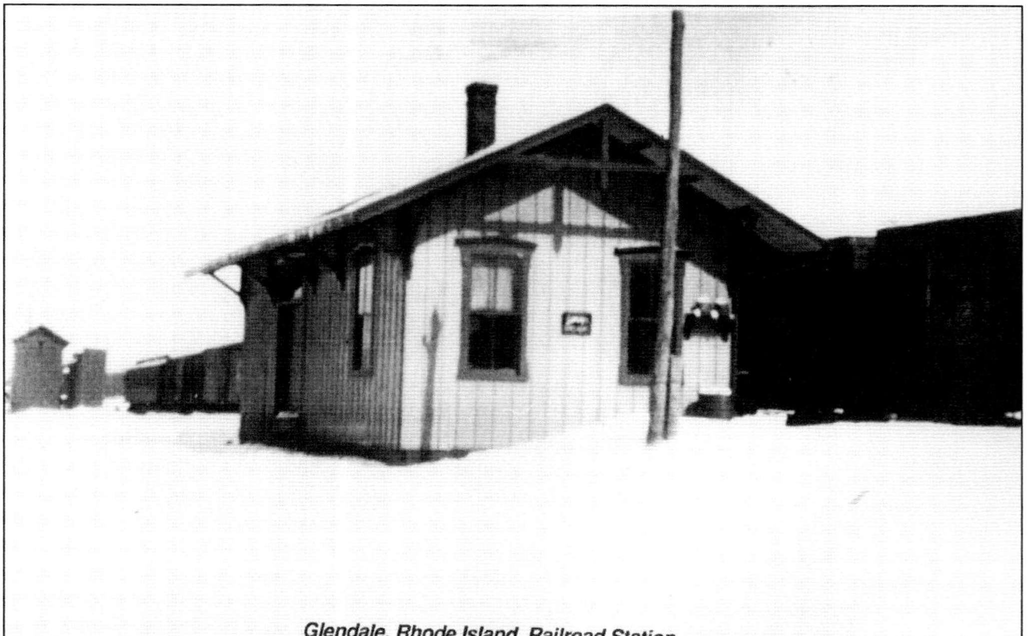

Glendale, Rhode Island, Railroad Station

The Glendale Station was eventually moved across the street and is now being used as the Glendale Post Office.

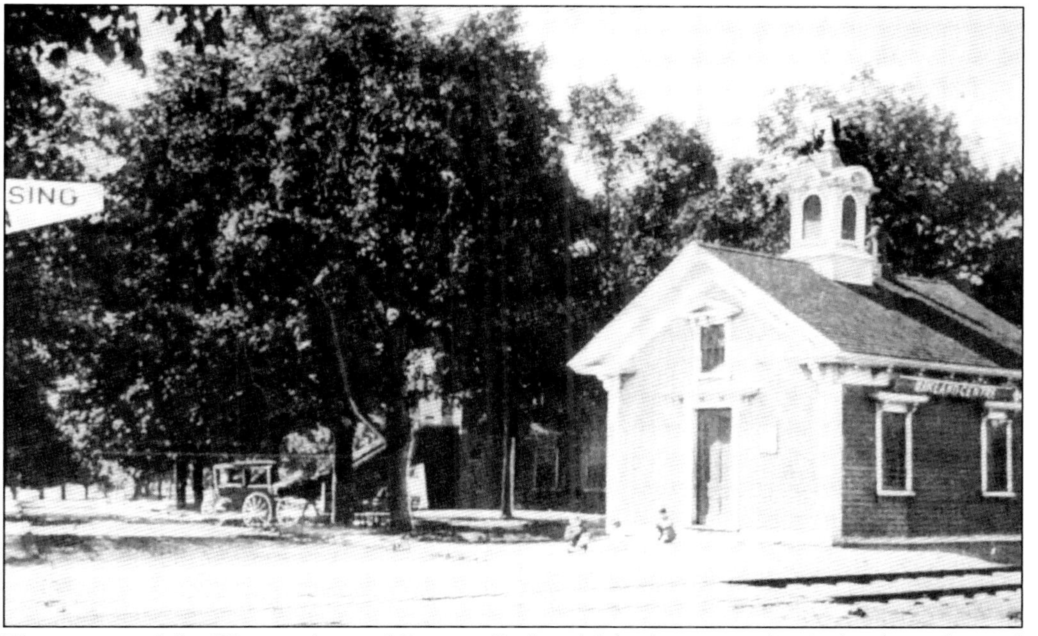

This station of the Woonsocket and Pascoag Railroad (also known as the Airline) was located near Recreation Hall in Oakland. It is now part of the garage at Brown's Funeral Home.

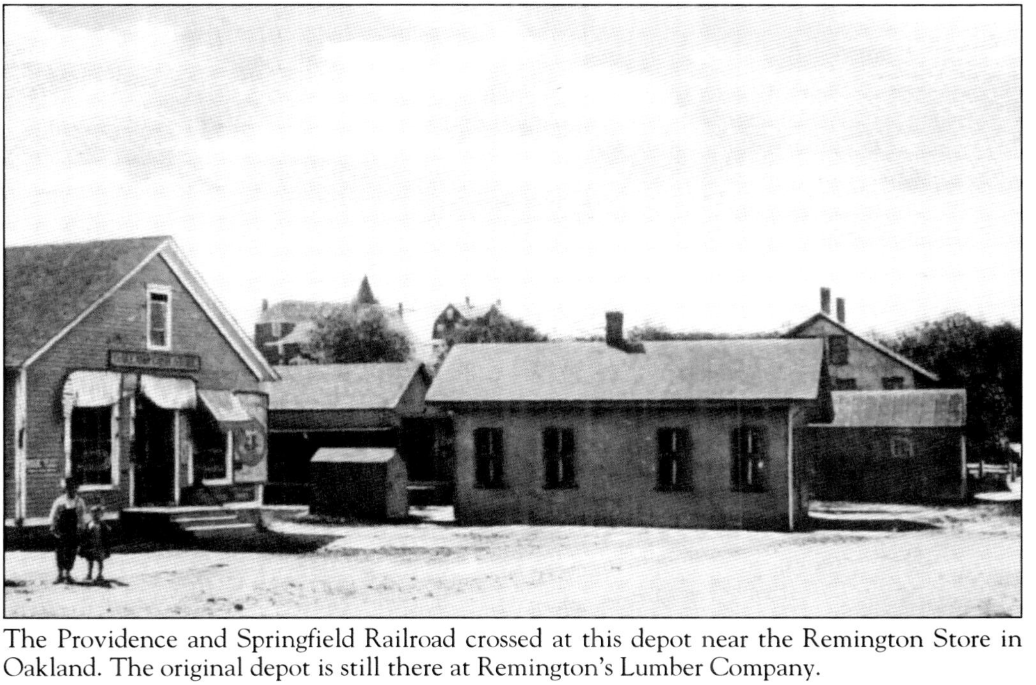

The Providence and Springfield Railroad crossed at this depot near the Remington Store in Oakland. The original depot is still there at Remington's Lumber Company.

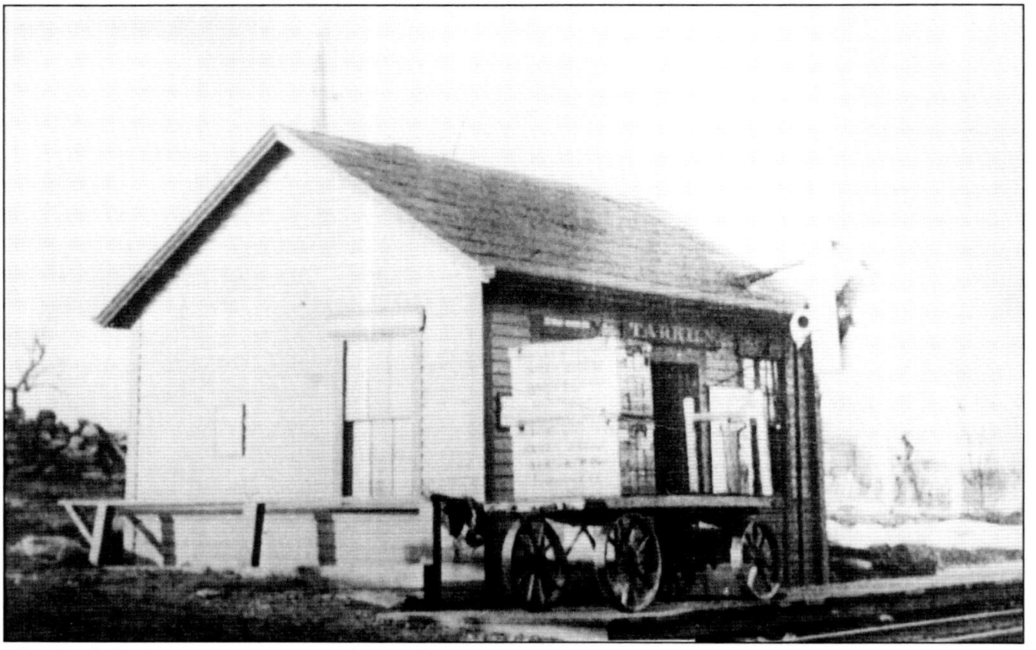

The Tarkiln Station was situated in a pleasant valley through which flowed the Tarkiln Stream. Two miles below, it united with the Branch River and continued to the mighty Blackstone.

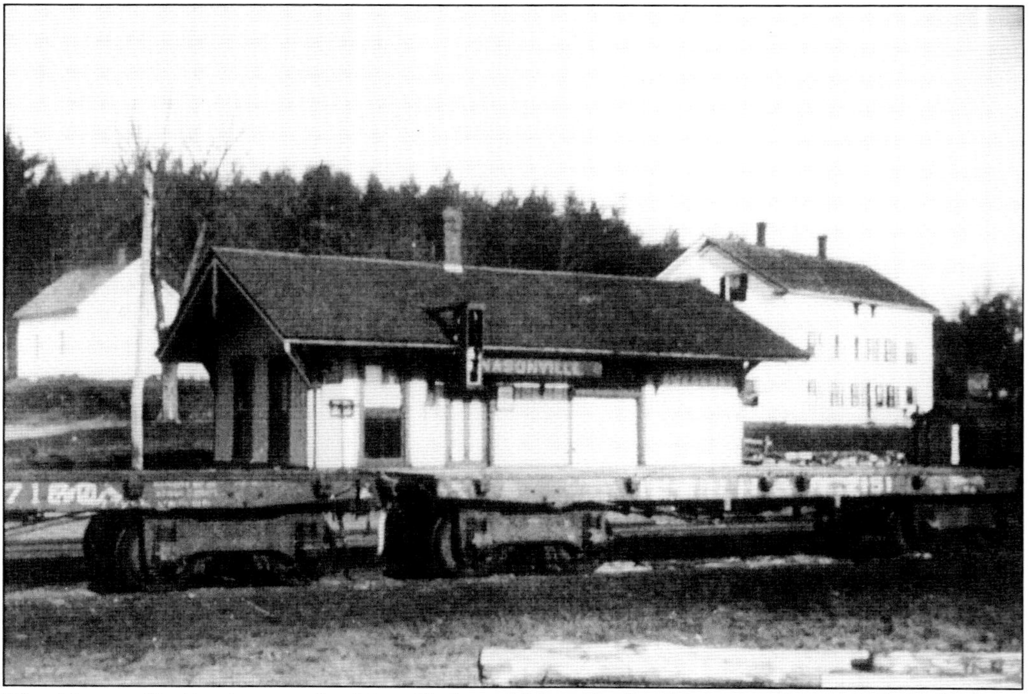

The Nasonville Station on the New York and New England line was located about halfway between Pascoag and Woonsocket.

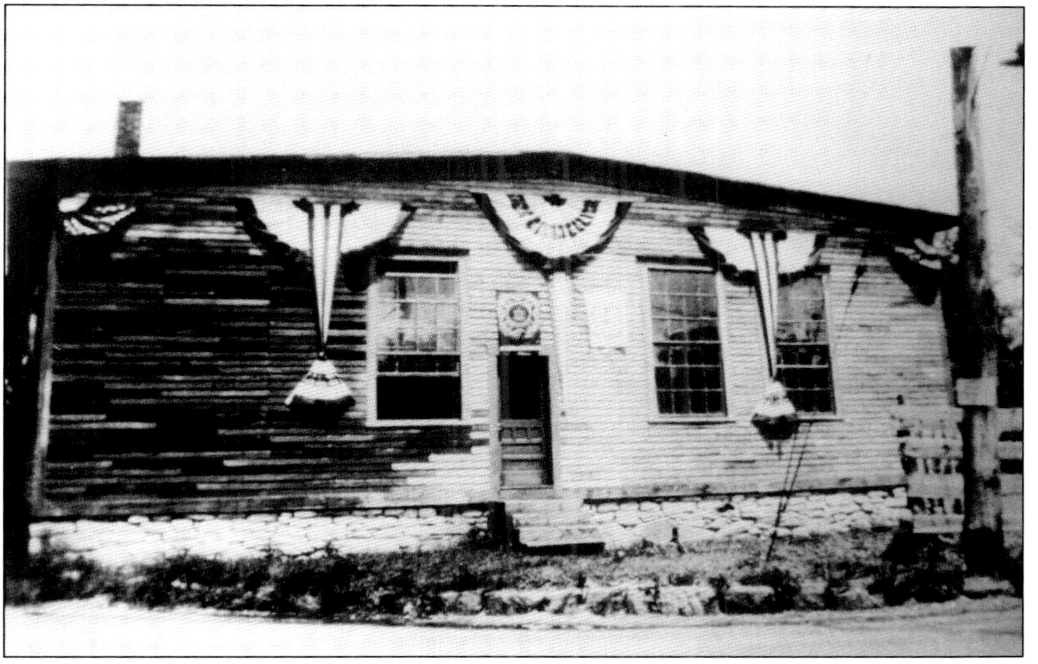

Jarvis's barn in Bridgeton was built in 1901, specifically for the storage and repair of the trolleys on the Woonsocket to Pascoag line. It is shown here decorated for the 1936 Rhode Island Tercentennial.

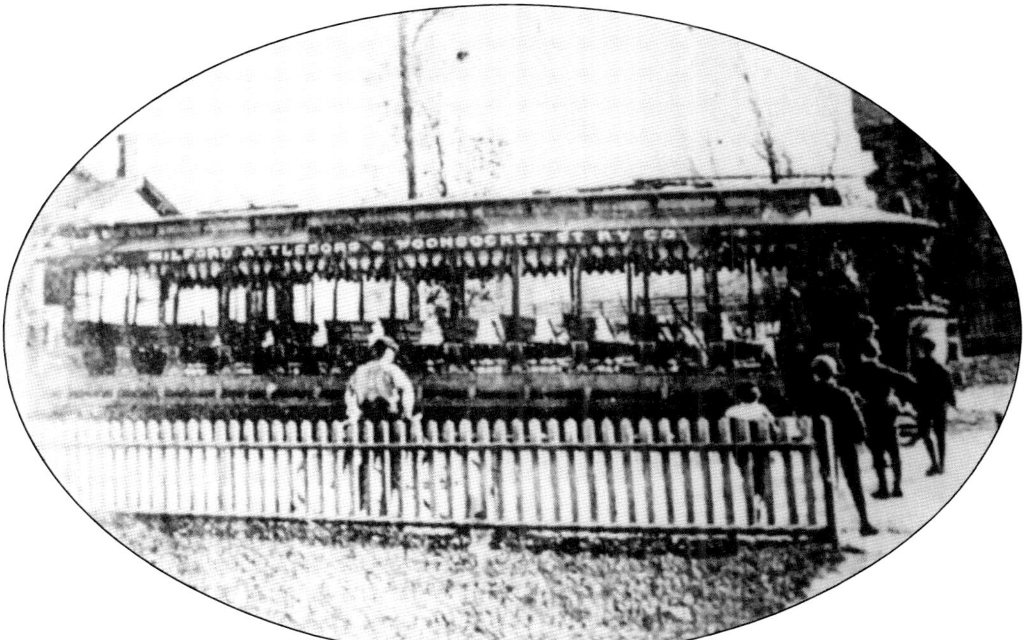

The first trolley on the Woonsocket to Pascoag line came to town on November 1, 1902. It was a great convenience for those who couldn't make the train connections. Trolleys and automobiles helped in the demise of the railroads in Burrillville.

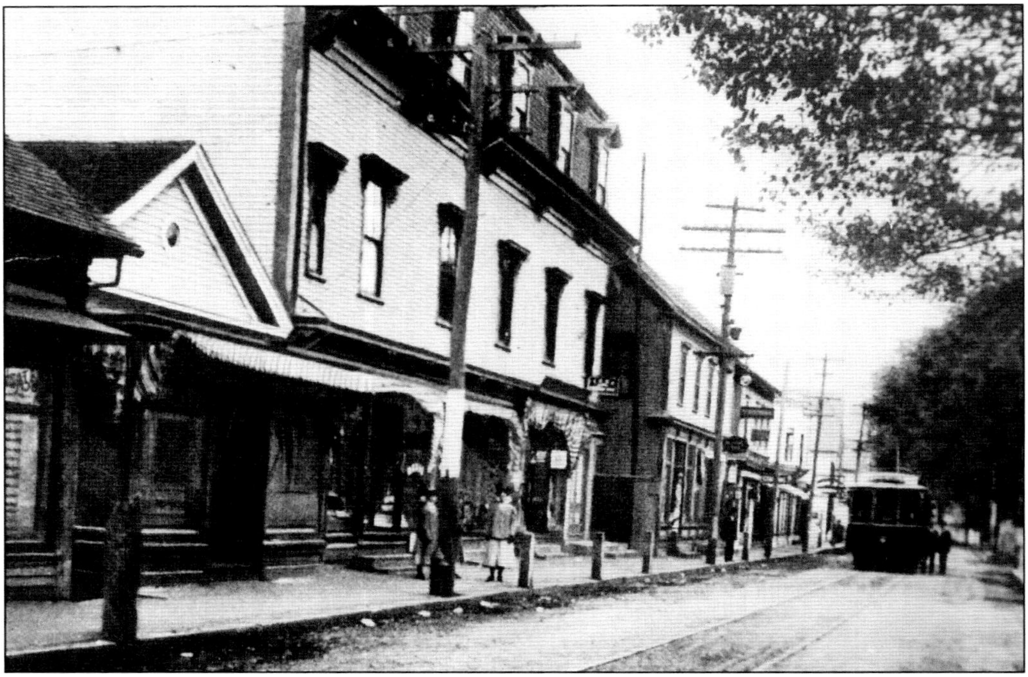

This *c.* 1910 photograph of a trolley on Main Street, Pascoag, shows the Smith Building and the Music Hall on the left. Some of the buildings on the right were destroyed by fire. Except for the trolley and tracks, it appears almost the same today.

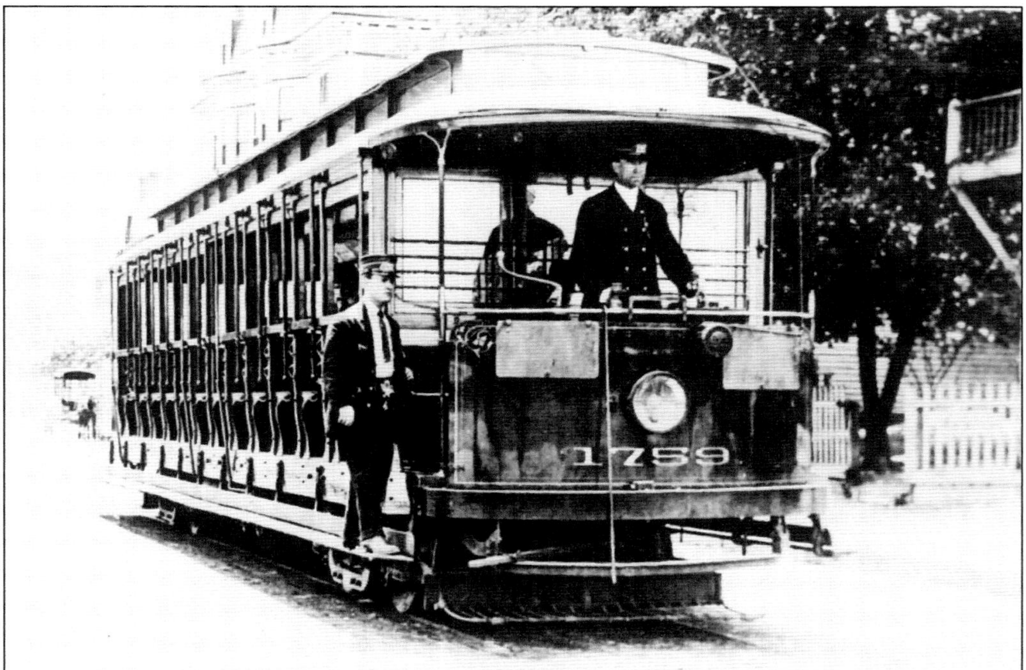

The Pascoag trolley was photographed at the end of its route in Woonsocket prior to 1928.

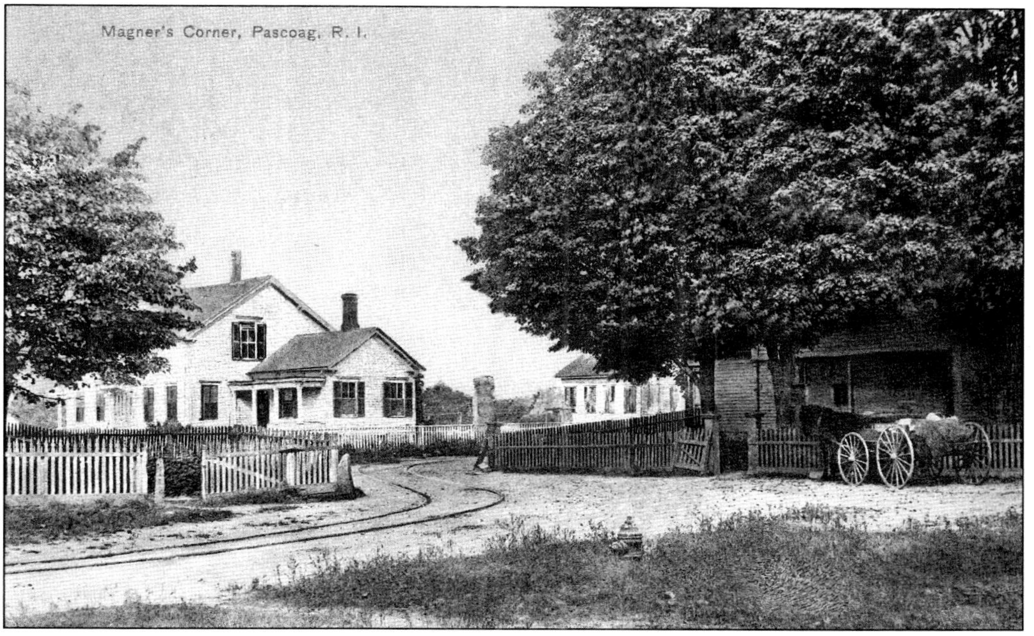

This photograph shows Magner's Corner and the trolley tracks off North Main Street in Pascoag. The Magner brothers operated the Silver Lake Worsted Mill, built in 1892, near here. A small weaving mill powered by steam, it was destroyed by fire in September 1895. The brothers then moved their operation to Glocester.

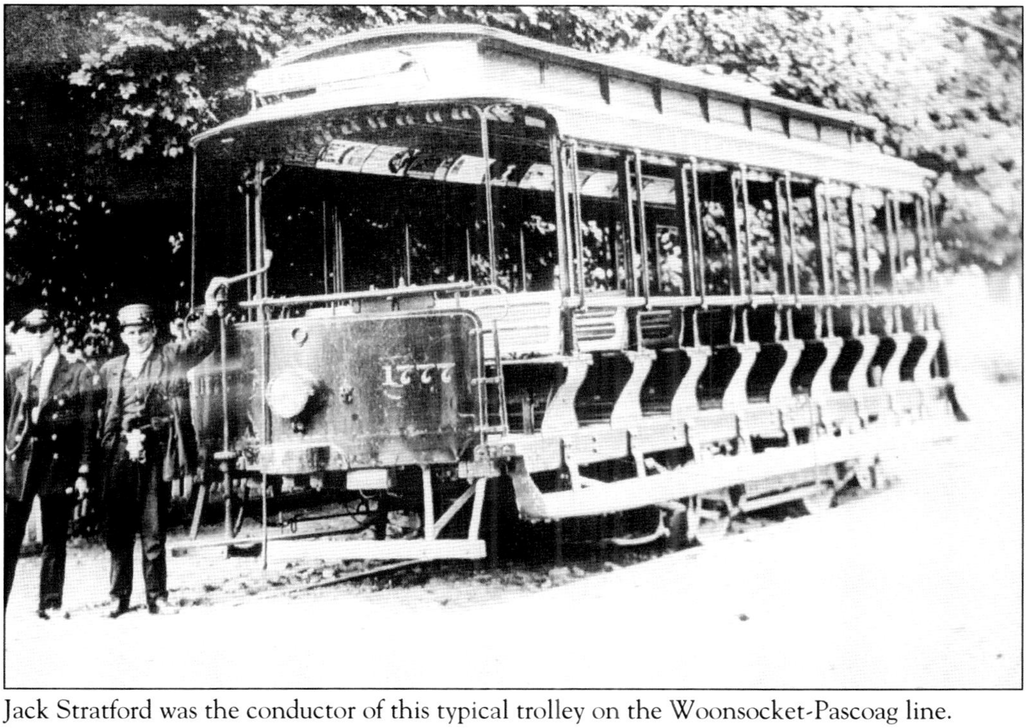

Jack Stratford was the conductor of this typical trolley on the Woonsocket-Pascoag line.

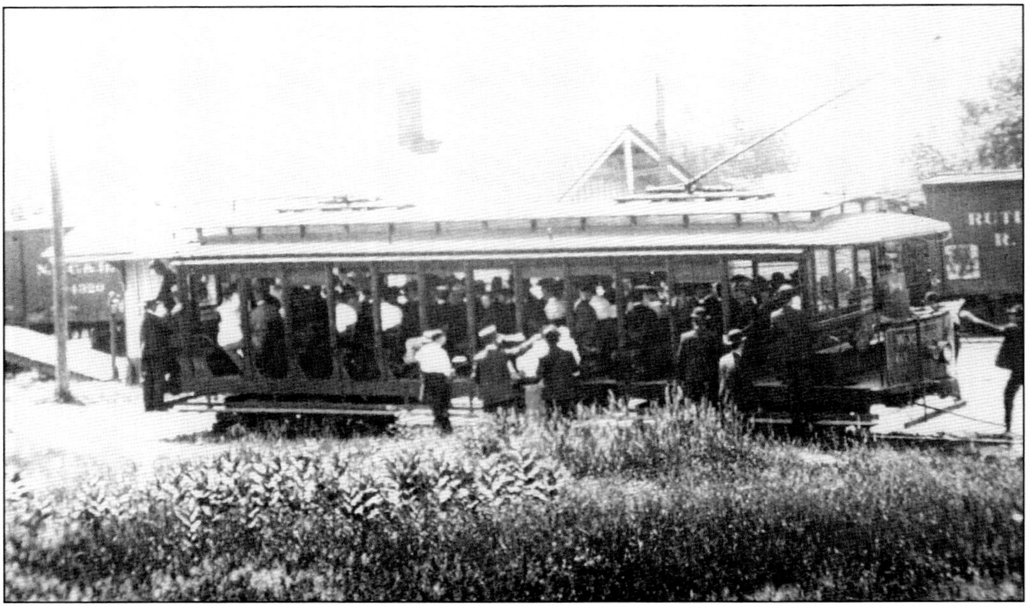

The Columbian Street Railway trolley line ran alongside the railroad tracks in Nasonville for a short distance. The railroad crossed the Branch River at this point, but the trolley line turned upward through Mohegan to continue its journey.

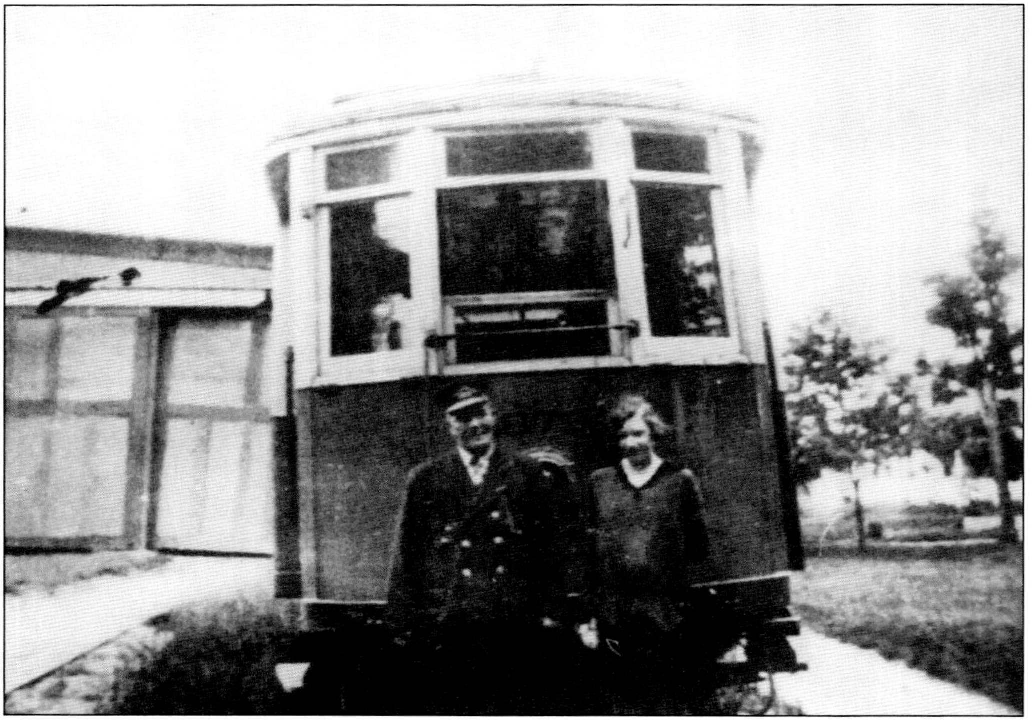

Ellery Mowry and Alice Keeling are shown here in front of the last trolley on the Woonsocket to Pascoag line, which departed the Bridgeton barn on September 17, 1928. Mr. Mowry was a motorman for years for the United Electric Railway Company.

Six

Parades and Entertainment

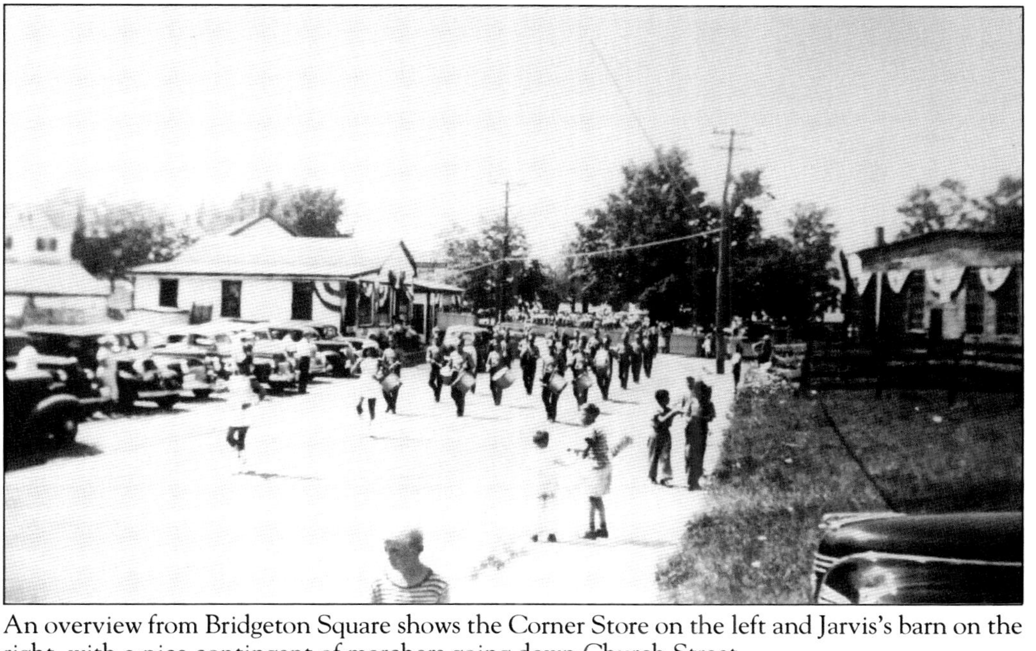

An overview from Bridgeton Square shows the Corner Store on the left and Jarvis's barn on the right, with a nice contingent of marchers going down Church Street.

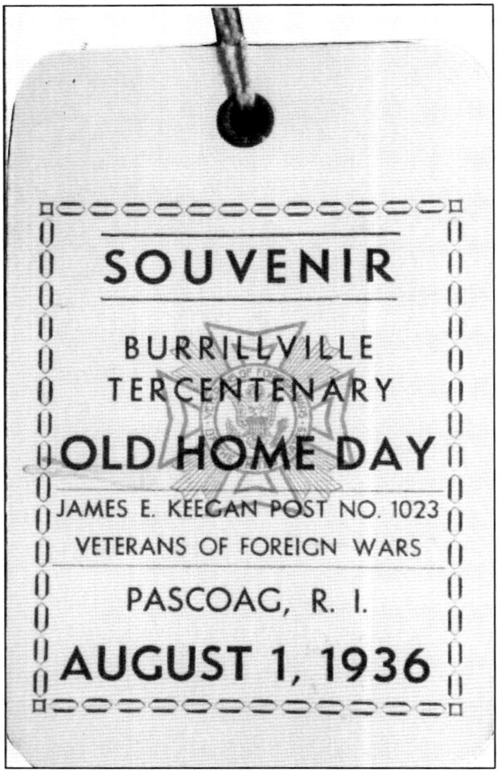

This Old Home Day tag is from Burrillville's celebration of the Rhode Island Tercentennial (1636–1936).

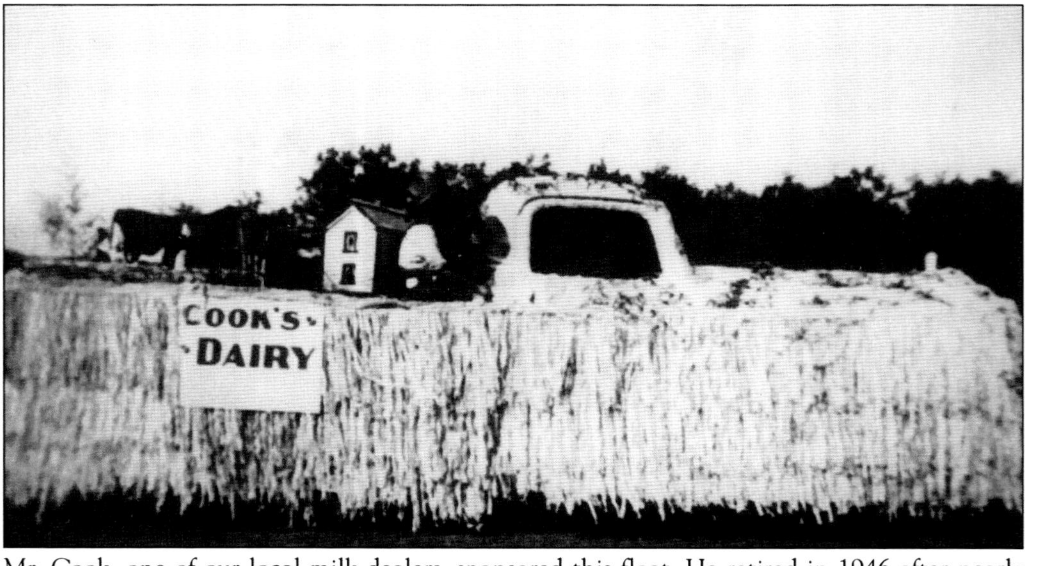

Mr. Cook, one of our local milk dealers, sponsored this float. He retired in 1946 after nearly thirty years in the business and sold out to the City Dairy of Woonsocket.

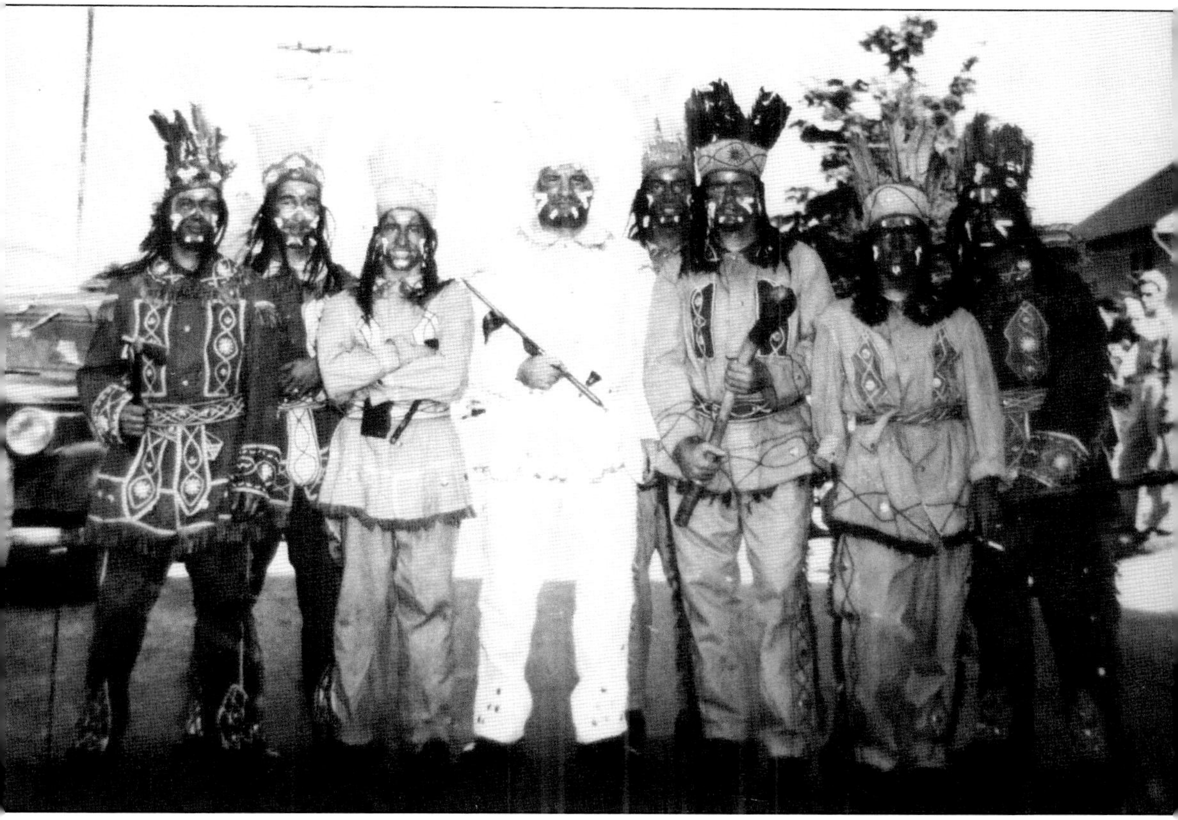

Members of the Ponagansett Tribe, the Improved Order of Red Men of Pascoag, stand ready to march in the Burrillville VJ Parade on August 16, 1948. John Kaczynski is dressed in white in the center.

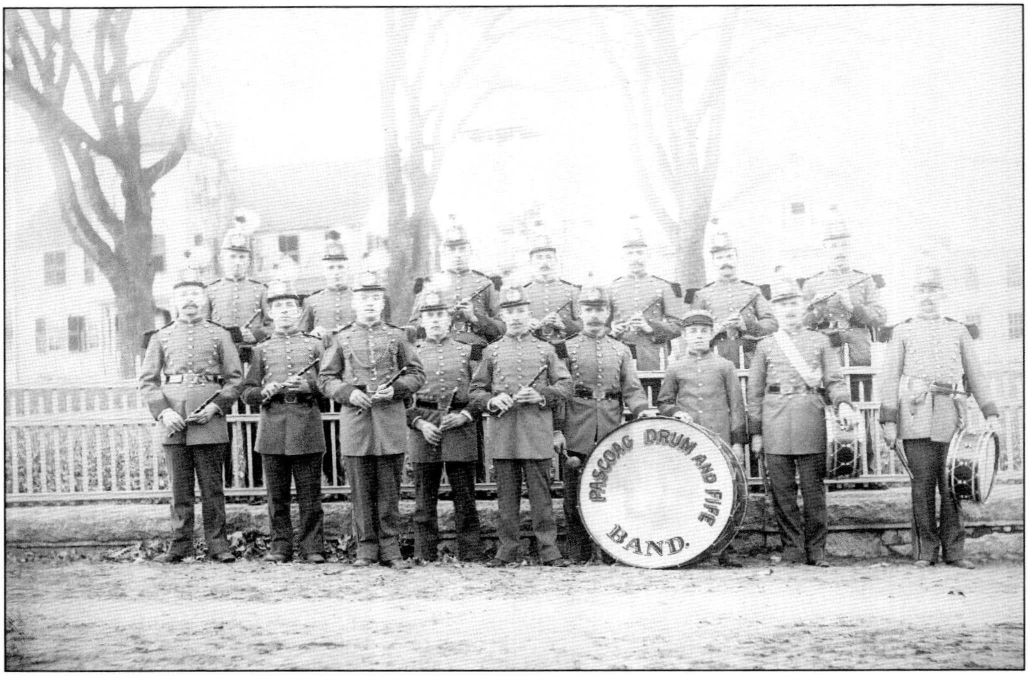

The Pascoag Drum and Fife Band made their first appearance on April 4, 1892. Each village had a band made up of amateur musicians who were proud to participate in every parade in Burrillville. When they first organized, quite a number of the members could not tell one note from another. After three weeks, they were ready to perform.

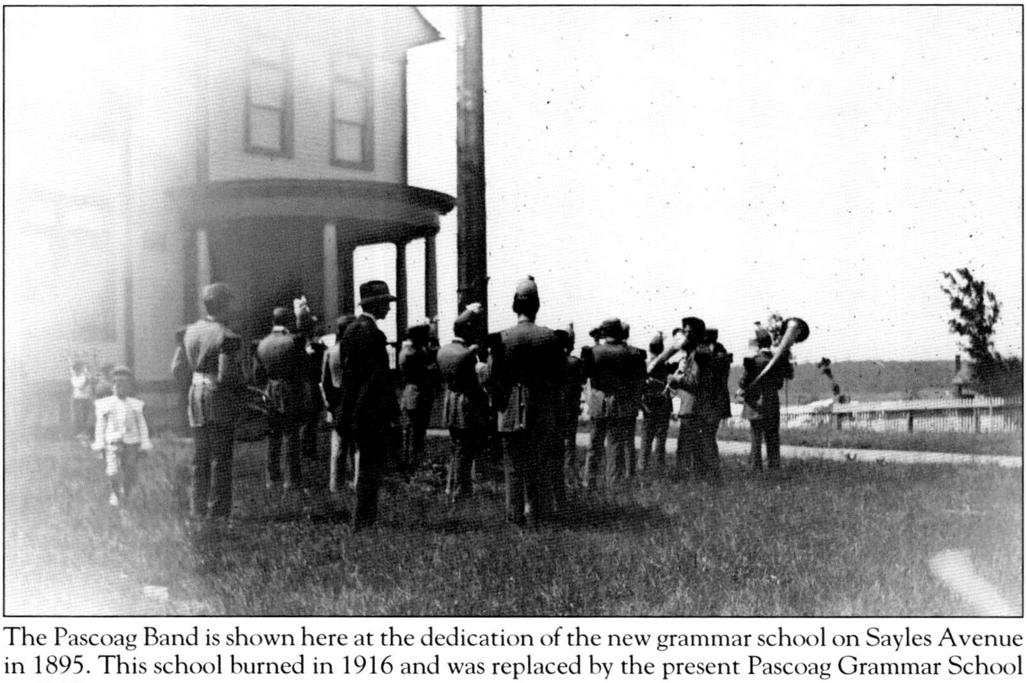

The Pascoag Band is shown here at the dedication of the new grammar school on Sayles Avenue in 1895. This school burned in 1916 and was replaced by the present Pascoag Grammar School in 1917.

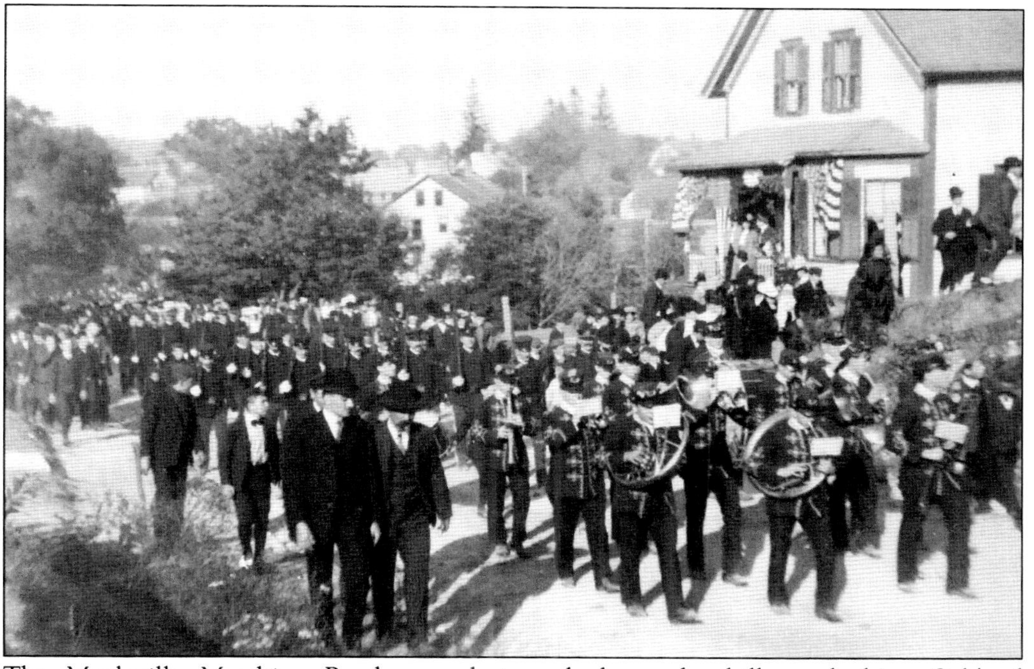

The Mapleville Marching Band was photographed on the hill overlooking Oakland and Mapleville.

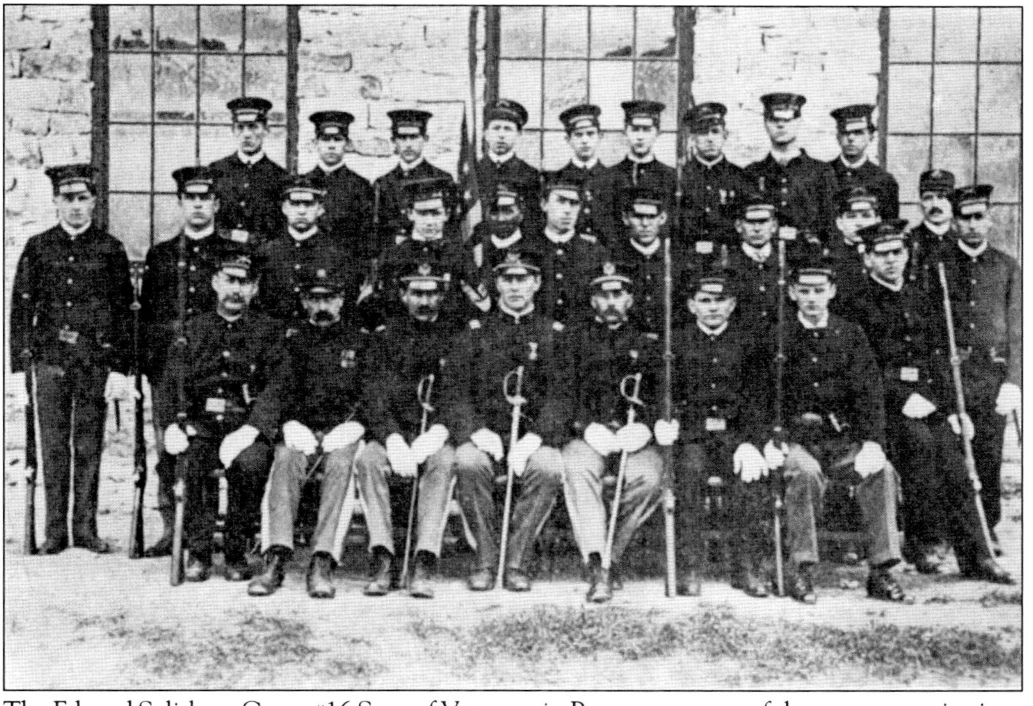

The Edward Salisbury Camp #16 Sons of Veterans in Pascoag was one of the many organizations in Burrillville which marched in the first Old Home Day Celebration in 1915.

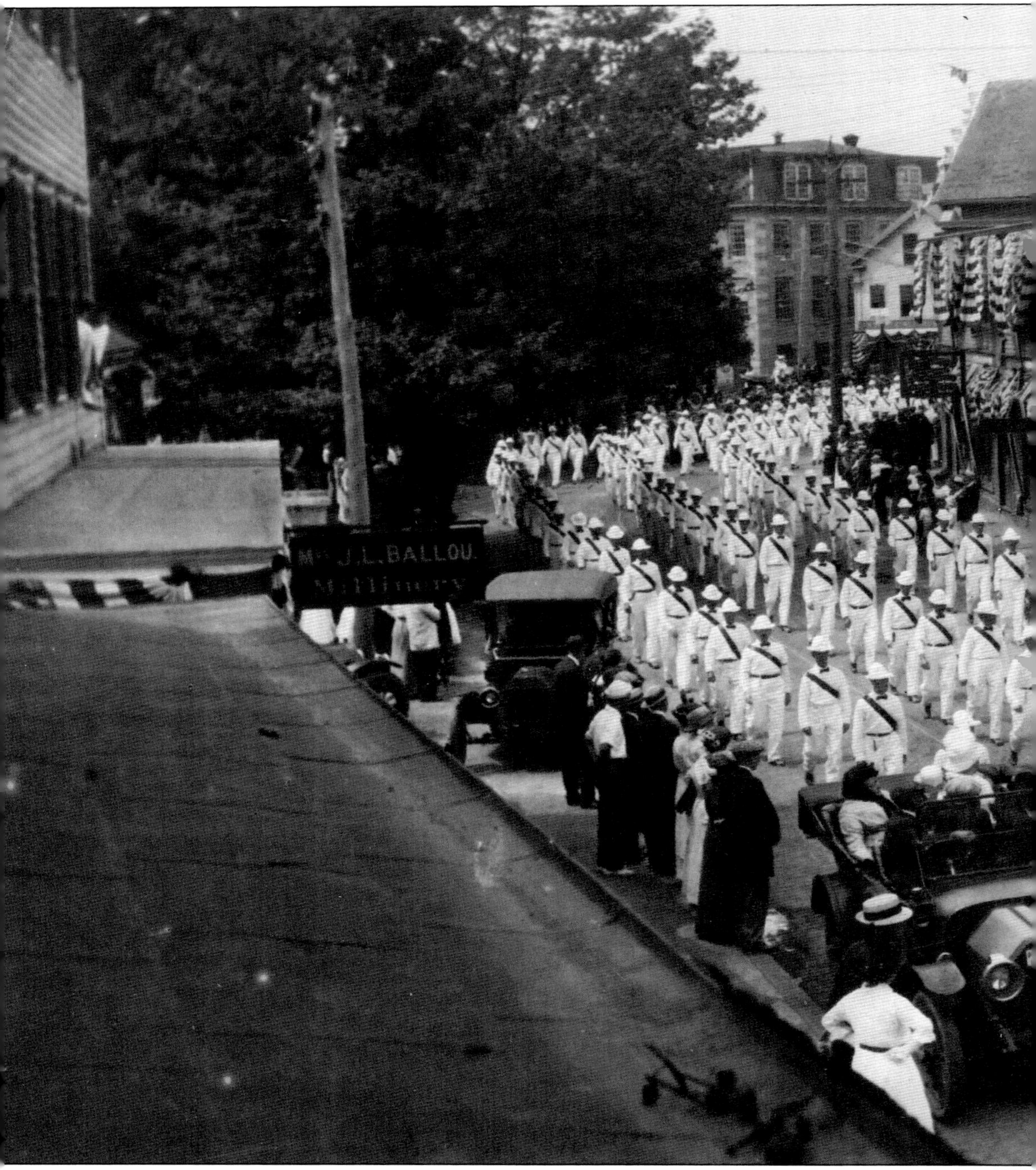

The 1915 Old Home Day Parade in downtown Pascoag was organized by the Pascoag Fire Department Companies #1 and #2. The large marching contingent is from the Granite Lodge of Pascoag. The street parade went from 9 to 10 am, starting from Fountain Square, Pascoag. A Rhode Island clambake was held at Griffith's Grove from 12 to 3:30 pm, supervised by Mr. Austin of Rocky Point, with at least three tables seating about five hundred people apiece. Speeches by the governor, the lieutenant governor, the congressman, etc. began at 3:30 pm.

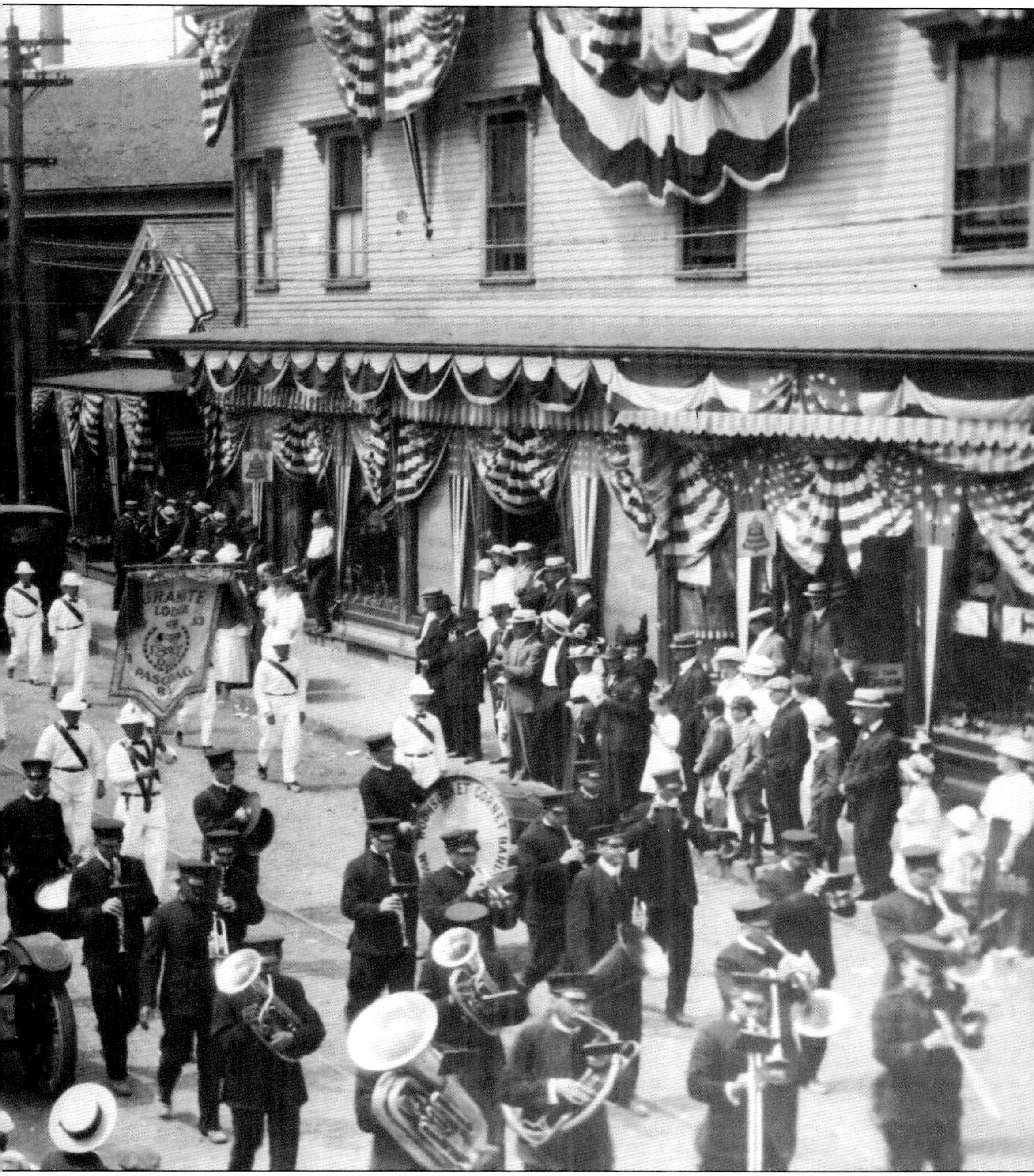

An aerial exhibition by "Jack" McGee in his Curtis biplane started at 5 pm. A promenade concert and dancing on the grounds, illuminated by electricity as well as by the moonlight from a full moon, occurred on the 26th. Prizes were given to the society making the best appearance, the society having the most members in line, and to the creators of the float or other vehicle making the best appearance.

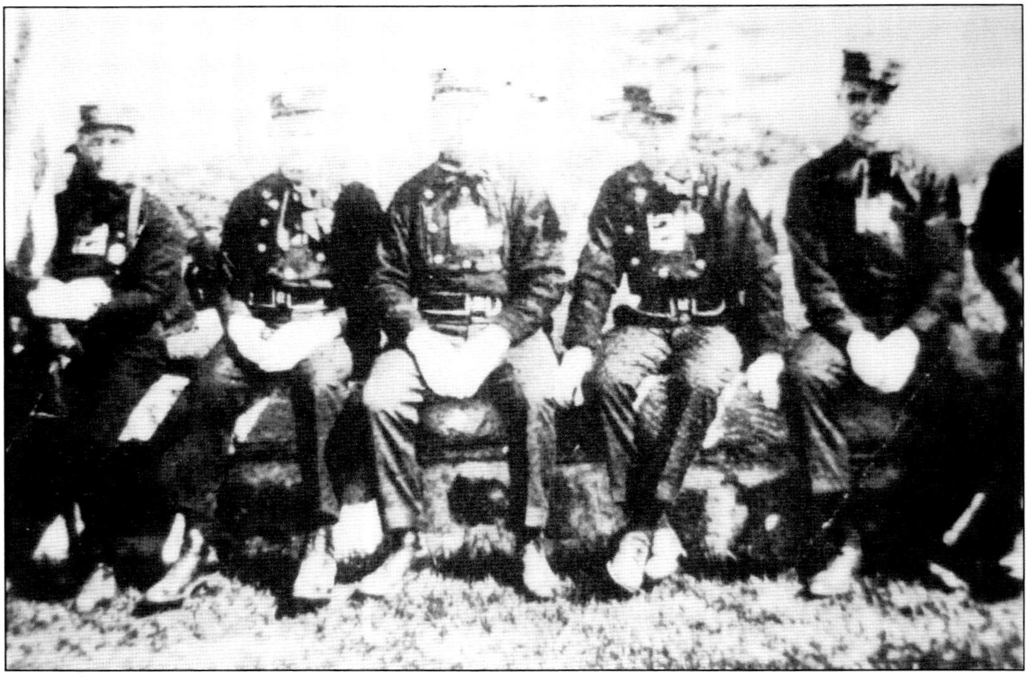

The uniform tops of the Bridgeton firemen were made of red felt and used for parades and celebrations. Milton Sherman (second from the left) was buried in his uniform when he died in 1989 at the age of ninety-six.

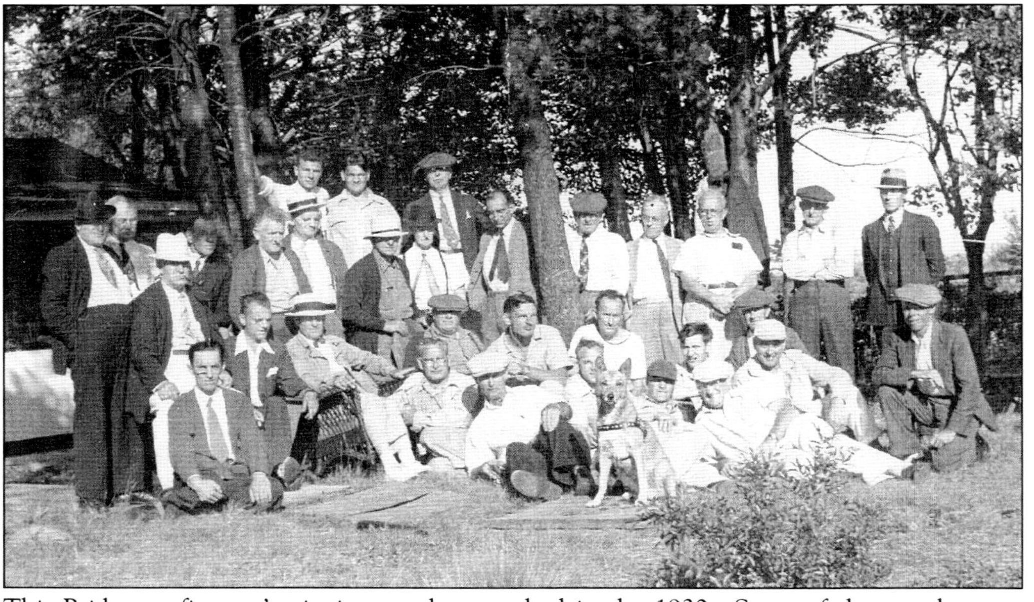

This Bridgeton firemen's picnic was photographed in the 1930s. Some of the members are Keyes, Charles and Vernon Bailey, George Dunn, Milton Sherman, James Nicholson, William Dickey, Harry Esten, Philip Rogers, "Tink" Angell, Peter Kapas, "Buddy" Patterson, Albert Green, and Marshal and Frank Shaw. All our fire departments were and are still today totally staffed by volunteers.

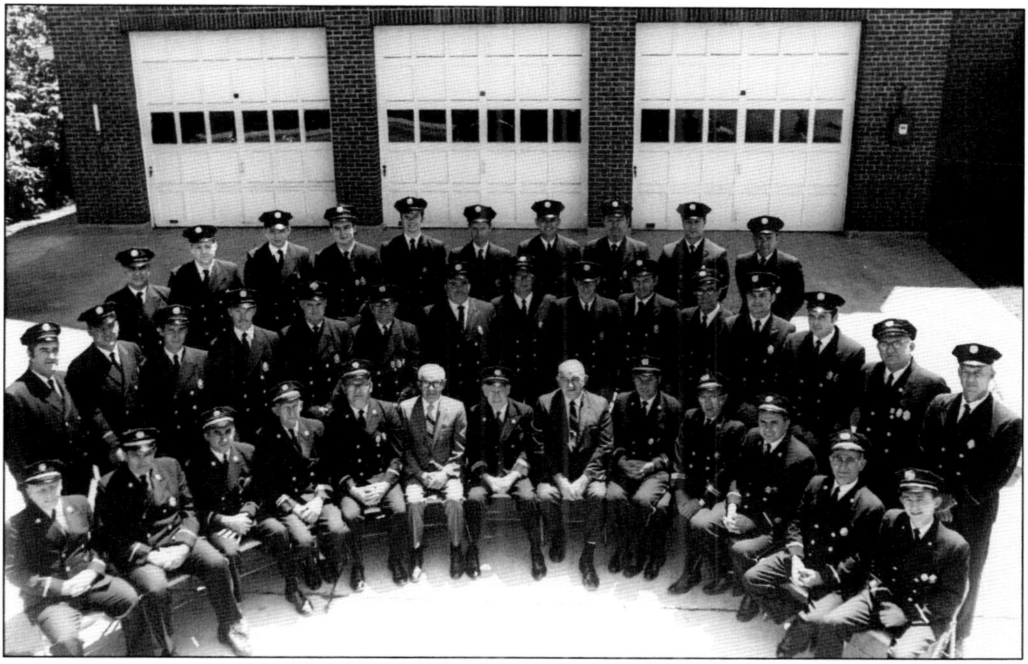

The volunteer members of the Pascoag Fire Department are shown here around 1952. Pascoag Hose #1 was started in 1903 after a disastrous fire. The building cost $50,000 in 1939 and was built with WPA funds.

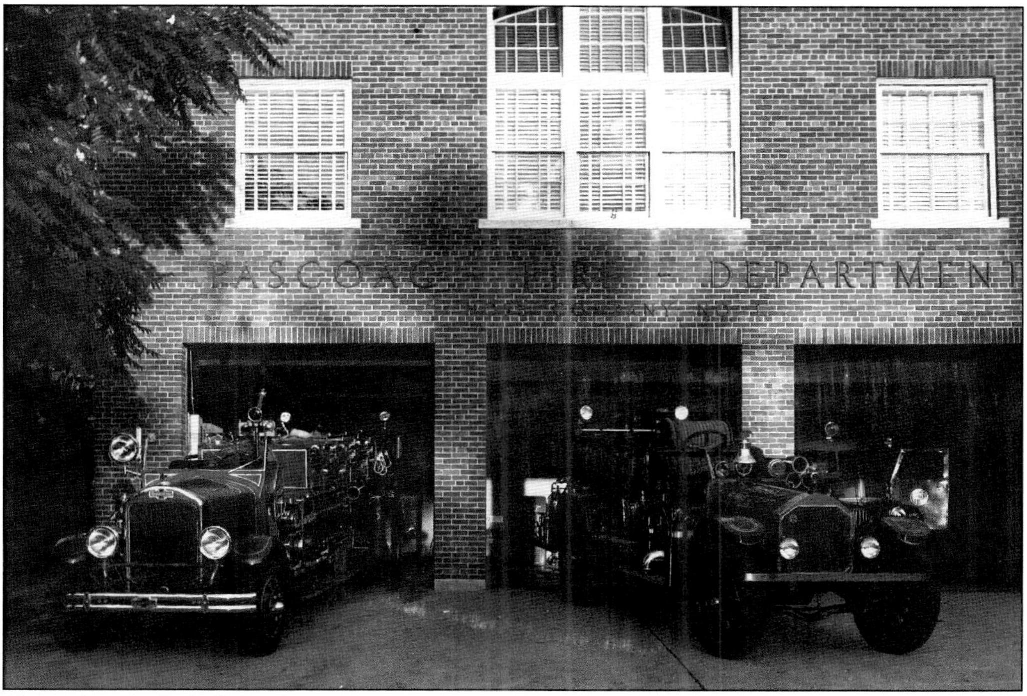

These fire trucks belonged to Hose #1 in Pascoag. Every village has their own fire department, manned by volunteers who dedicate their lives to protect our homes and families.

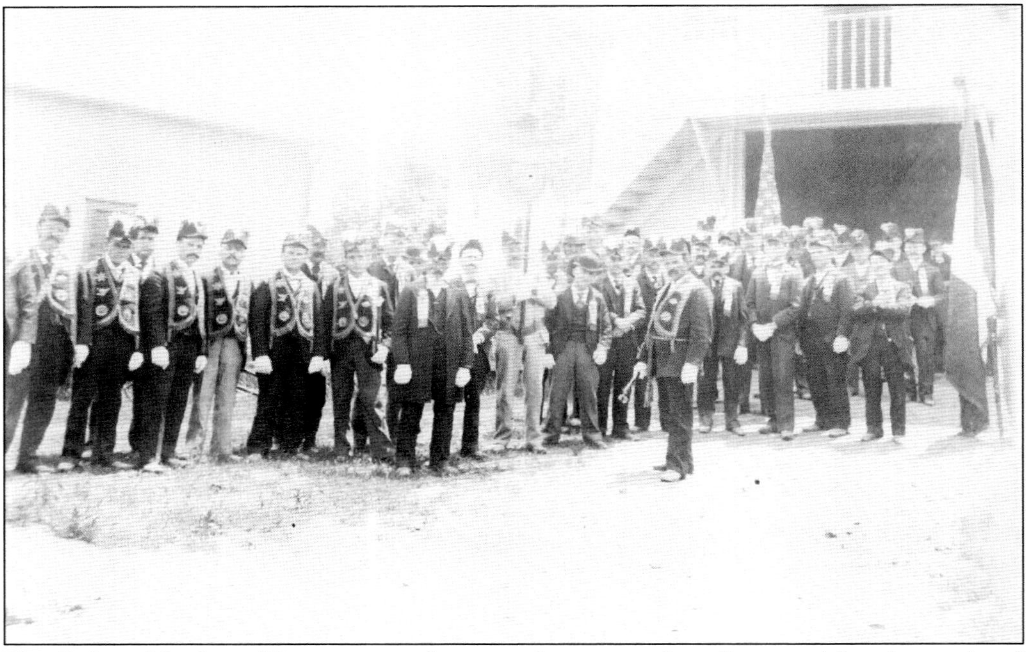

The Order of St. Jean d'Baptists is ready to march in a parade in Pascoag. Most fraternal and religious organizations participated in community celebrations.

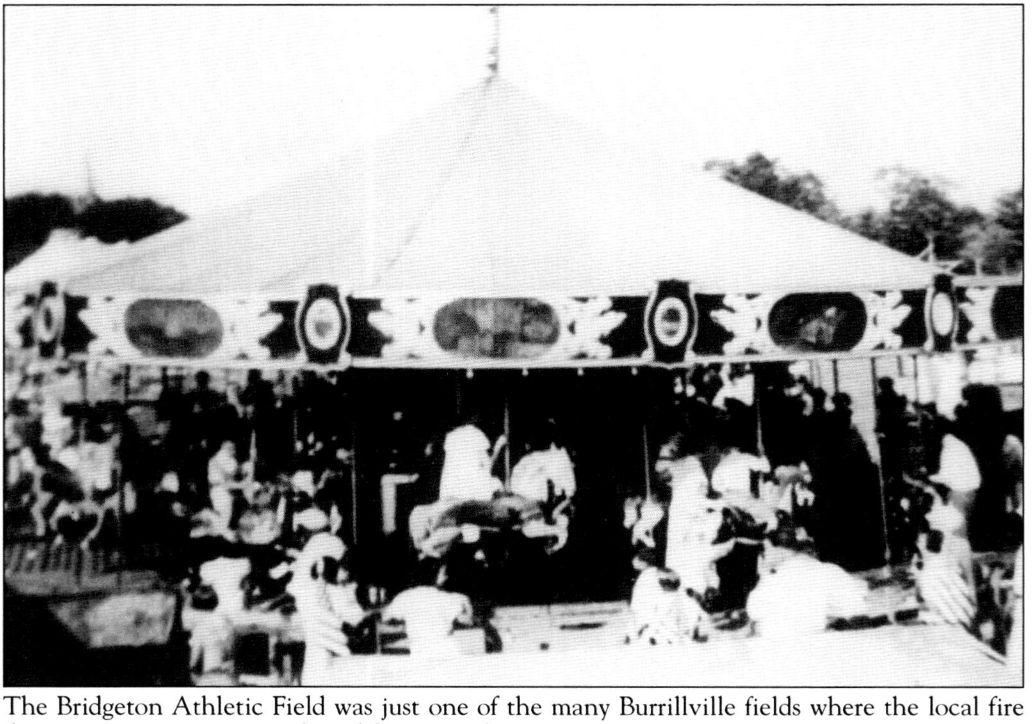

The Bridgeton Athletic Field was just one of the many Burrillville fields where the local fire departments put on carnivals and fairs over the years.

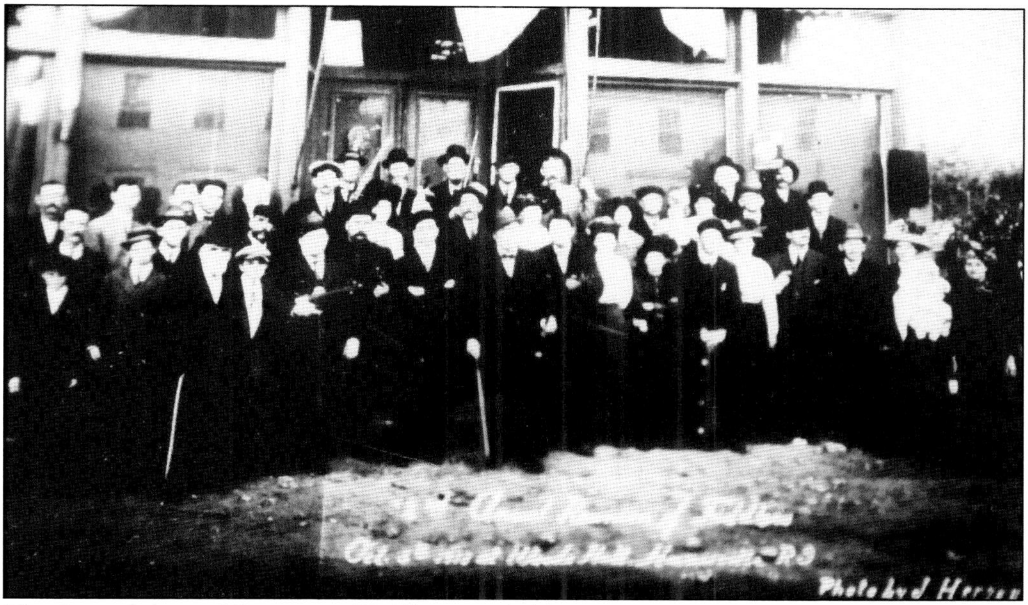

The Second Annual Reunion of Fiddlers was held in Otis Wood's hall in Harrisville in 1913. Many Burrillville fiddlers, including the Angells, the Spinks, and the Mitchells, made their own instruments. Stephen Mitchell is the baby in his mother's arms on the right.

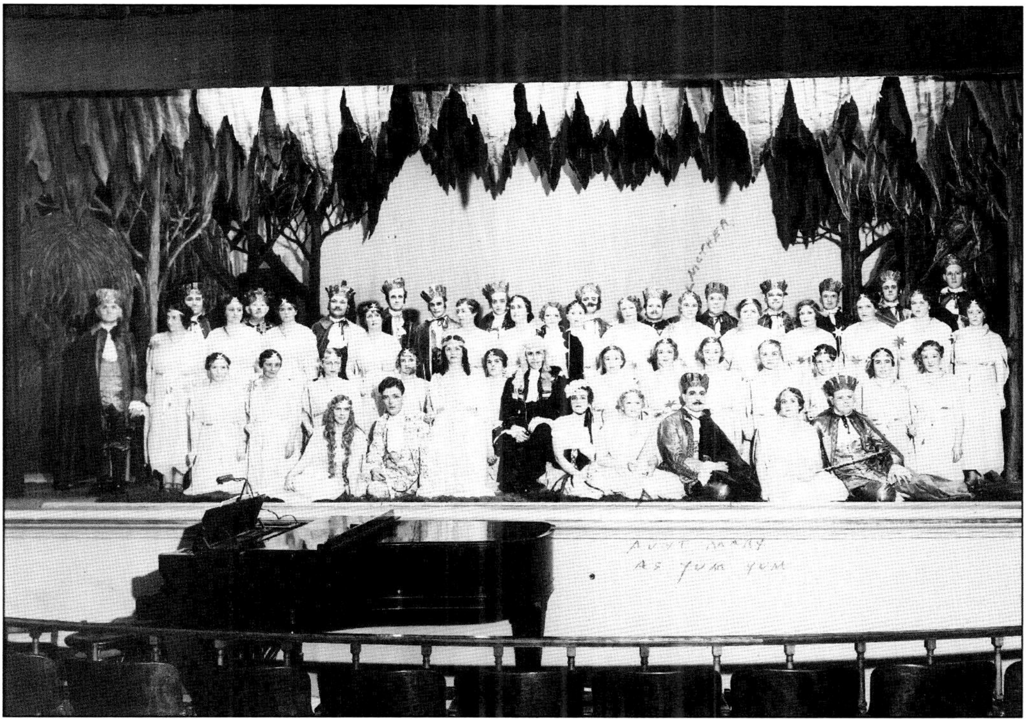

This show was put on at the new Assembly Theatre in Harrisville in 1935. It was one of the many grand productions that combined local talent with professional directors (hired by Austin T. Levy) to bring entertainment to the citizens of Burrillville.

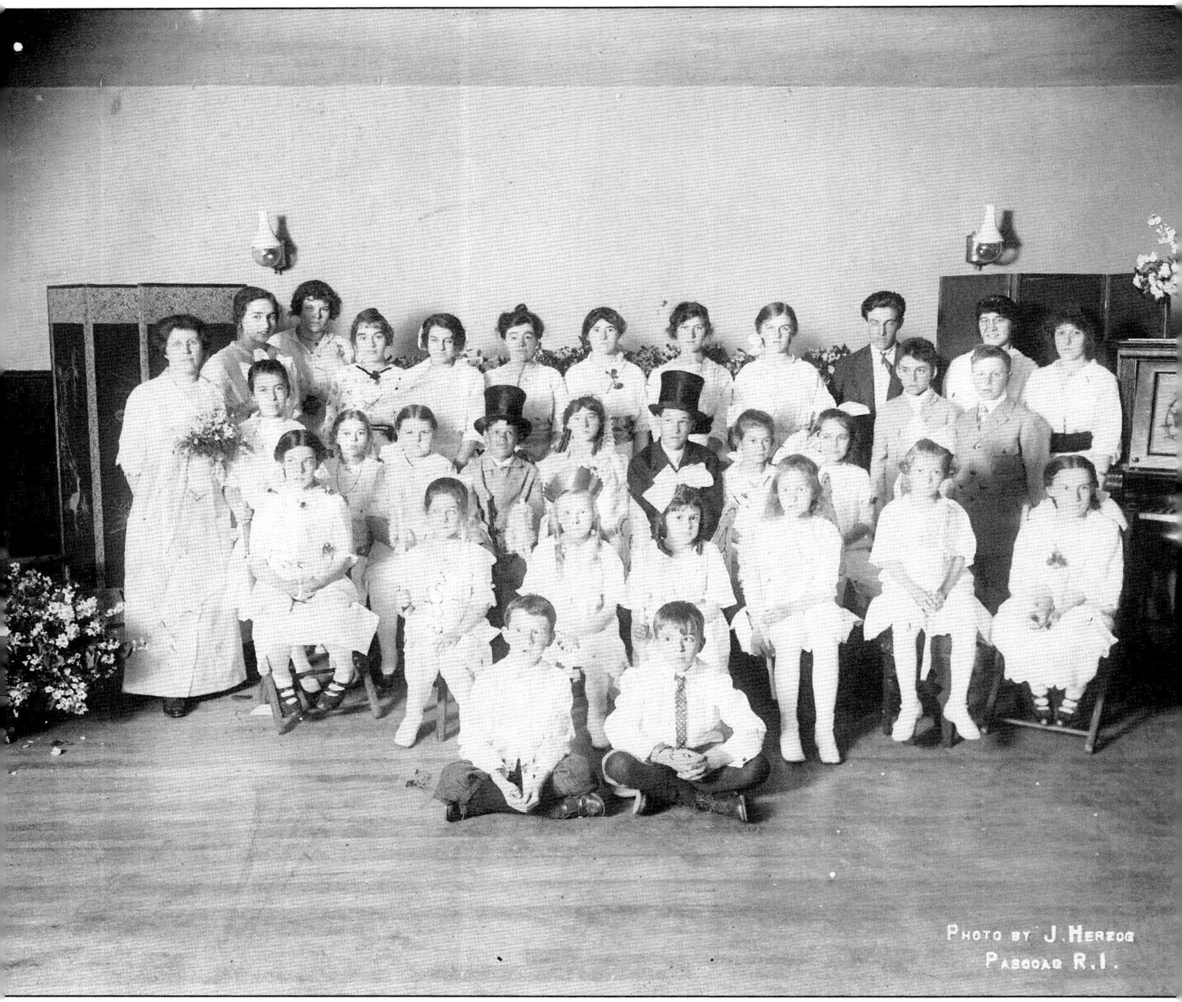

This recital was given in 1914 in the Golden Cross Hall above the New York Department Store in Pascoag. From left to right are: (first row) Wendell Wade and Edward Lovejoy; (second row) Rosa Burnett, Etta Mowry, Alice Miester, unknown, Winifred Hinchliffe, Alice Burnam, and Viola Green; (third row) teacher Winifred Hopkins, Siliva Silvia, Editha Lovejoy, Ethel Wilcox, ? Taft, Ivy Sayles, George Shea, Emma Inman, Blanche Silvia, unknown, and George Coleman; (back row) Stella Rogers, unknown, Emma Rogers, unknown, Erminie Hill, Marion Hill, Vesta Carpenter, ? Shea, Franklin Green, unknown, and unknown.

Seven

Village Streets

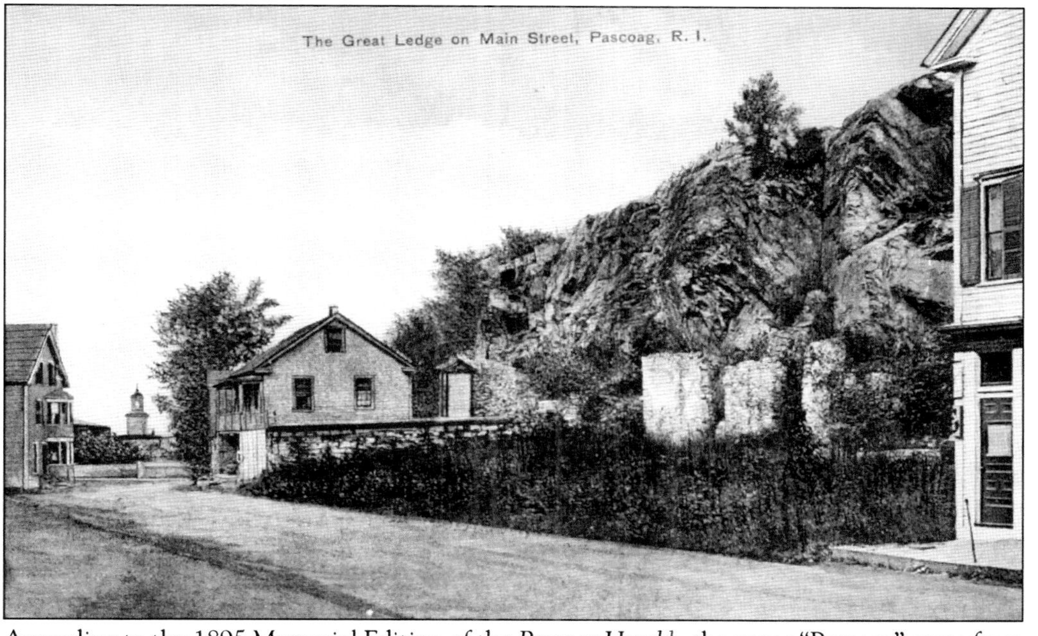

According to the 1895 Memorial Edition of the *Pascoag Herald* , the name "Pascoag" came from the Indian name of the stream which flows in the area of what is now the Reservoir. "Coag" signified "snake" in the Indian tongue; because of the many ledges in the area, there were many snakes. "Pas-coag" means "to pass a snake." Stone from this particular ledge was used in building the foundations of some of the local mills.

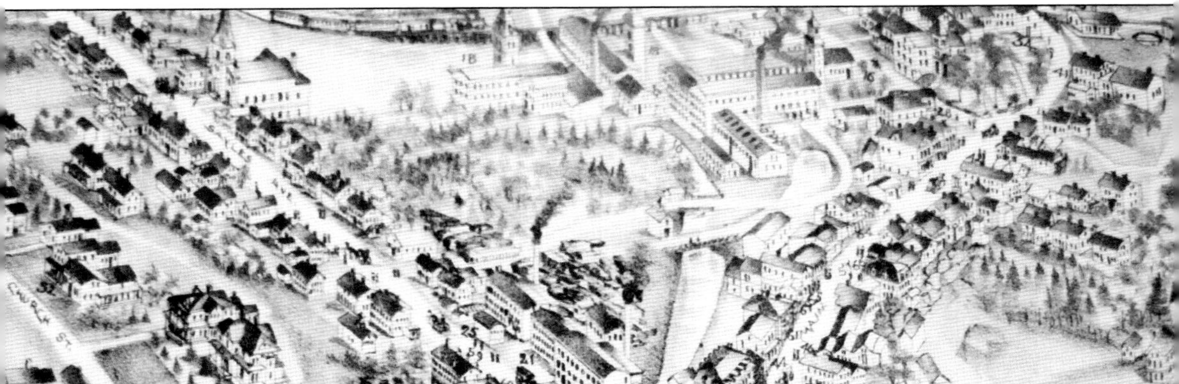

This overview of the downtown Pascoag mills and Main Street is from the 1895 *Pascoag Herald* map. Union Pond is in the lower middle facing the Sayles Mill. Sayles Avenue joins South Main Street at Main Street cutting diagonally across the picture from the left top. A mill sits on the site of what is now the Bridgeway. All the mills shown here have disappeared over the years, either due to fire or demolition, but much of the rest has stayed basically the same.

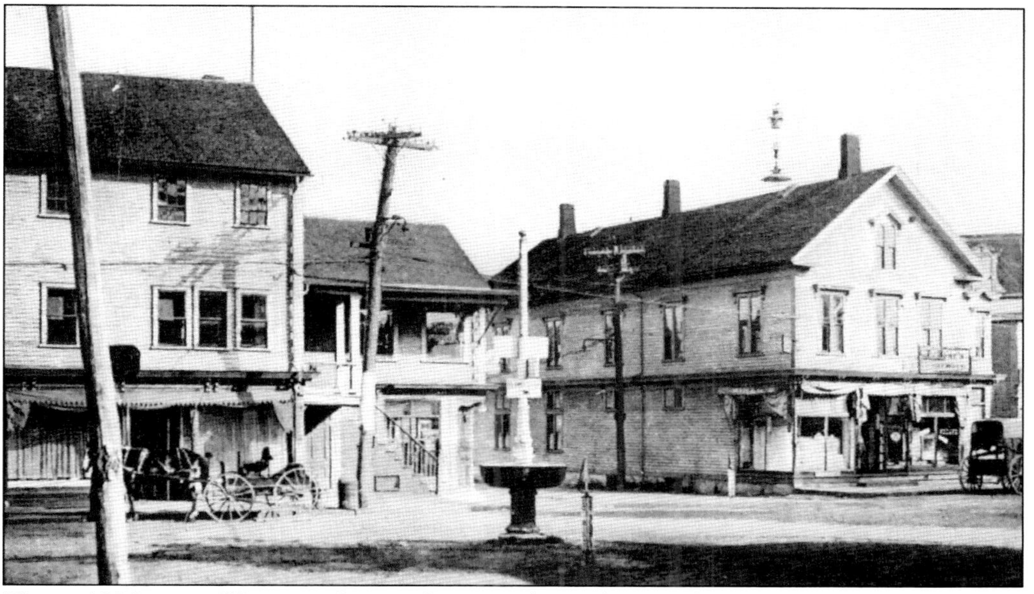

This *c.* 1906 view of Fountain Square, Pascoag, shows the complex of buildings known later as the New York Department Store on the left. A W.W. Logee Insurance sign can be seen on the second floor at the right. Rosenberg's closed the store and sold the building in 1975.

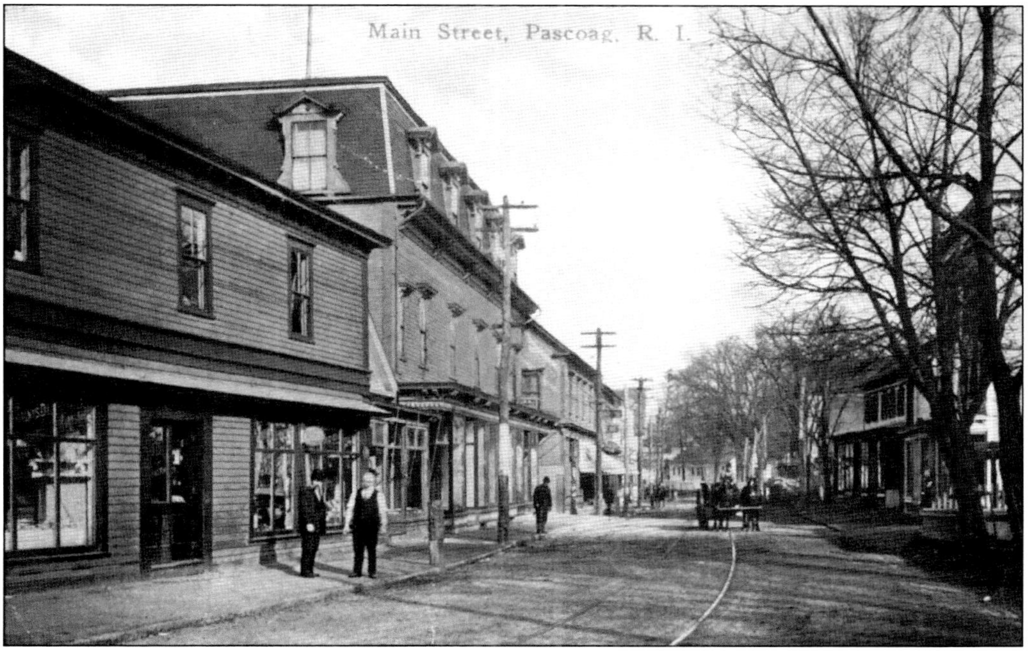

Downtown Pascoag was photographed during the era of the horse and buggy. Smith Hardware is on the left.

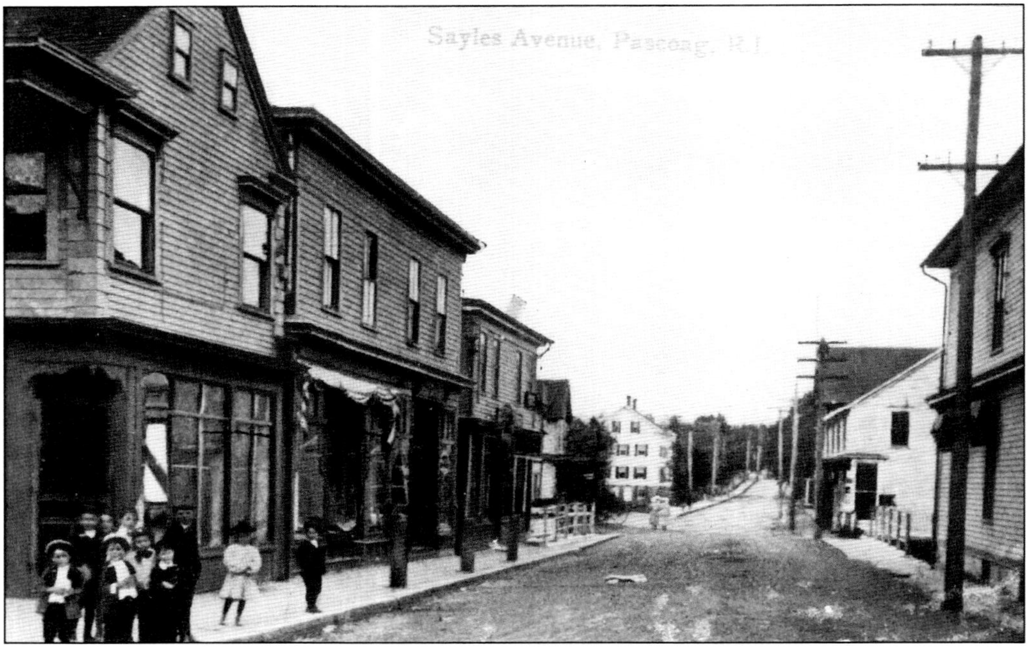

The seven small buildings on the left in this view, looking up Sayles Avenue from Fountain Square around 1906, were eventually all combined into one. The right side has changed very little.

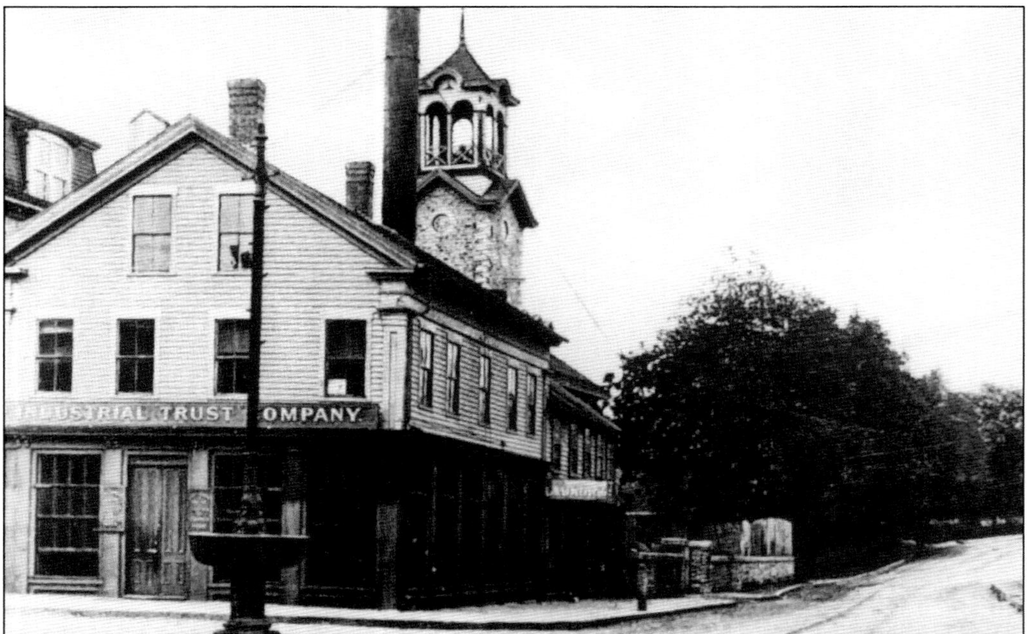

This building, built in 1903 on the corner of South Main and High Street, housed several businesses over the years: the Industrial Bank, the Ford Motor Company, and Gautreau's Restaurant. The building was razed in the spring of 1948. Gautreau's then moved to Chepachet.

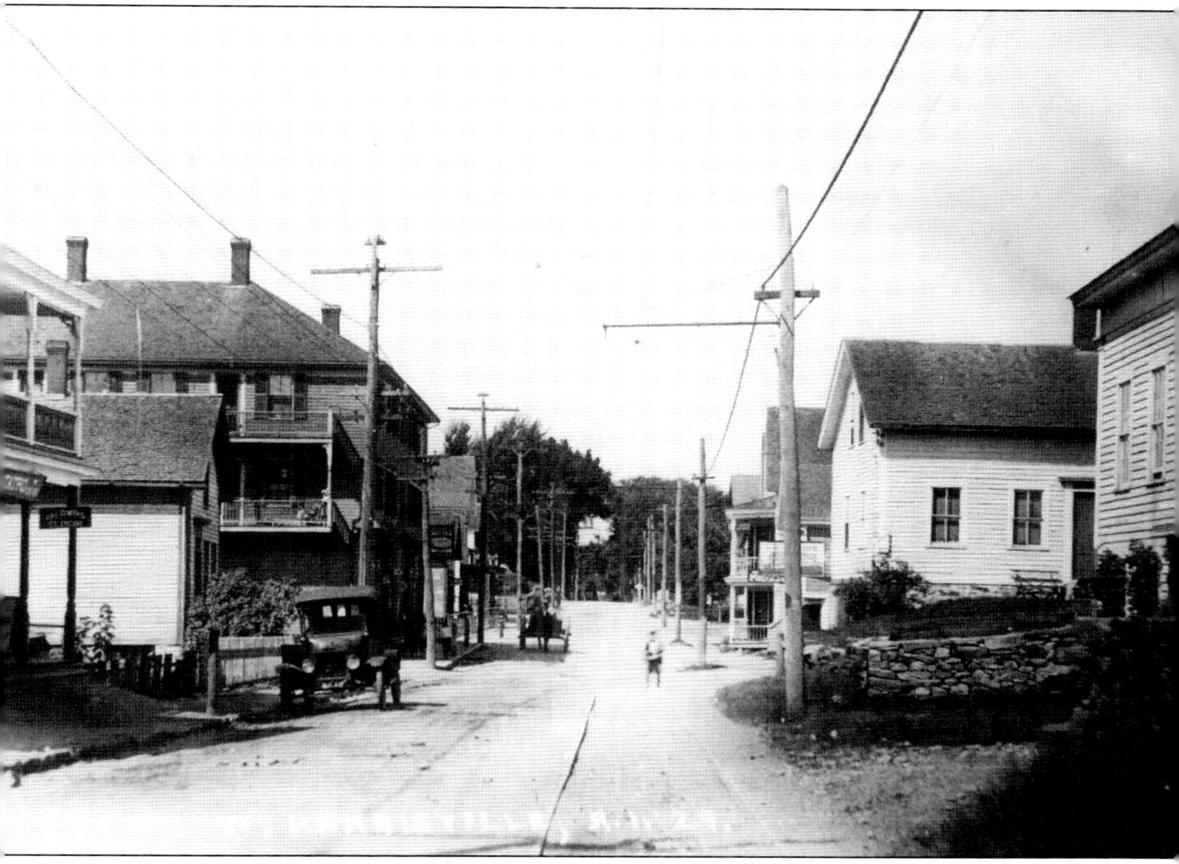

Chapel Street in Harrisville was photographed in the 1920s. Tatro's store is on the left. Horses and buggies as well as automobiles shared the road with trolleys. There always had to be someone posing in the middle of the road whenever the photographer came to town. The houses in the right foreground were moved by Mr. Levy and replaced by newer homes for his supervisors. Because of Mr. Levy's influence, the village of Harrisville is on the National Register of Historic Places.

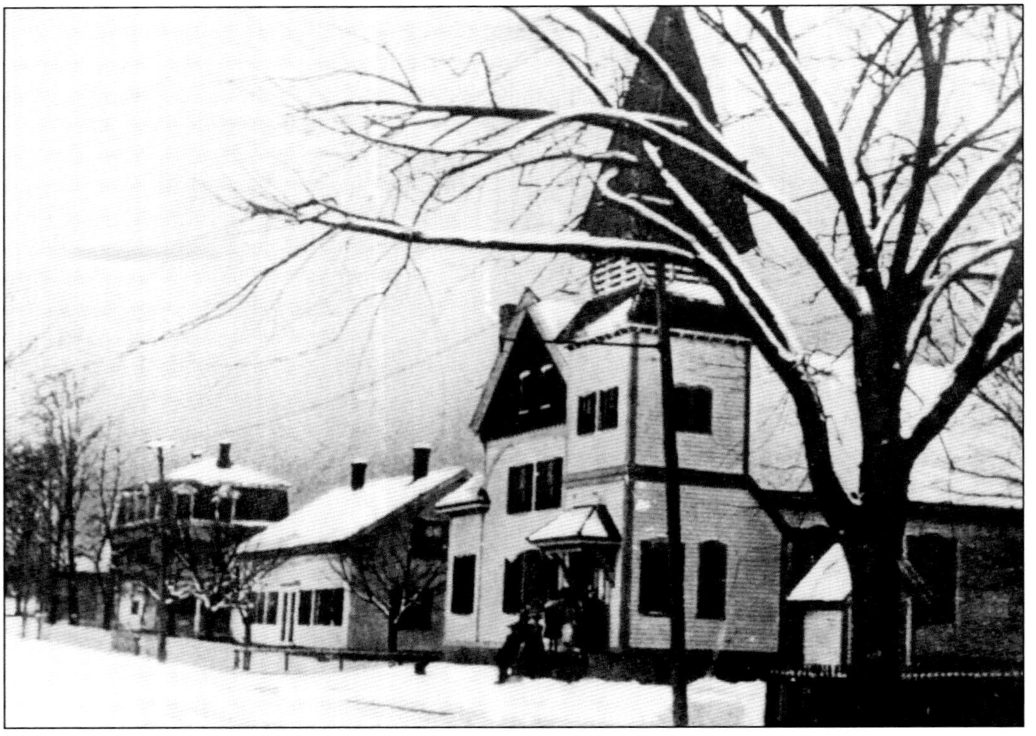

Chapel Street, Harrisville, is shown here prior to the changes made in the Berean Baptist Church in the 1930s by Mr. Levy. The Burrillville Town Hall was built on the lot to the right of the church.

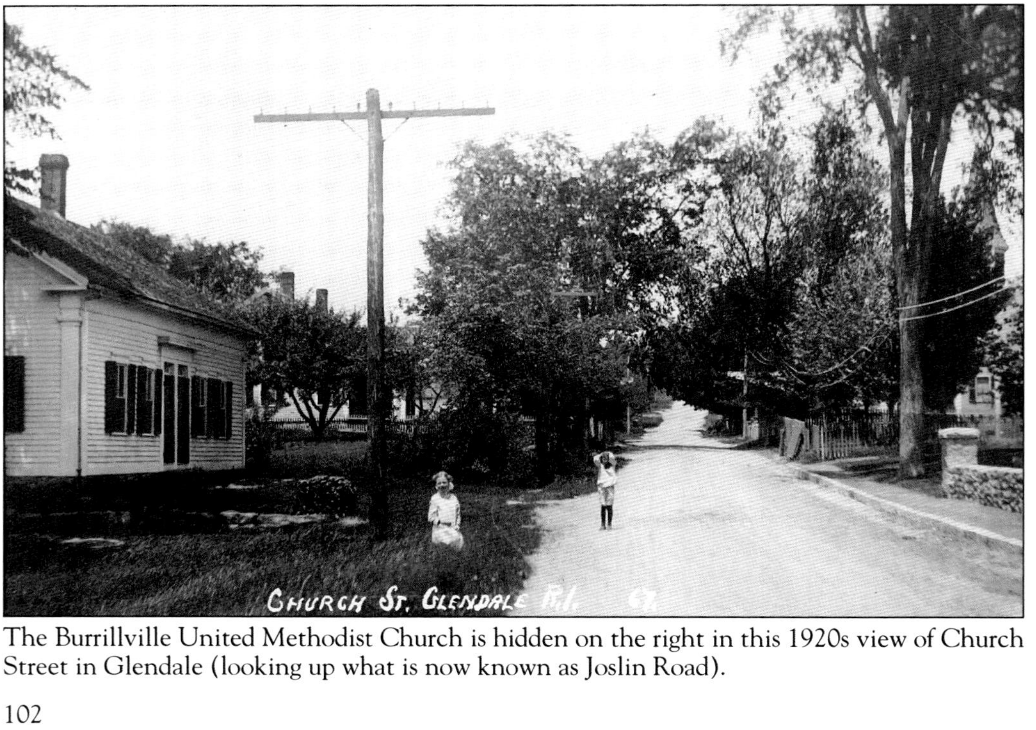

The Burrillville United Methodist Church is hidden on the right in this 1920s view of Church Street in Glendale (looking up what is now known as Joslin Road).

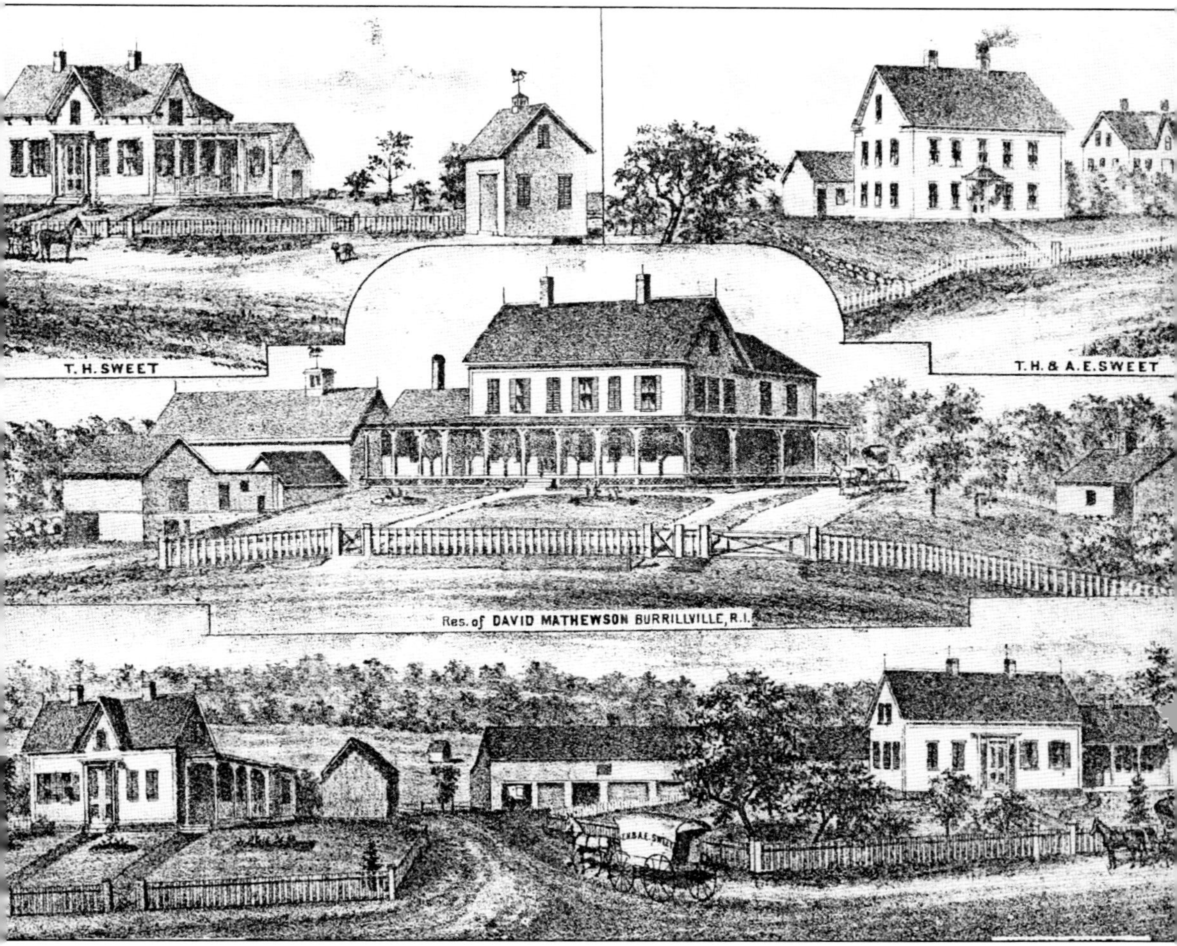

This etching shows Mathewson Avenue (now East Avenue) in Harrisville. The house in the middle was the residence of Welcome Mathewson, a local gunsmith whose family settled the original farm. In later years, it was known as Sweet's Dairy Farm and furnished beef and milk to the town. It was demolished in the early 1990s, but the other houses remain. In back of this farm was a quarry where stones were cut and sent by rail to Providence for building purposes.

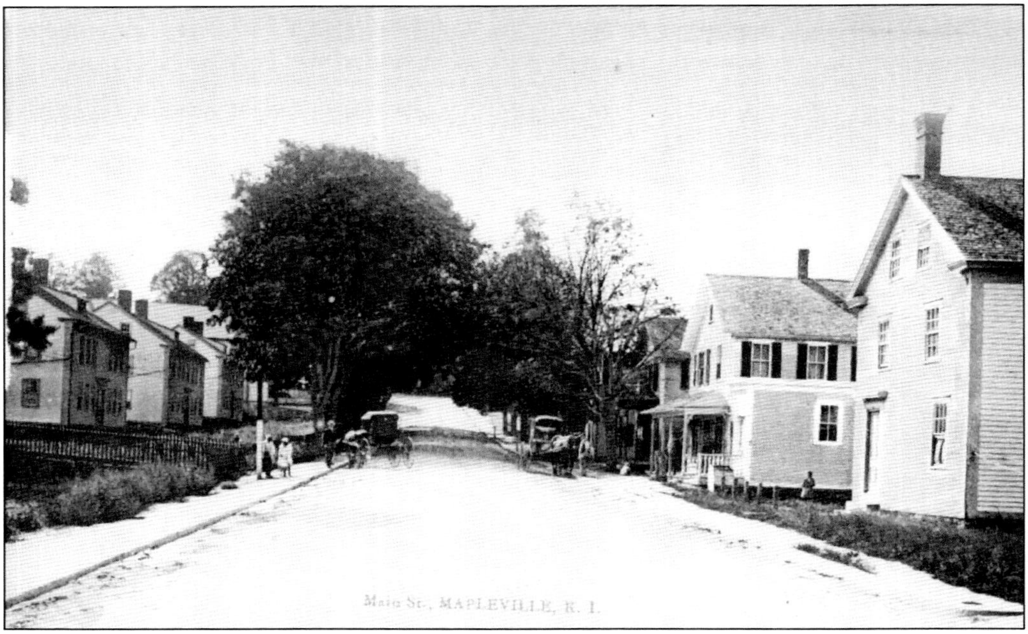

Horses and buggies abound in this *c.* 1915 view of Main Street in Mapleville. Every other house on the left was moved to make more yard space for the remaining houses.

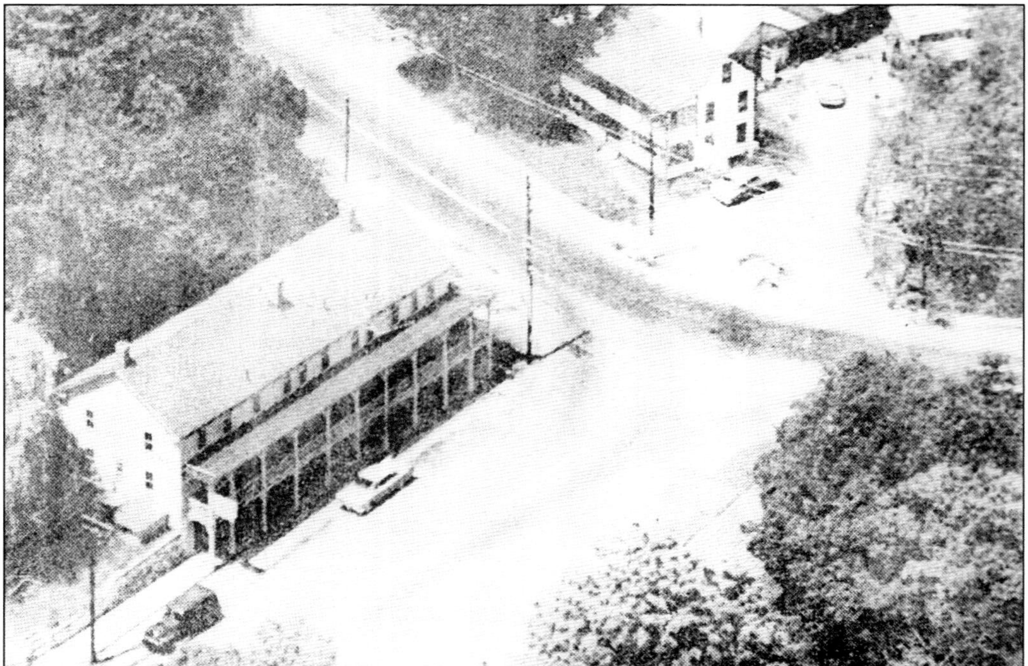

The Western Hotel in Nasonville, formerly the Walling Hotel, was an important stagecoach stop on the old Douglas Turnpike from the early 1800s and is still operating today as a restaurant.

Eight

Lakes, Camping, and Picnics

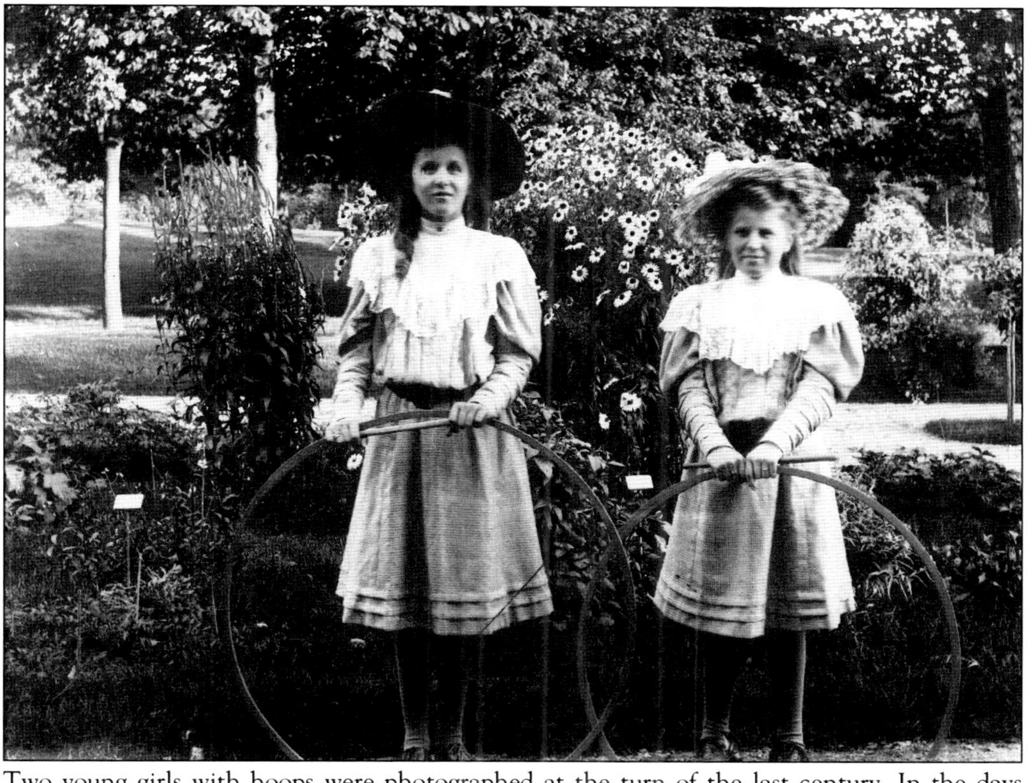

Two young girls with hoops were photographed at the turn of the last century. In the days before radio and TV, this was one of the few amusements available to the young.

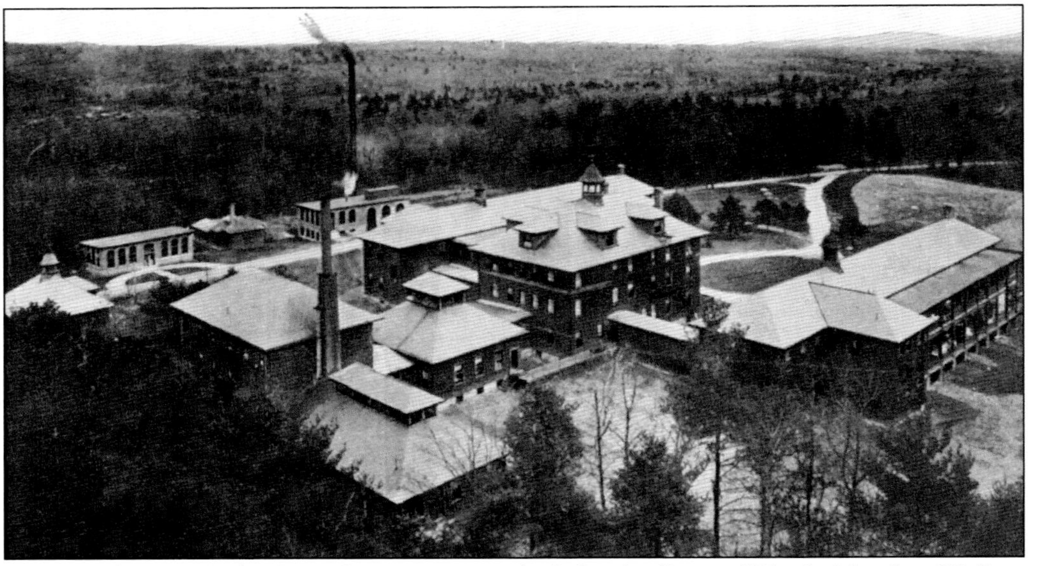

In November 1905, the State Sanatorium was built by the State of Rhode Island at Wallum Lake for the express purpose of treating tubercular patients. Dr. Harry Lee Barnes was the administrator. It was believed the purity of the water at the lake would help to cure that dreadful disease.

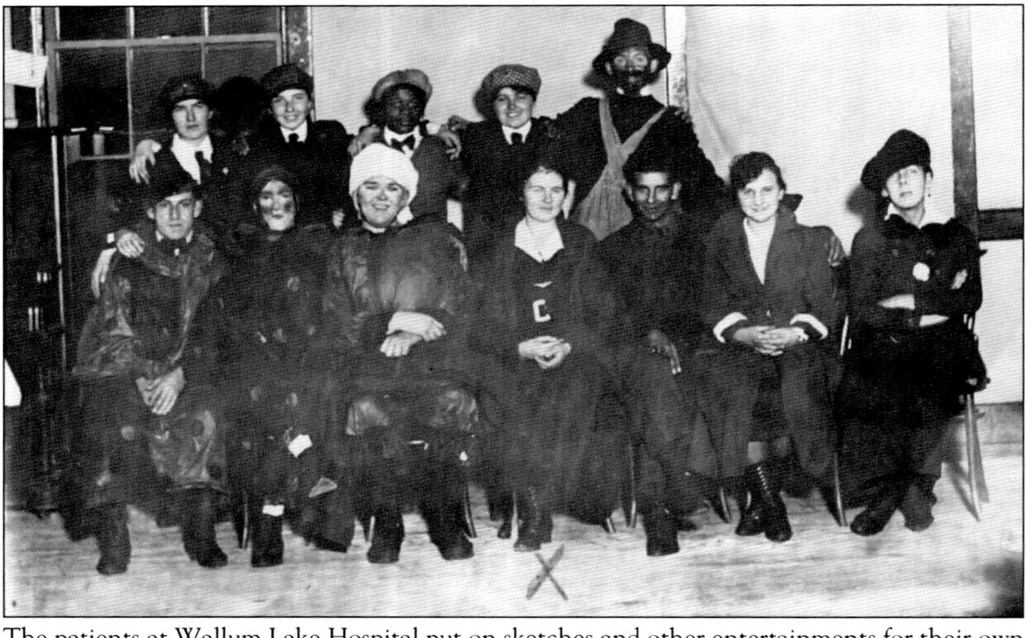

The patients at Wallum Lake Hospital put on sketches and other entertainments for their own amusement, including this typical Halloween party. The "X" indicates Idella Almon, who died from tuberculosis in 1921.

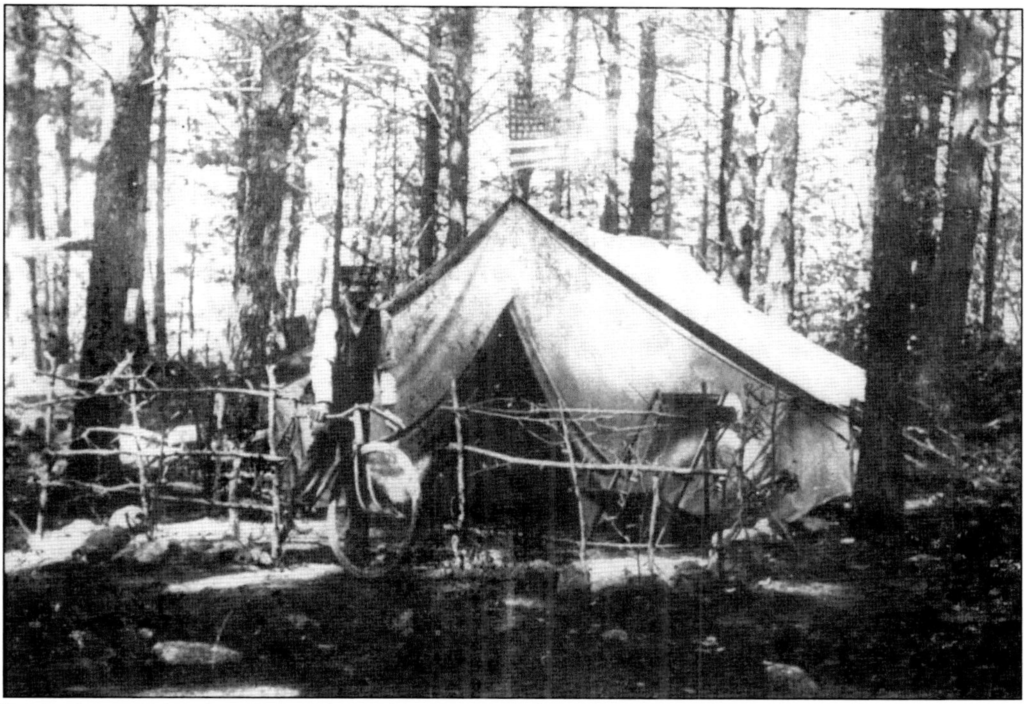

In the late 1890s, there were about thirty summer boarders living in Salisbury's camps and tents at the north end of Wallum Lake. Some were from the city, and others were from the town.

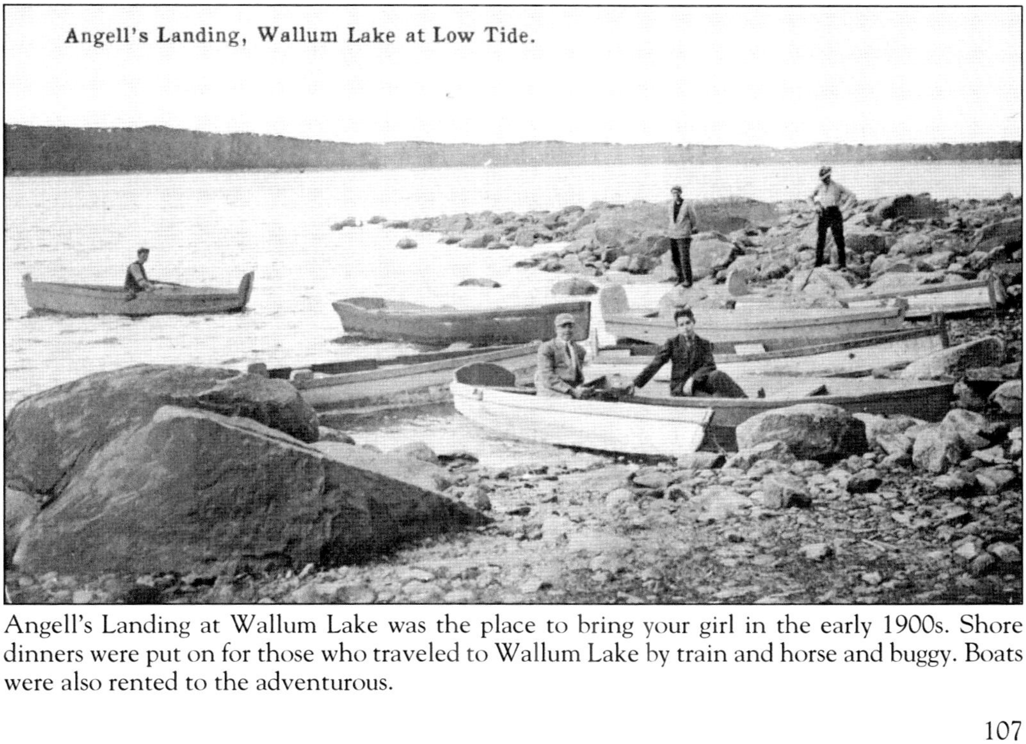

Angell's Landing at Wallum Lake was the place to bring your girl in the early 1900s. Shore dinners were put on for those who traveled to Wallum Lake by train and horse and buggy. Boats were also rented to the adventurous.

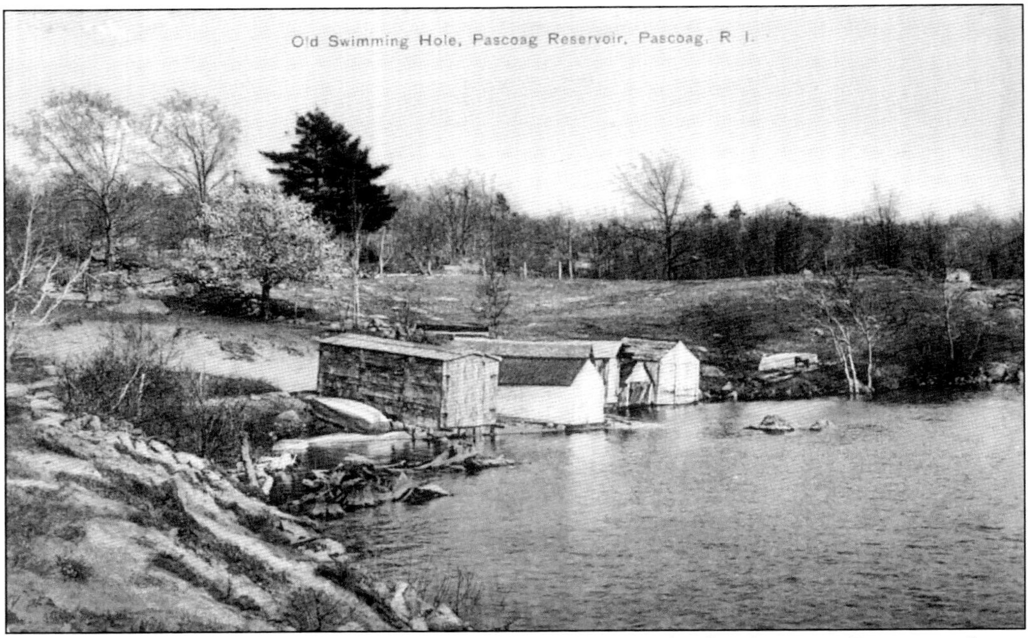

This photograph of the Flat Rock area on the Reservoir Road side of Pascoag Reservoir shows the boathouses near the dam. This was a favorite swimming spot for young and old alike for many years.

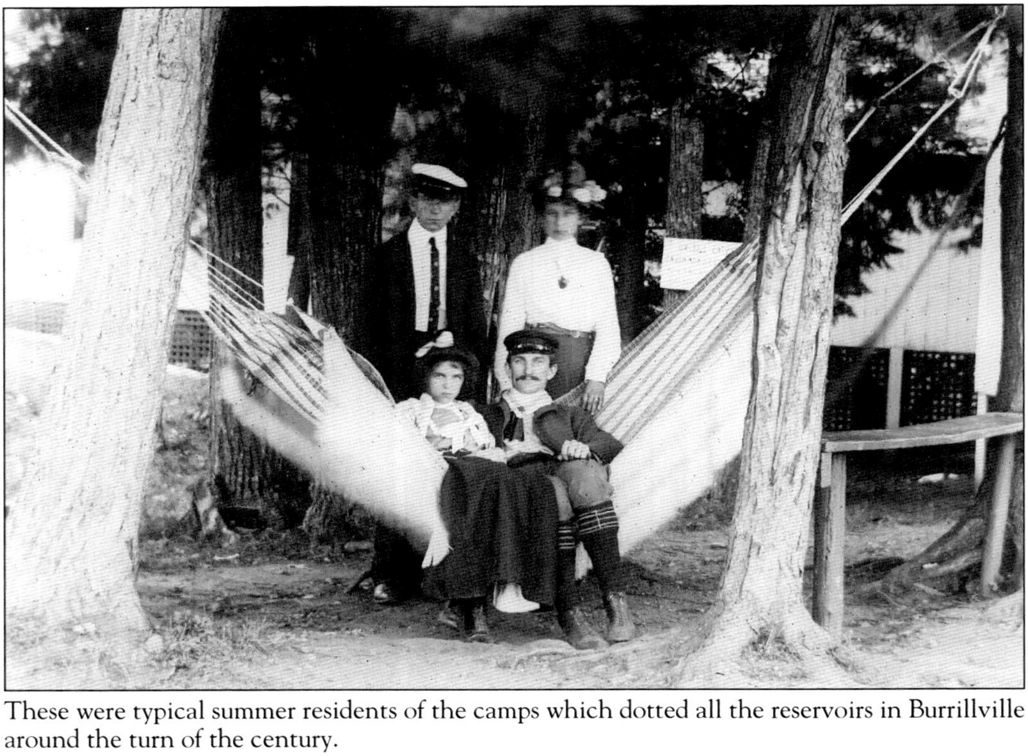

These were typical summer residents of the camps which dotted all the reservoirs in Burrillville around the turn of the century.

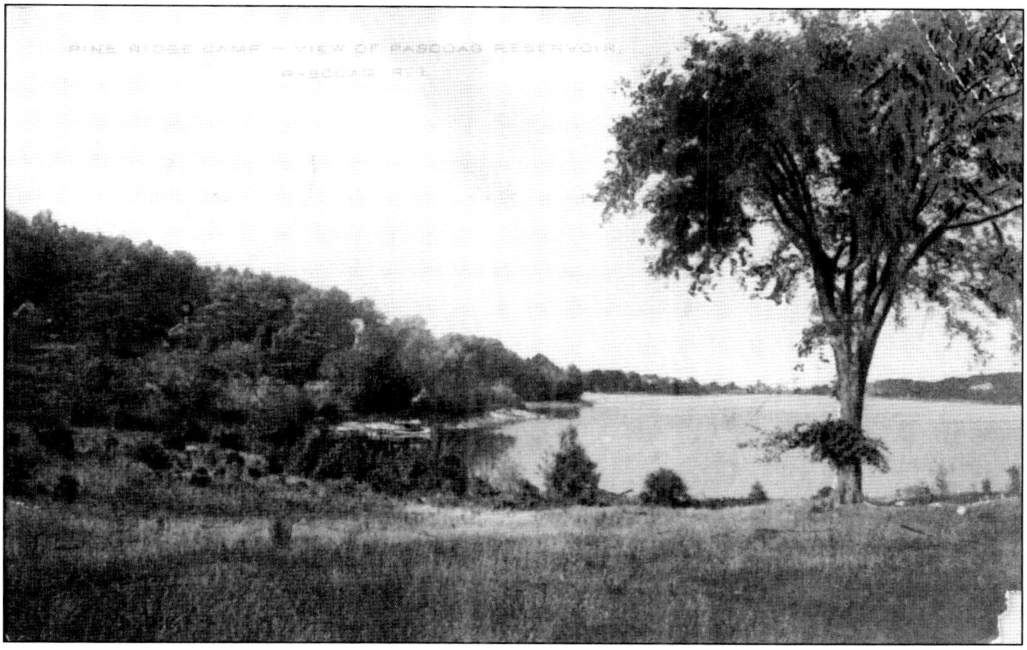

The Pine Ridge Camp, near the Canada Rocks Dam at Pascoag, was one of many camps on the shores of the lake where tents could be pitched and life enjoyed to its fullest.

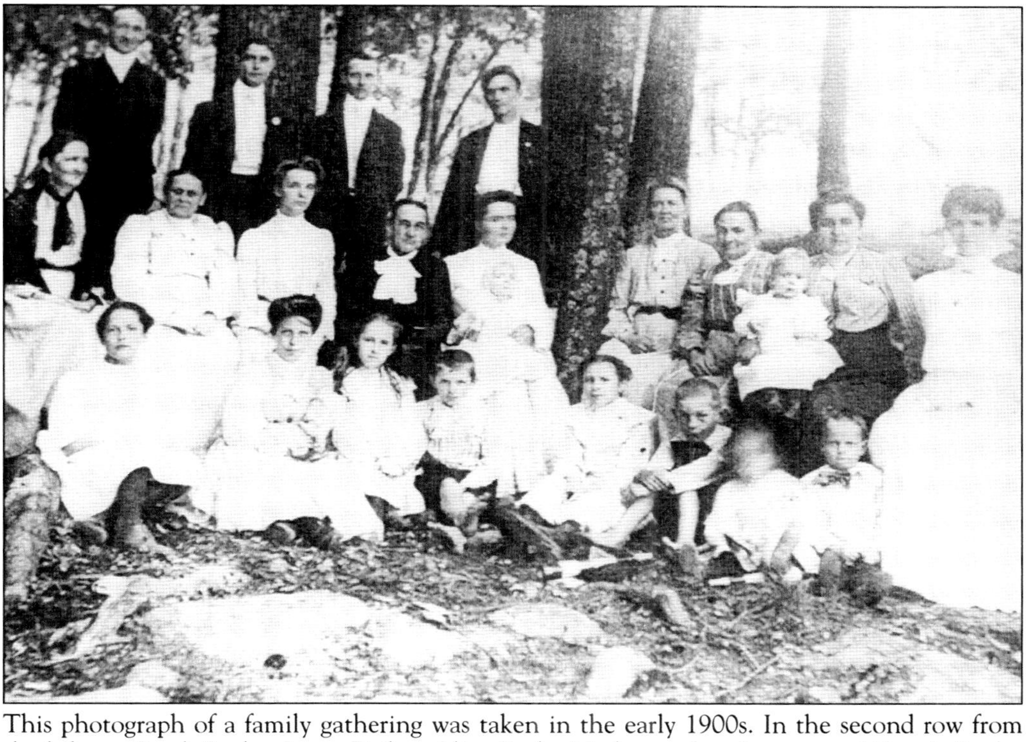

This photograph of a family gathering was taken in the early 1900s. In the second row from the left are: Sarah Sayles, Laura Bailey, Alice Sayles Underwood, unknown, and Fannie Sayles Knight (holding Harold Knight).

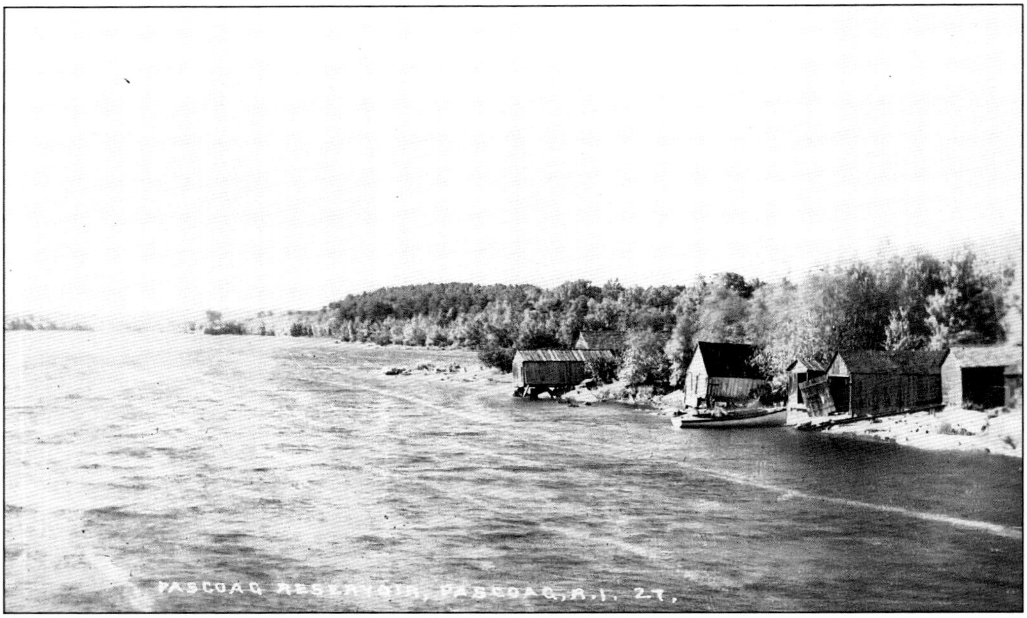

These old boathouses at the Pascoag Reservoir were photographed in the 1920s. The Reservoir was enlarged in 1860 by Albert Sayles and the Pascoag Reservoir Association to furnish power to all the mills downstream from the Pascoag, Clear, and Branch Rivers.

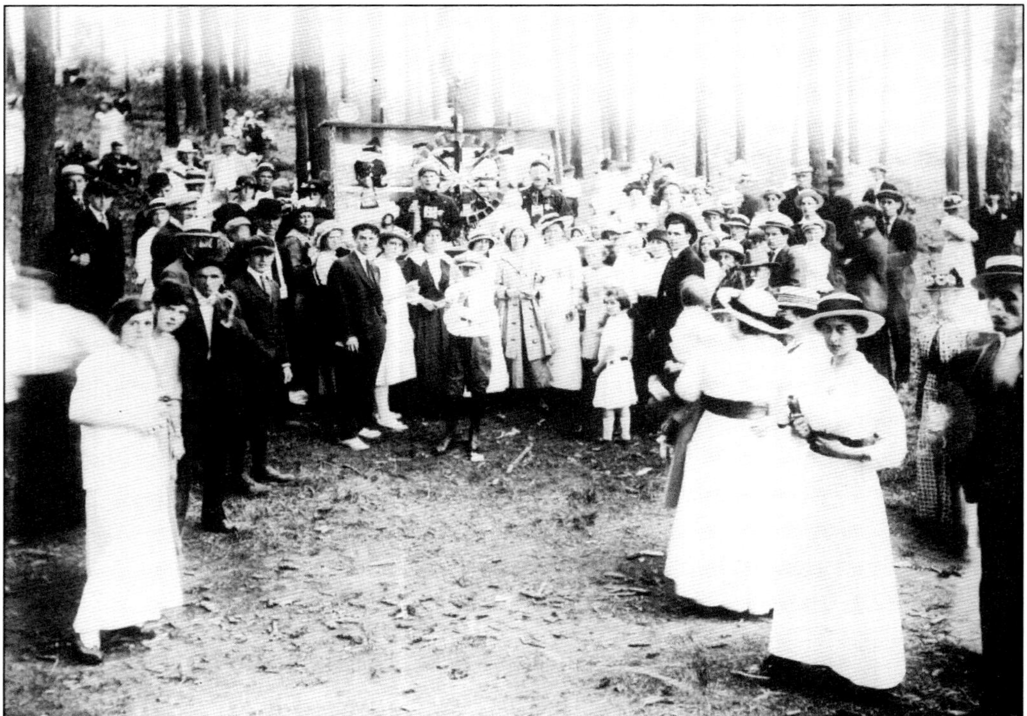

Keyes Bailey is the fireman on the right in the back working the wheel of chance during this *c.* 1910 firemen's carnival.

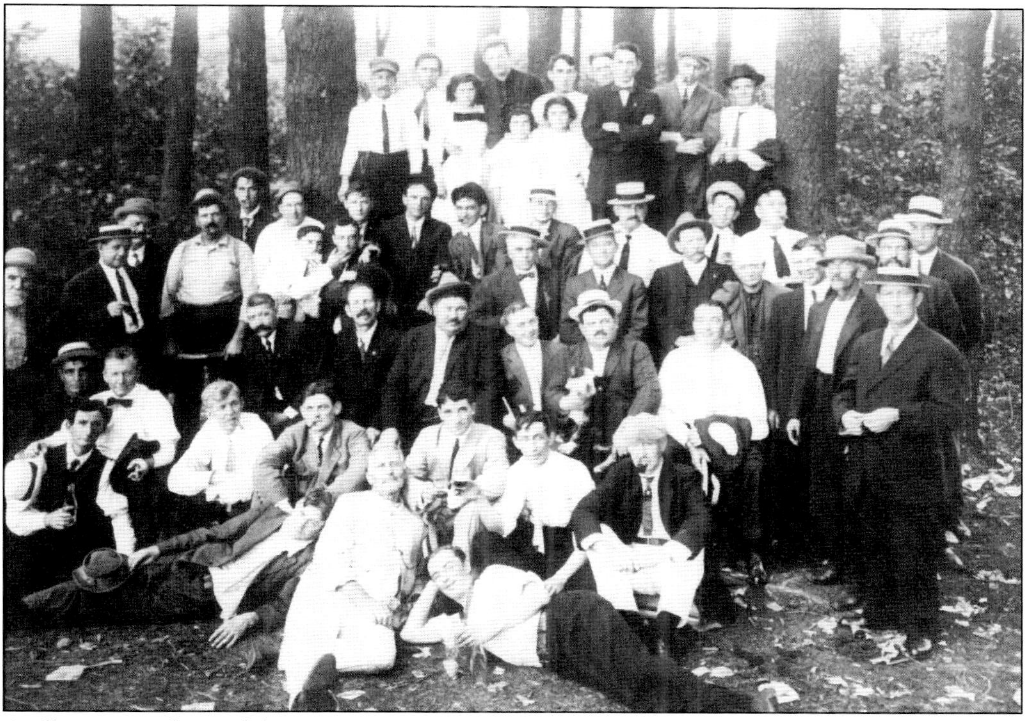

Griff's Grove, located between Pascoag and Harrisville, was the site of much recreation. Providence trains going to Pascoag made special stops here to drop off passengers going to picnics, baseball games, etc.

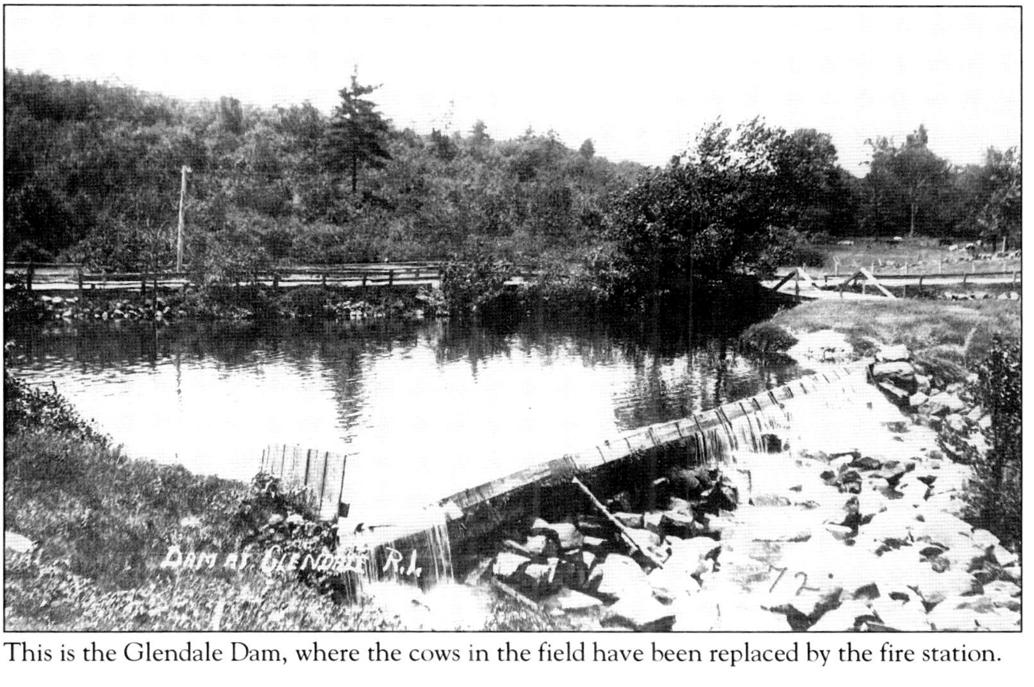

This is the Glendale Dam, where the cows in the field have been replaced by the fire station.

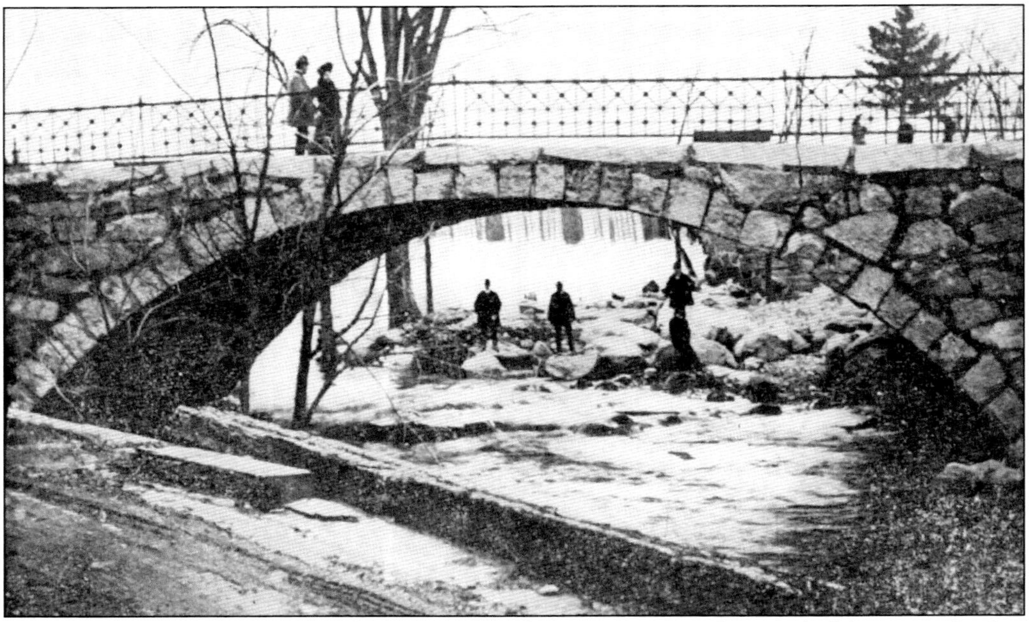

The old Stone Arch Bridge was built by Mr. Mathewson c. 1910 after much debate on whether to spend the extra money for a stone bridge. Keystone construction was used and it endured until 1995, when the Rhode Island Department of Transportation rebuilt it.

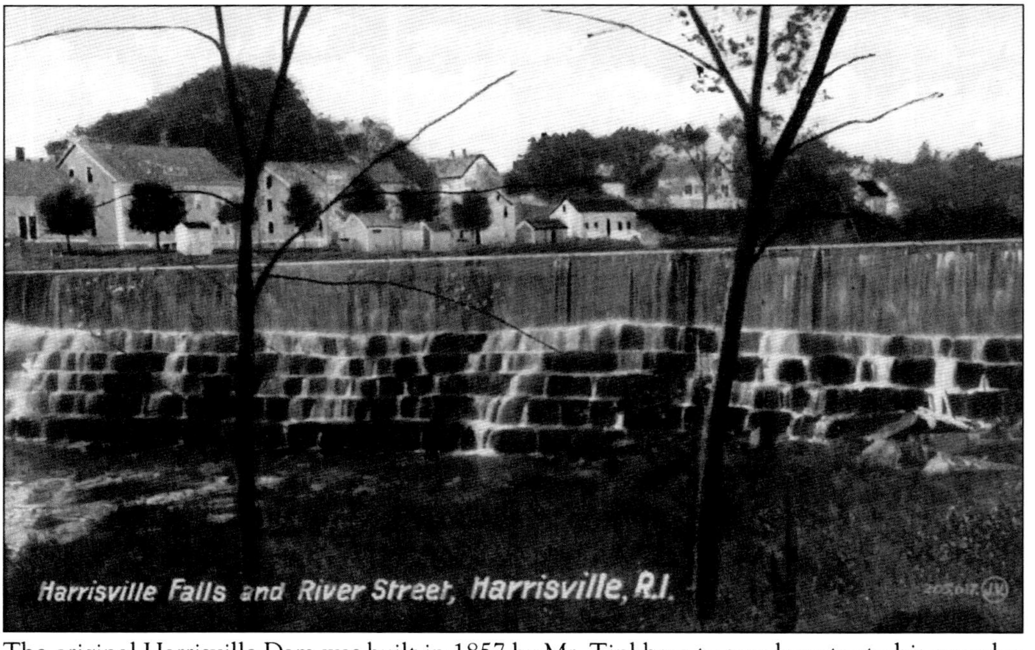

The original Harrisville Dam was built in 1857 by Mr. Tinkham to supply water to his complex of mills. The tenements in the background were moved by Austin T. Levy in 1933 and replaced by the Assembly Building.

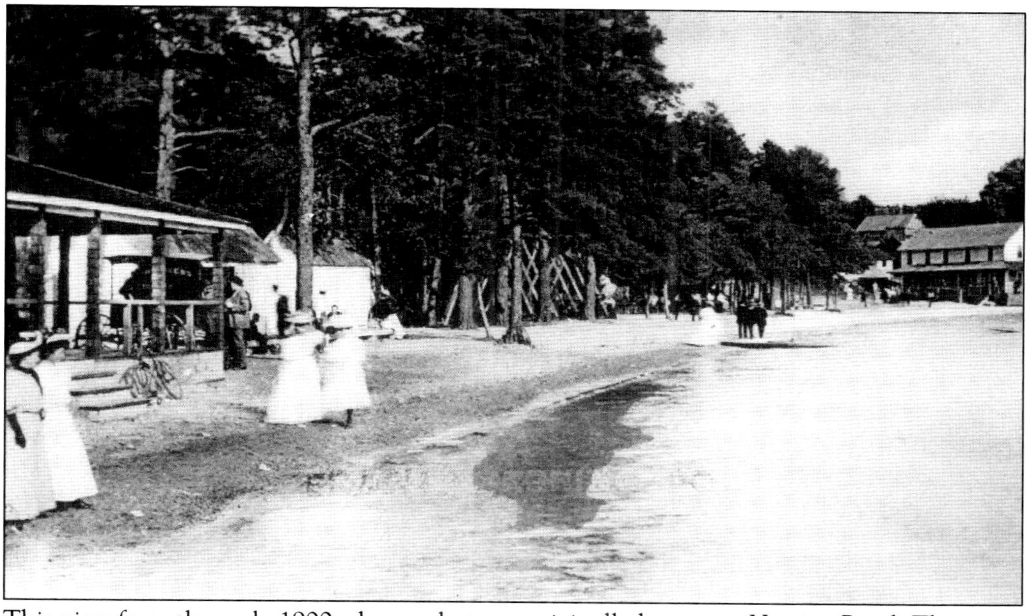

This view from the early 1900s shows what was originally known as Herring Pond. The name came from the Indians, who said that there were so many herring here they could walk across the backs of the fish from one side of the lake to the other.

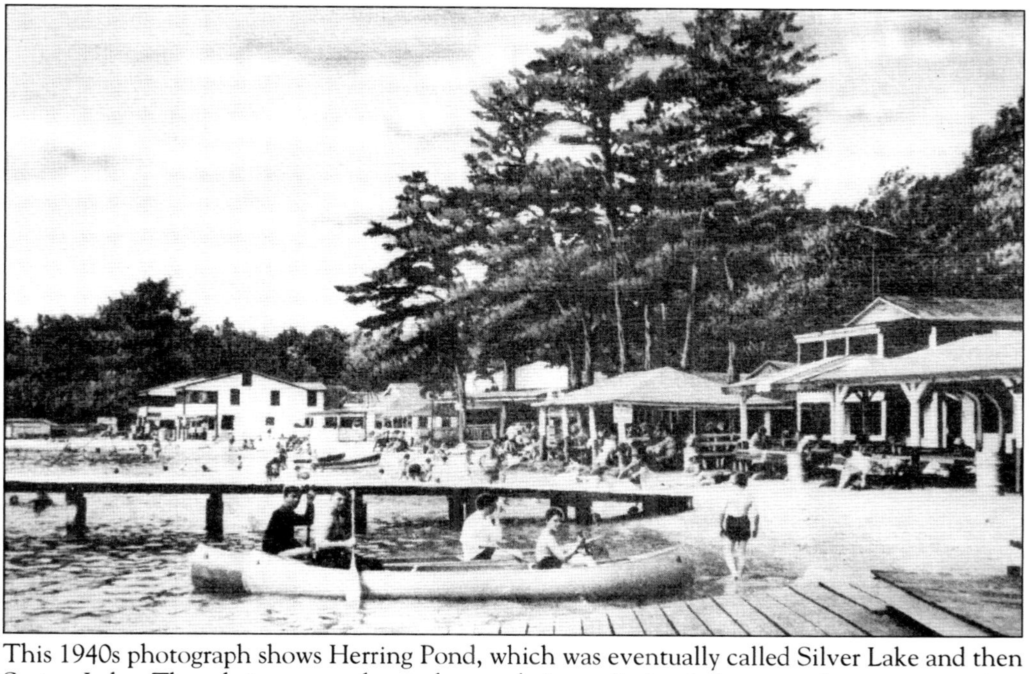

This 1940s photograph shows Herring Pond, which was eventually called Silver Lake and then Spring Lake. Though its name changed several times, Spring Lake seemed most appropriate because of the cold springs which fed it. It is now owned by the town of Burrillville.

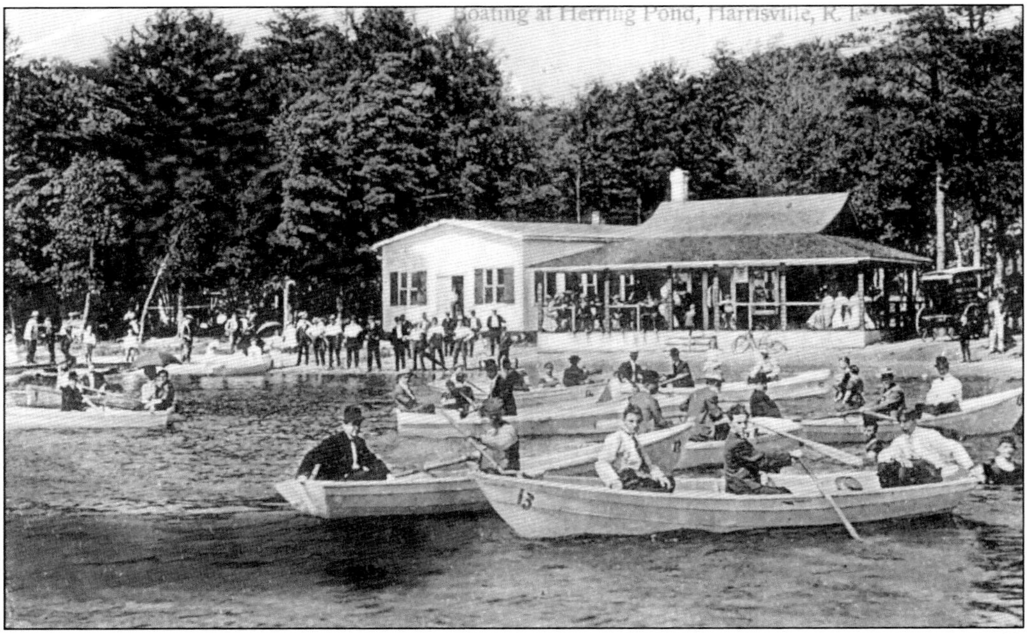

People would come from the city by trolley to the end of the road and then take jitneys or walk the short distance to enjoy the opportunities for fun that the lake provided.

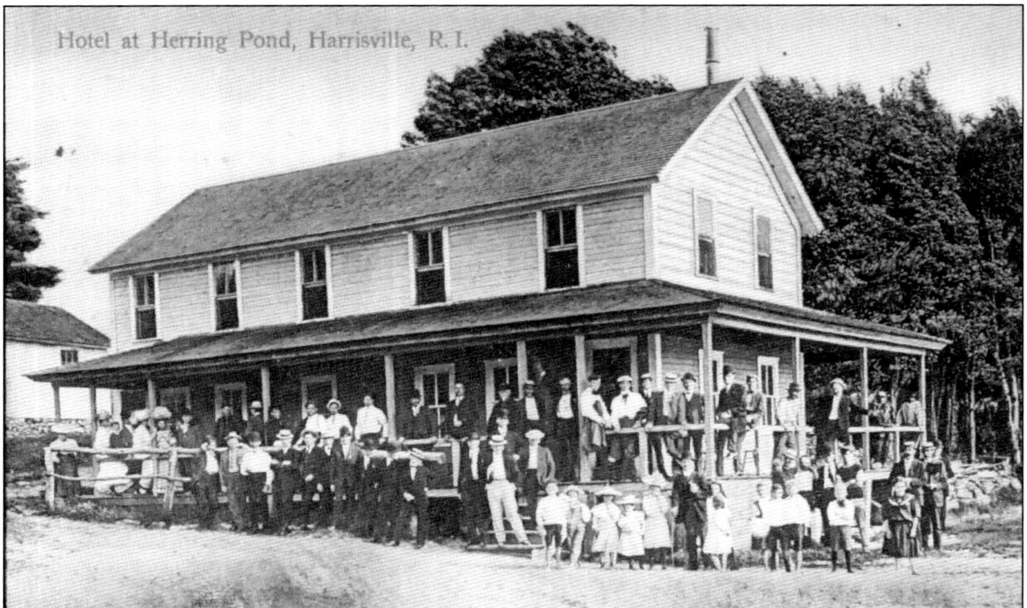

From the turn of the last century until today, Spring Lake holds a place in the hearts of those who love to swim, boat, picnic, and just enjoy life.

Nine

Old Churches and Schools

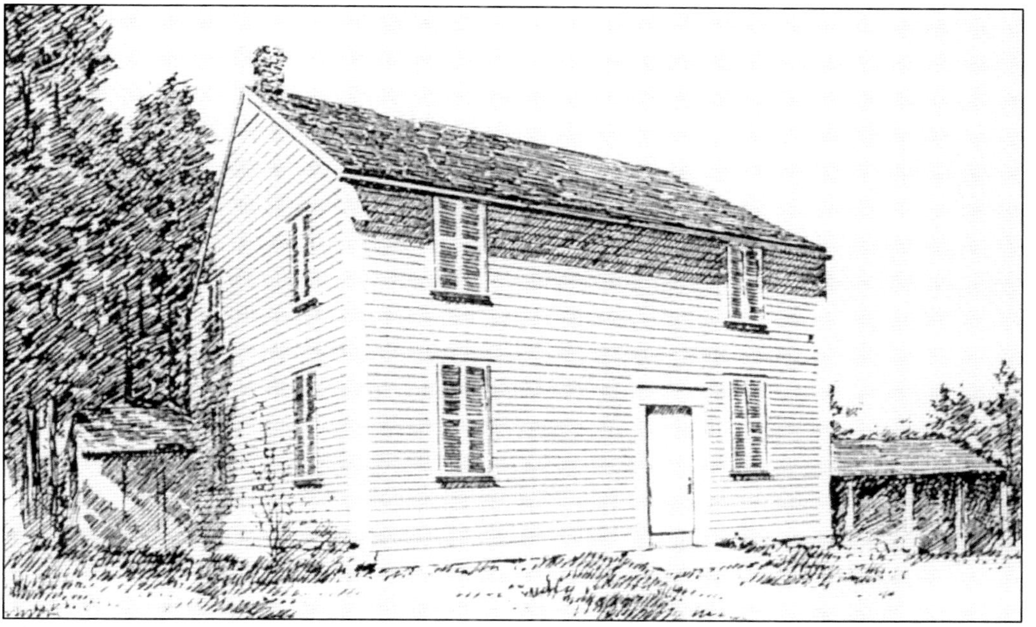

The Friends Meeting House, built in Mapleville in 1791 on a lot donated by Moses Cooper, belonged to the oldest religious group in Burrillville, the Society of Friends. It cost 109 pounds and 12 shillings. The building was remodeled in 1848. In 1902, after being unused for several years, it was sold to Joseph Fletcher, who owned the Mapleville Mills.

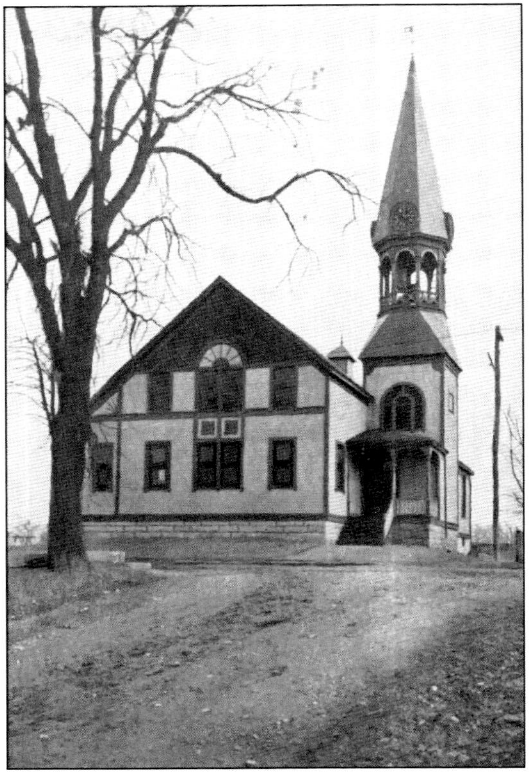

The Laurel Hill Methodist Episcopal Church was located in Bridgeton. The first church was built here in 1852. It was refurbished in 1891 and again in 1911. The first Methodist preacher held meetings in 1813 in the Huntsville Emporium near the White Mill in Bridgeton.

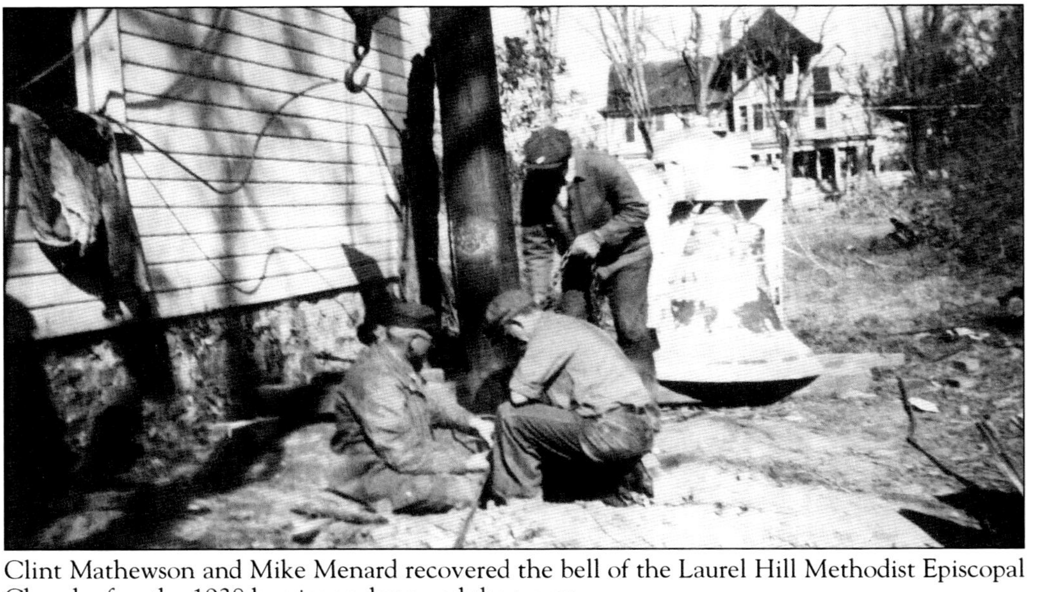

Clint Mathewson and Mike Menard recovered the bell of the Laurel Hill Methodist Episcopal Church after the 1938 hurricane destroyed the tower.

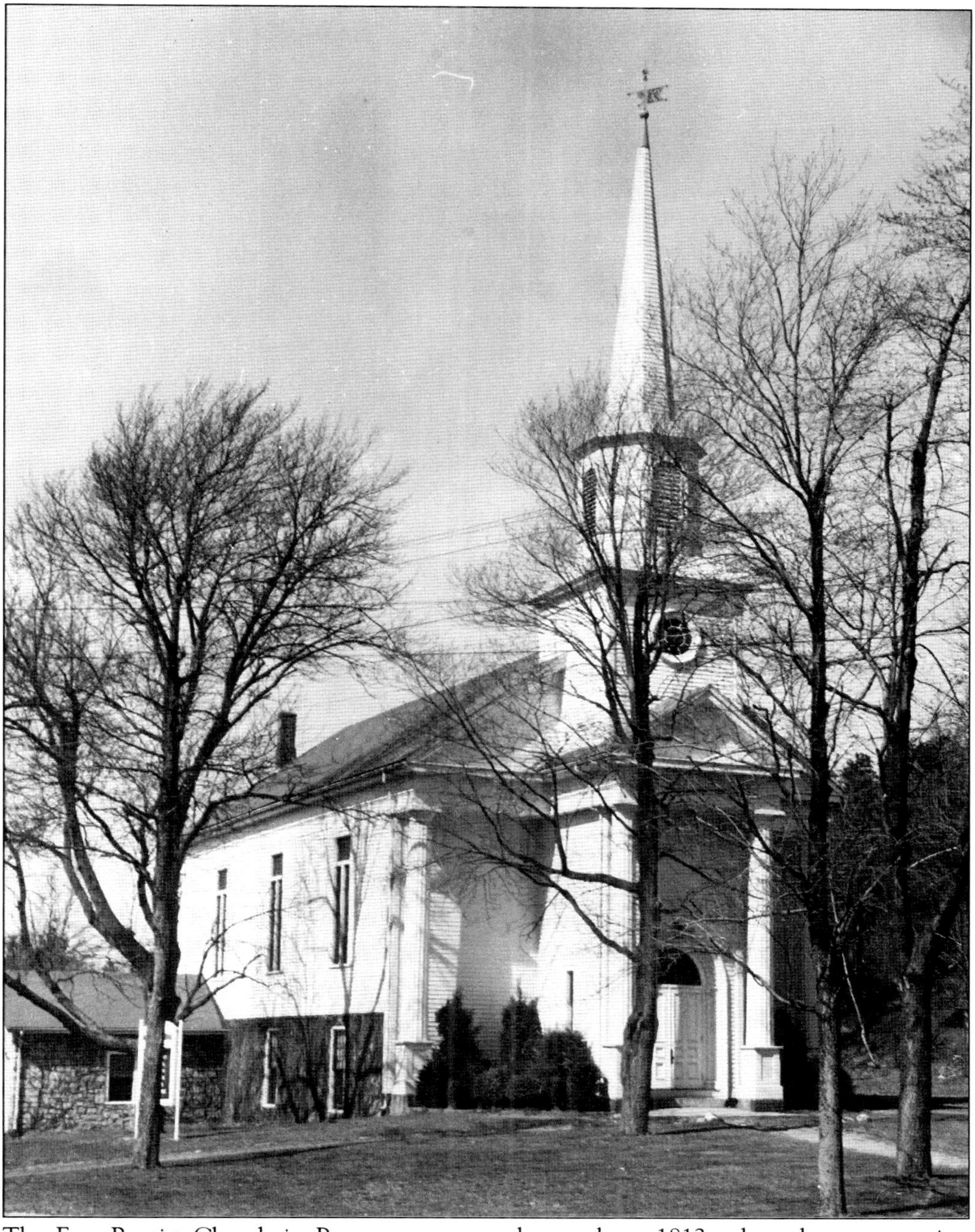

The Free Baptist Church in Pascoag was started as early as 1812, when the congregation worshiped in various places, including the old Town House on the Pascoag-Harrisville Road. This church was built in 1839. The pews originally faced the entrance, but in 1857 they were changed to face north. The impressive building is still standing and serving its congregation more than 150 years later.

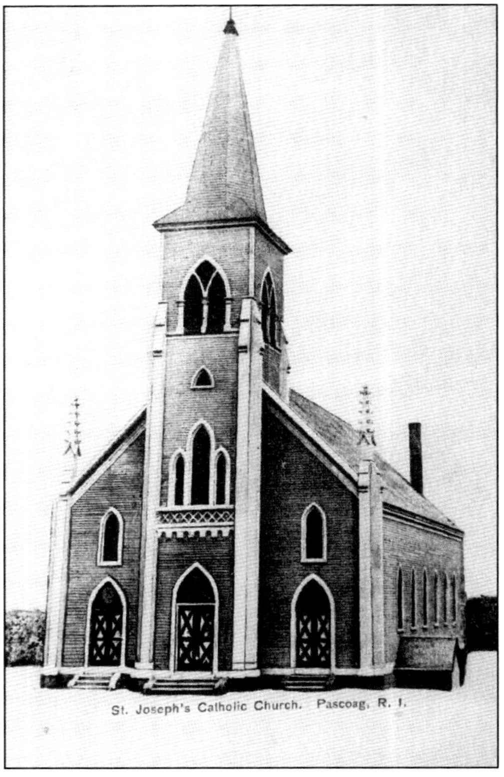

The original wooden St. Joseph's Church in Pascoag burned in 1919, and services were held in the Pascoag Grammar School until the church basement was completed in 1932. The new stone church was dedicated in 1938, with another fire in 1948 causing $150,000 worth of damage.

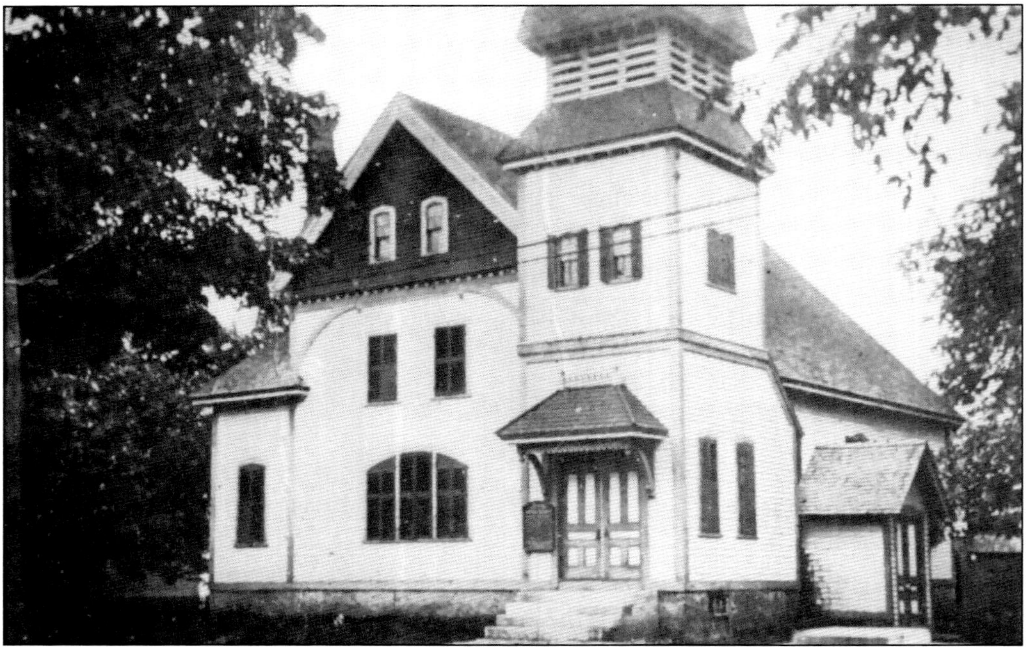

The Berean Baptist Church in Harrisville was dedicated on April 27, 1881. The entire cost of the lot, grading, edifice, and furniture reached the sum of $4,500.

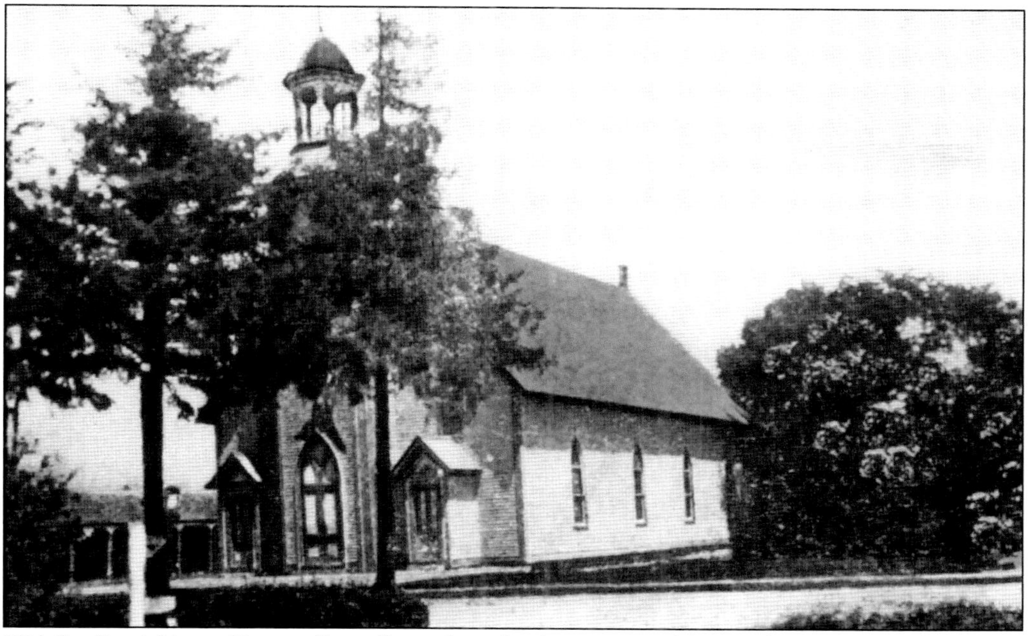

Old St. Patrick's in Harrisville collapsed in the hurricane of September 1938. Dedicated in 1858, it was the first Catholic church in Burrillville. Fortunately for the congregation, a brick church was already in the process of being built across the street to replace the original church.

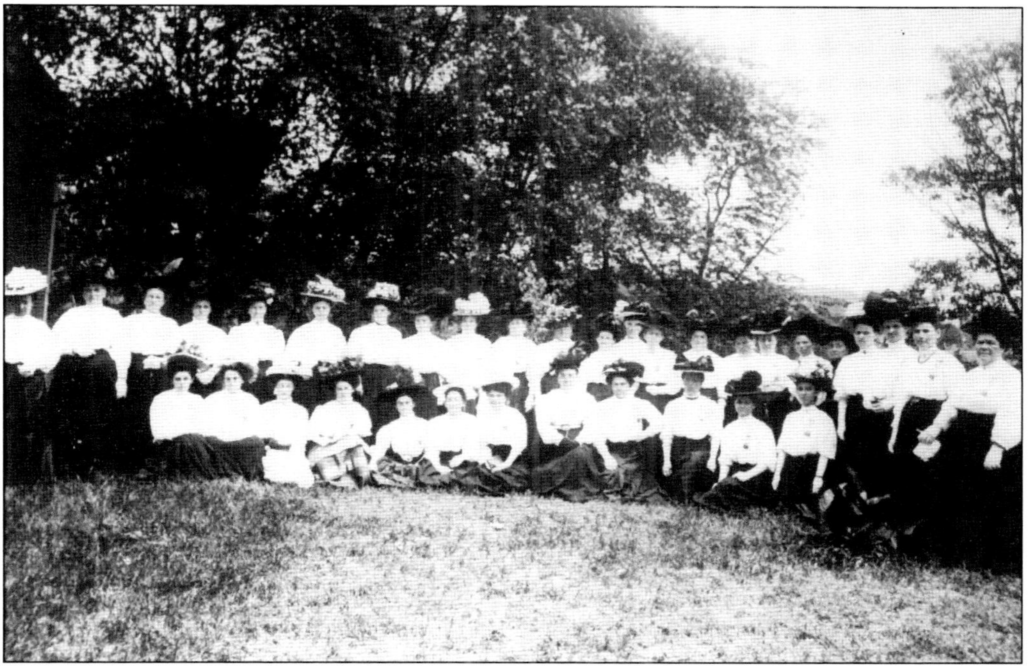

These ladies were from the Rosary and Altar Society of St. Patrick's Church in Harrisville, one of the many religious organizations in town around the turn of the century.

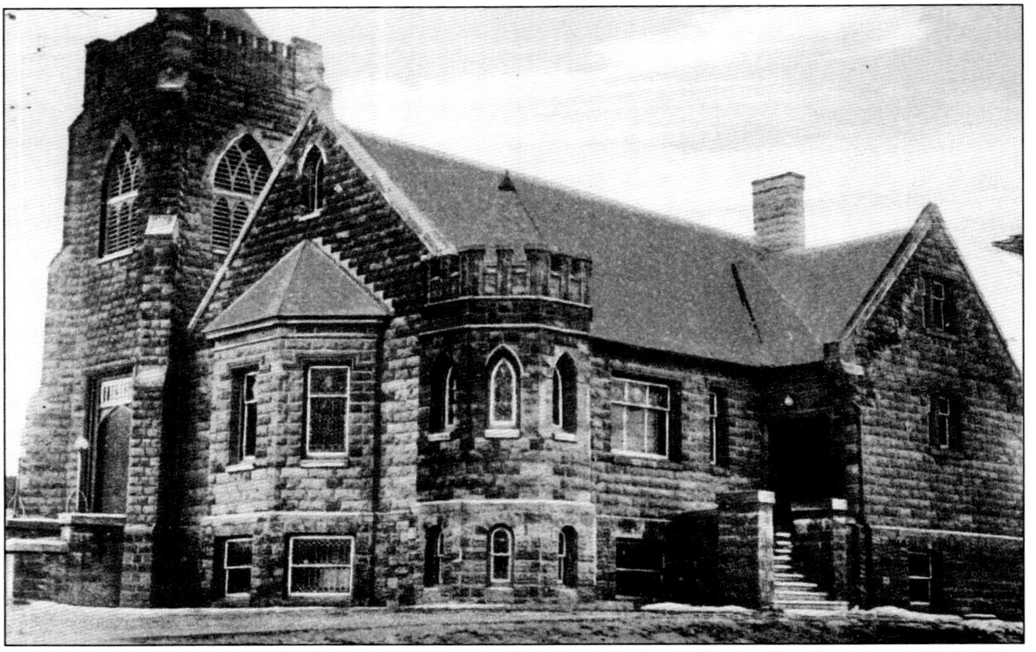

The Methodist Episcopal Church in Mapleville was dedicated on October 24, 1909. The parishioners donated $1 for each molded concrete block used in the construction. Andrew Carnegie contributed $500 toward the cost of the $1,400 pipe organ.

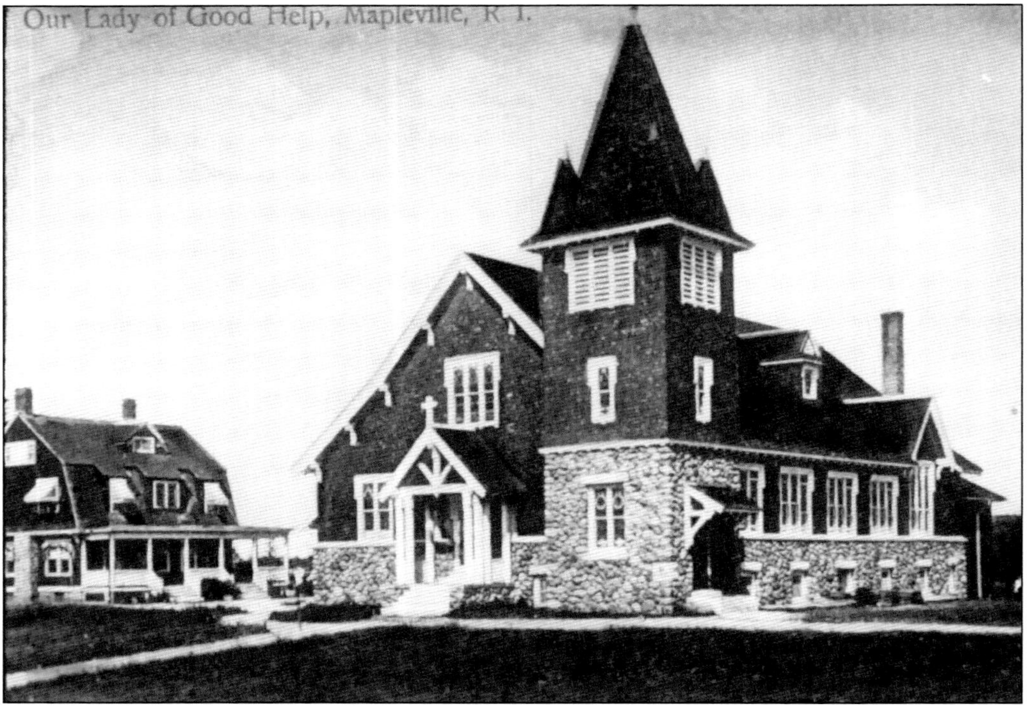

The cornerstone for the Our Lady of Good Help Church in Mapleville was laid on October 14, 1906, and the church was dedicated on May 30, 1907. The rectory was built in 1906.

The cornerstone for the Zion Primitive Methodist Church on South Main Street in Pascoag was laid in November 1891, and the building was dedicated in April 1892.

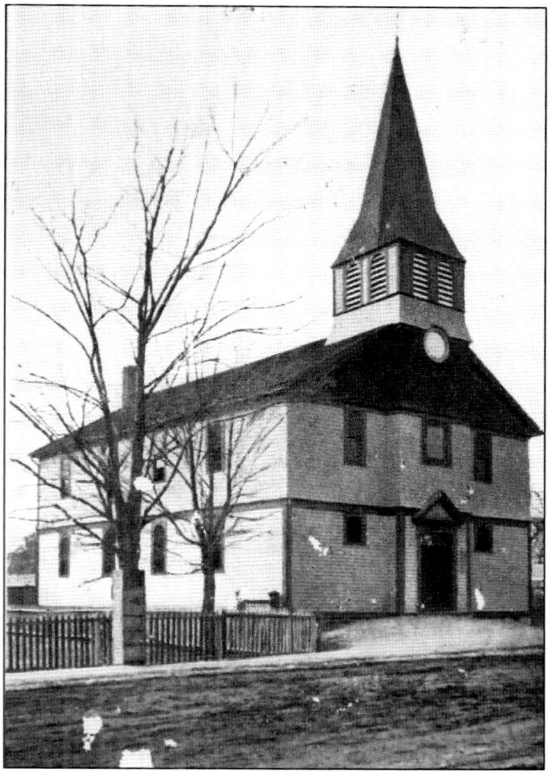

The old Esten Schoolhouse was built in 1806 in the vicinity of "Cripple Corner." During the winter of 1868, because the school was badly in need of repairs and there was only one pupil, it was closed permanently.

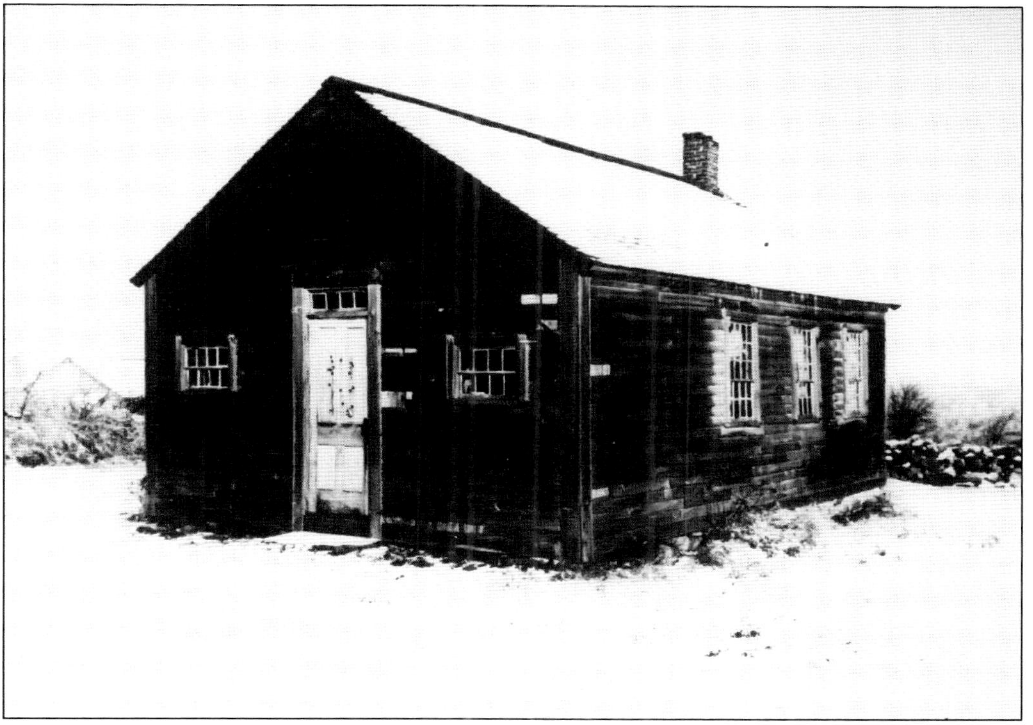

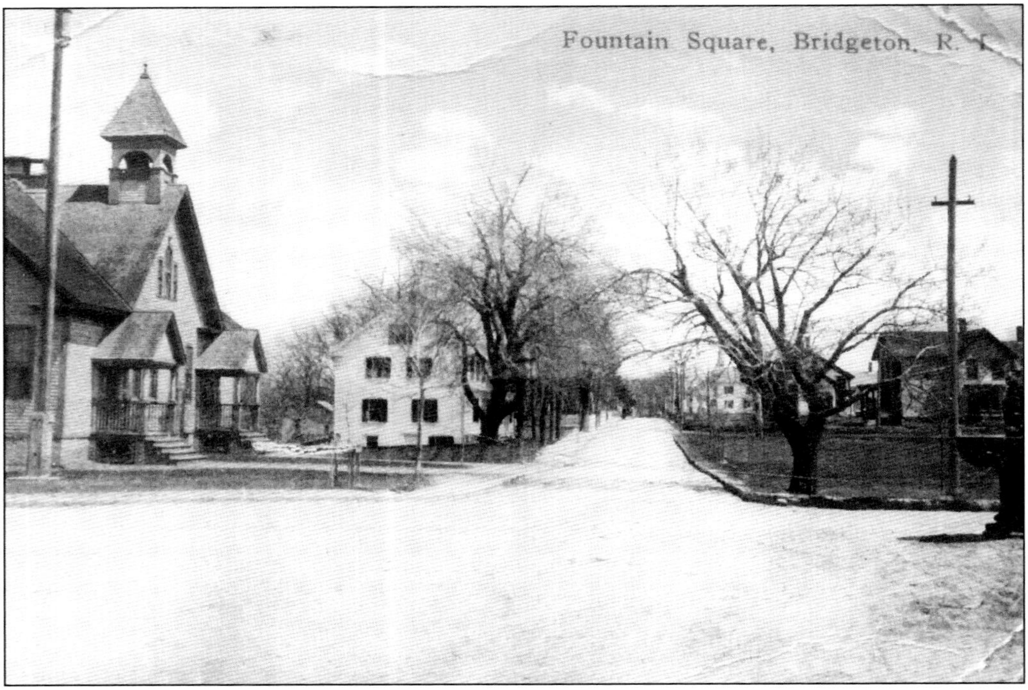

In this view looking down Laurel Hill Avenue, the Bridgeton Schoolhouse (built in 1897) can be seen on the left, with the fountain and Jarvis's barn on the far right. The land for the square was donated by Mr. Prendergast and Mr. Kimball, manufacturers.

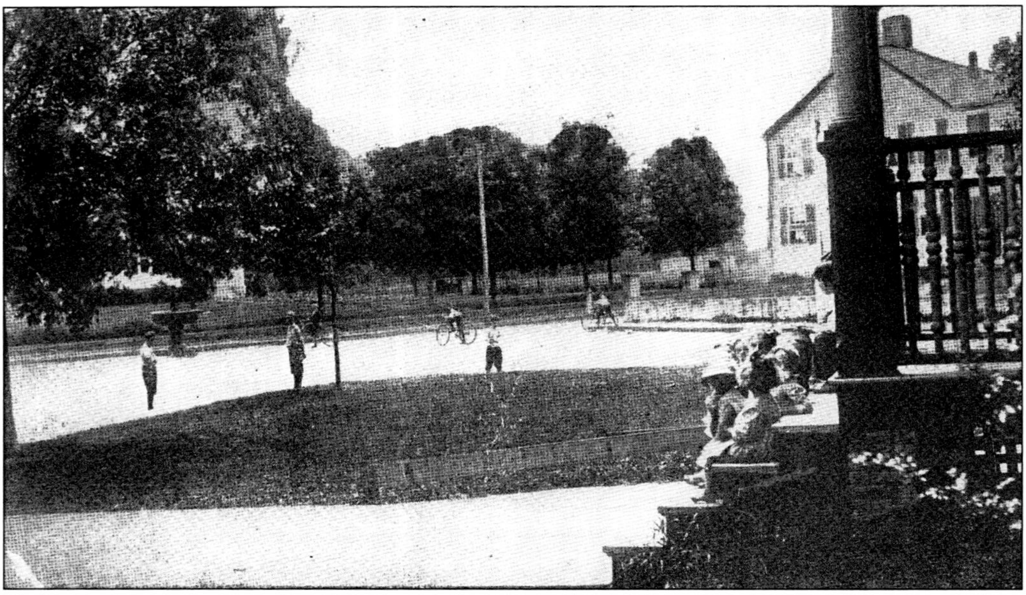

Fountain Square is shown here from the steps of the Bridgeton Schoolhouse. The children played in the square in the foreground. Carnivals were held here before the Bridgeton Athletic Field opened.

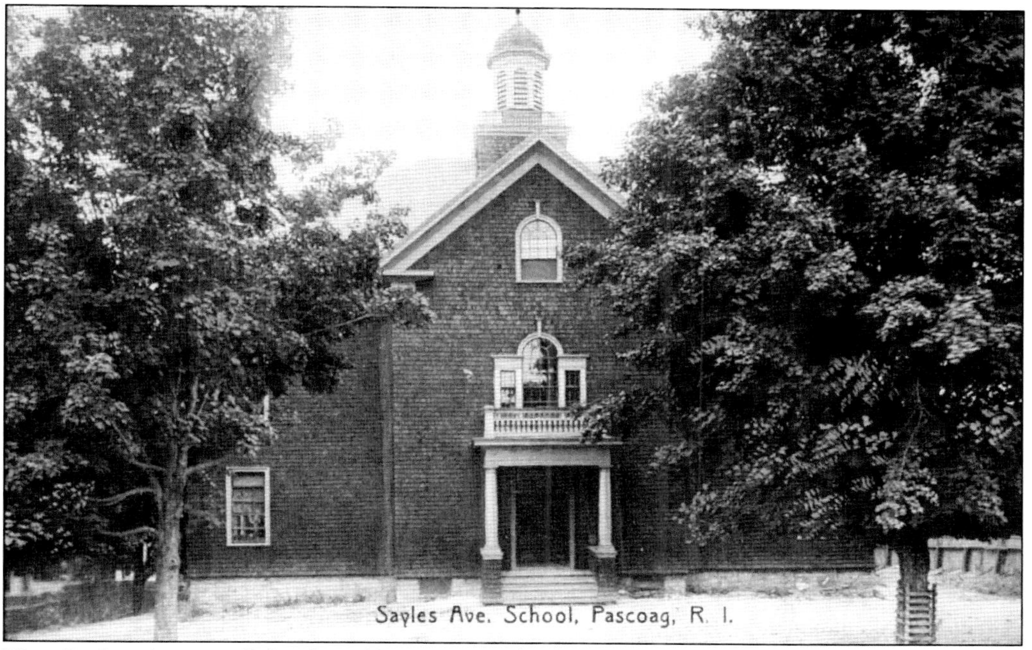

The Sayles Avenue School in Pascoag was built in 1905. Closed in 1966, it is now a private dwelling.

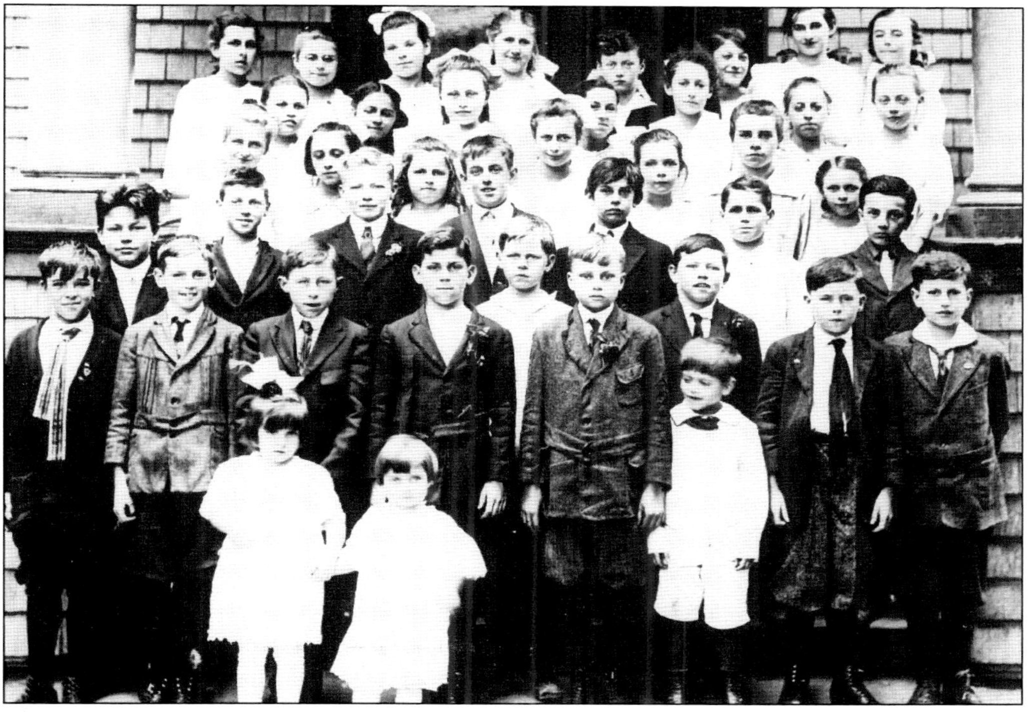

These Sayles Avenue schoolchildren were photographed c. 1912.

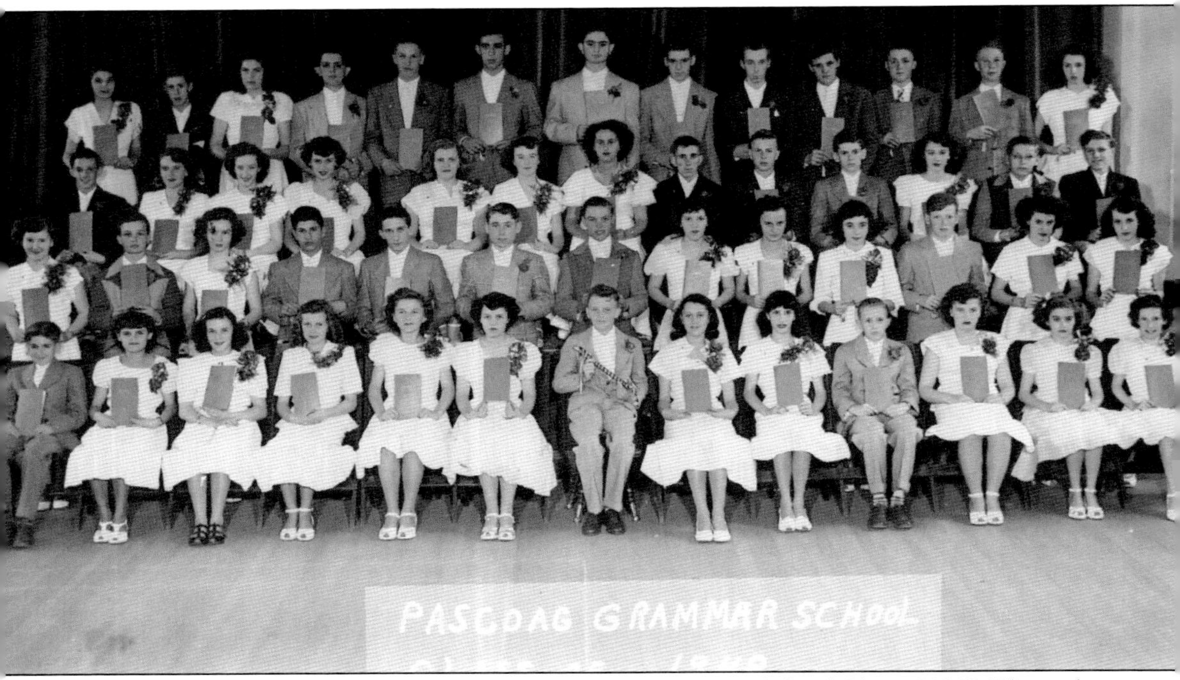

These eighth-grade graduates were from the Pascoag Grammar School Class of 1948. The author is second on the left in the front row. Each village had its own individual schools with the students meeting each other for the first time at their eighth-grade graduation. This fact alone helped to keep the villages separate from each other until most of the older schools disappeared and the students were bused together to newer facilities. The assimilation of students led to the demise of the village concept for school purposes, but not in the minds of those who grew up under the advantages of being from various sections of the town of Burrillville.

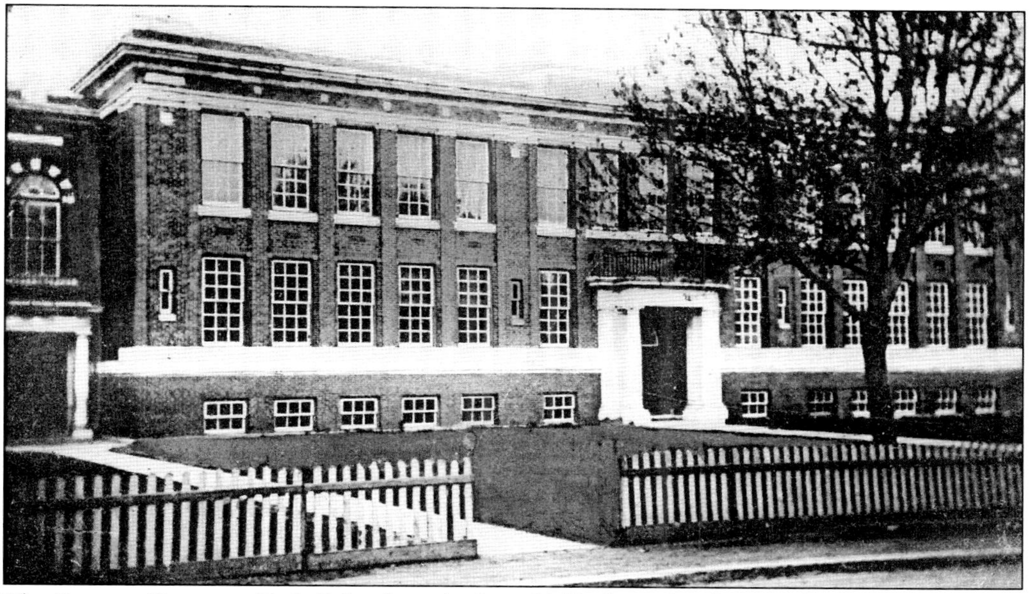

The Pascoag Grammar High School was built in 1917 after a fire destroyed the previous school in 1916. The cost for the building and equipment was $63,000. Grammar and high school classes were held here until Burrillville High School was built in 1937 in Harrisville. This building was then used as a grammar school until it was closed by the town in June 1995.

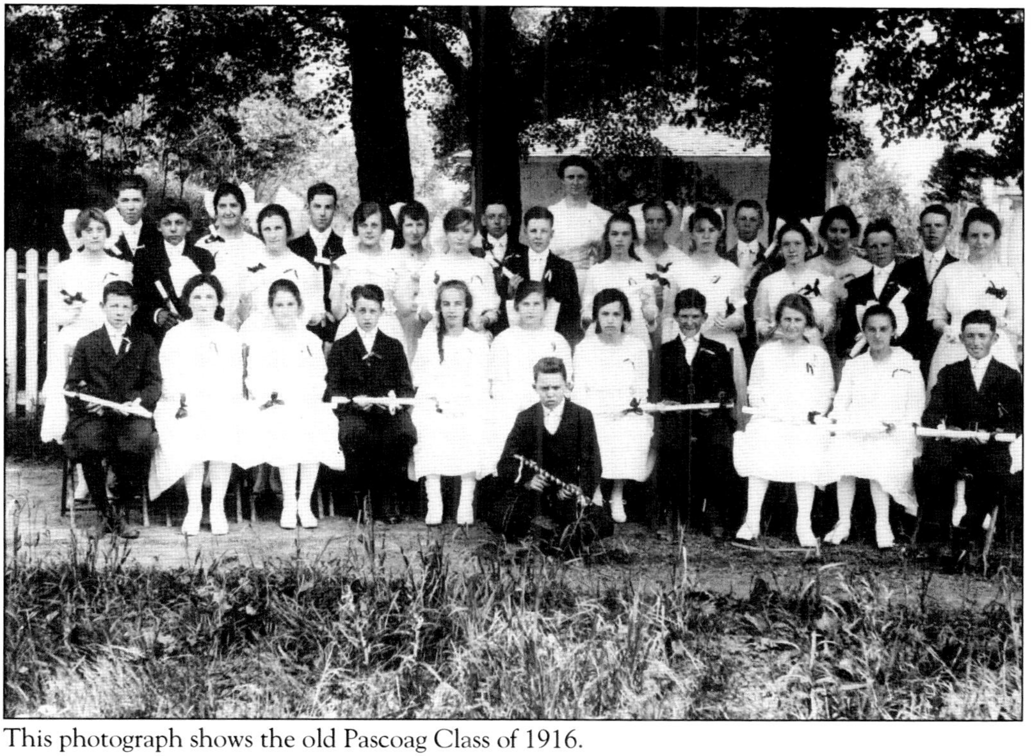

This photograph shows the old Pascoag Class of 1916.

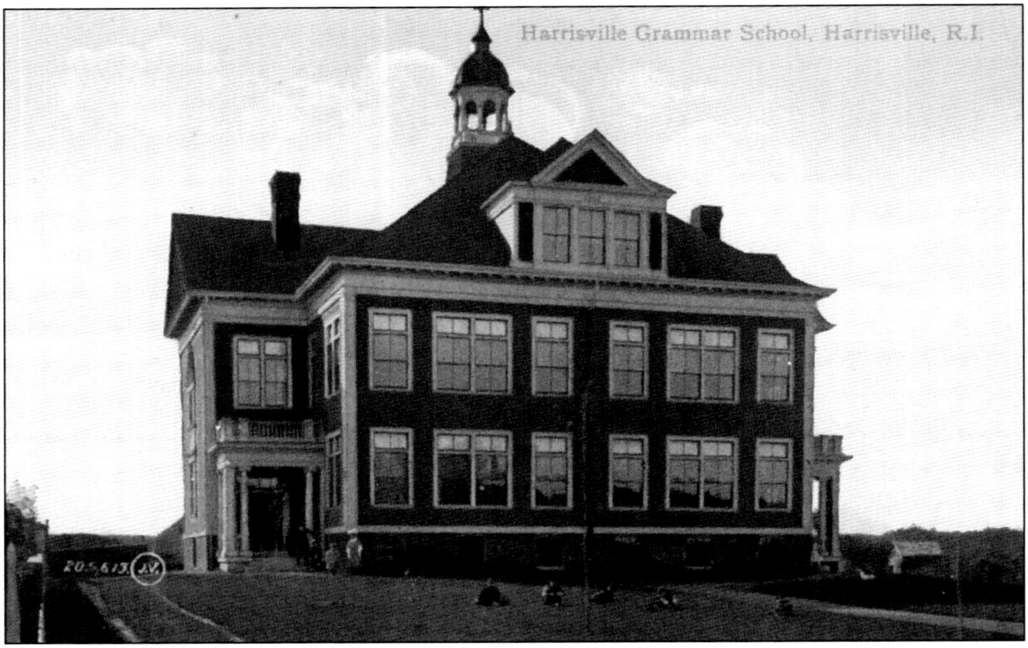

The Harrisville Grammar School was dedicated in November 1902, and known as "the handsomest structure of its kind in this section of the state." It was demolished in 1968 and replaced by the Harrisville Fire Station.

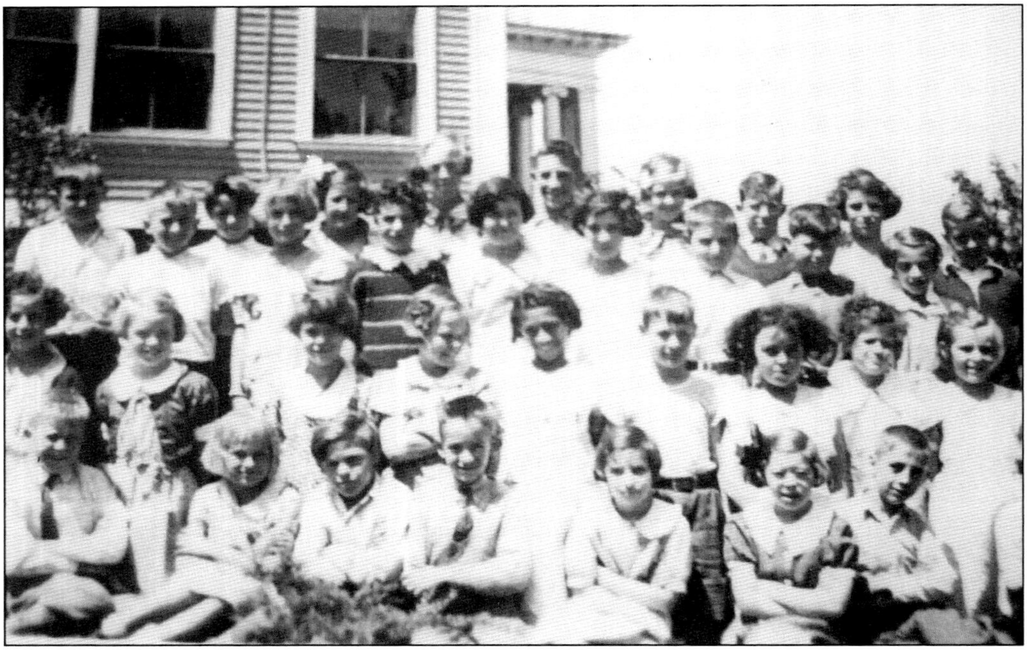

These Harrisville Primary School pupils were photographed in the 1930s.

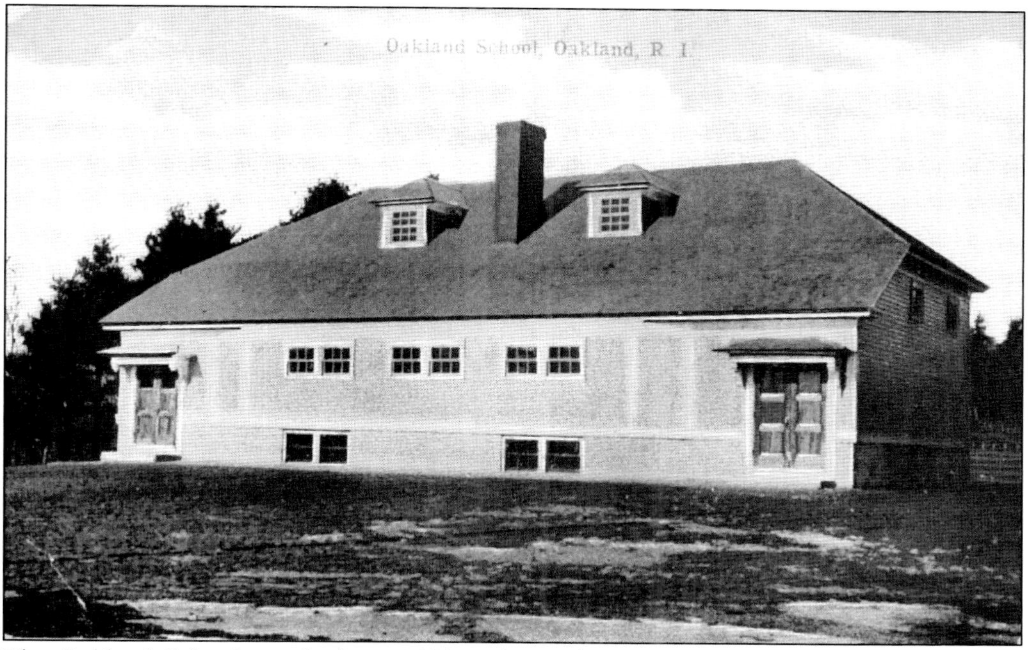

The Oakland School was built in 1873 and cost $2,000. It was located halfway between Plainville (Whipple) and Oakland. The erection of this schoolhouse put an end to the practice of using private dwellings for schools.

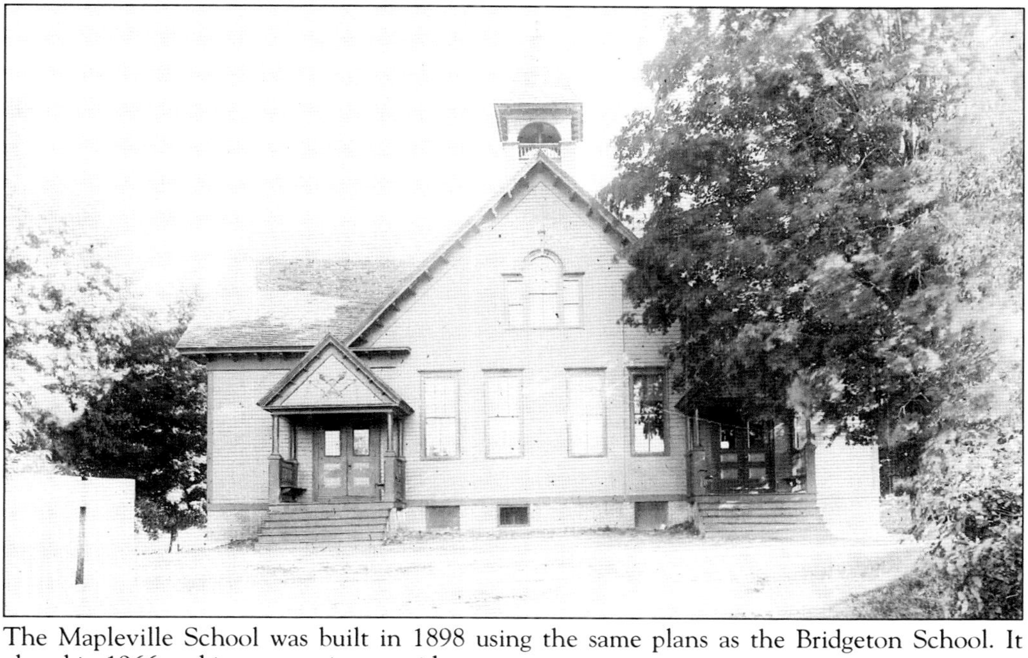

The Mapleville School was built in 1898 using the same plans as the Bridgeton School. It closed in 1966 and is now a private residence.

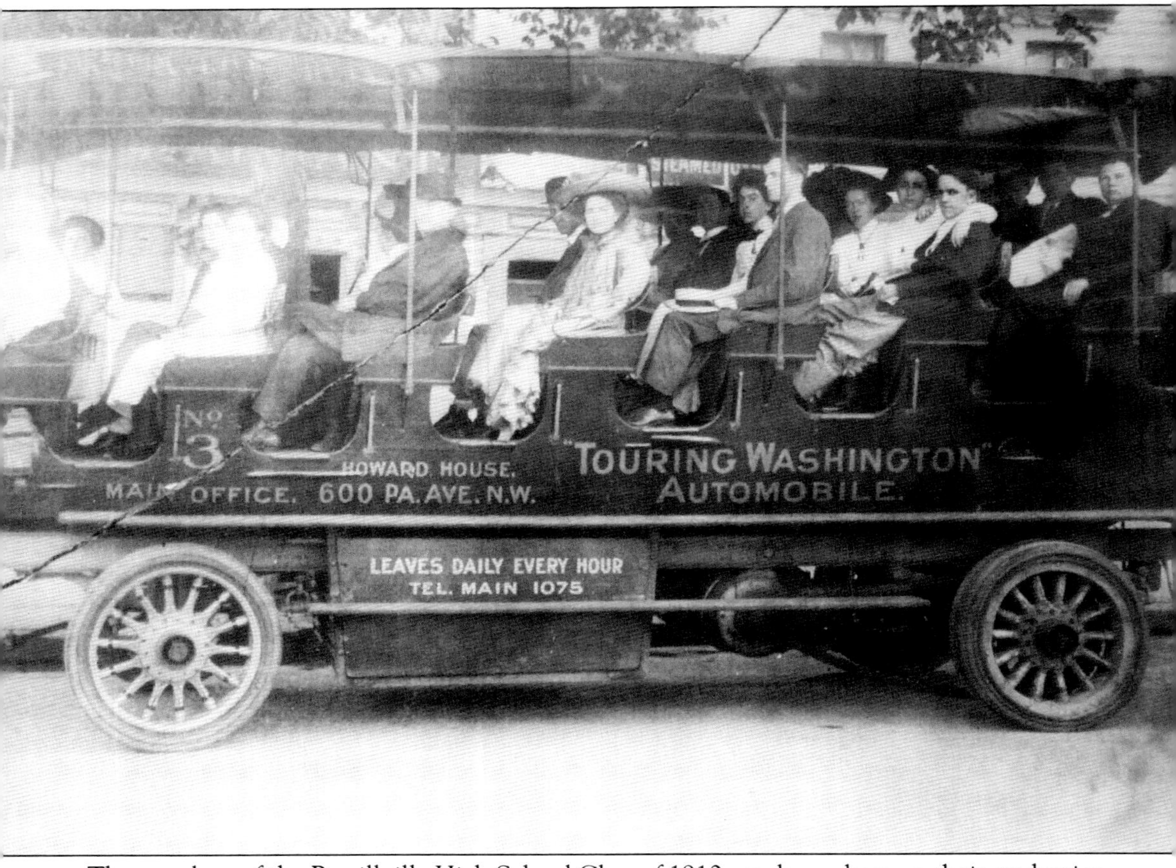

The members of the Burrillville High School Class of 1910 are shown here on their graduation trip to Washington, D.C. Some of the graduates were Josephine Fitz, Gertrude Campbell, Elizabeth Piche, Francis Corbin, Corrine Blanchard, William Fagan, Charles Whiting, Forrest Ross, Waldo Randall, Clothilda Clavin, and Joseph Sweeney (advisor).